THEY'RE COMING FOR YOU

THEY'RE COMING FOR YOU

How Deep State Spies, NGOs, and Woke Corporations Plan to Push You Out of the Economy

JASON CHAFFETZ

BROADSIDE BOOKS

HarperCollins books may be purchased for educational, business, or sales promotional use. For information, please email the Special Markets Department at SPsales@harpercollins.com.

Broadside Books™ and the Broadside logo are trademarks of HarperCollins Publishers.

FIRST EDITION

Library of Congress Cataloging-in-Publication Data has been applied for.

ISBN 978-0-06-338758-4

25 26 27 28 29 LBC 5 4 3 2 1

Dedicated to our future generations.

Our world is what you make it.

Civilization is the progress toward a society of privacy. The savage's whole existence is public, ruled by the laws of his tribe. Civilization is the process of setting man free from men.

—Ayn Rand

Freedom is never more than one generation away from extinction. We didn't pass it to our children in the bloodstream. It must be fought for, protected, and handed on for them to do the same.

—Ronald Reagan

Contents

Preface

Our government's unhealthy obsession with collecting vast troves of information about every single American is not benign. We know that now. After countless Americans have been politically prosecuted, censored, and debanked for failure to conform to official government narratives, we seem to have a US version of Chinese social credit scores.

Regardless of who sits in the White House, permanent Washington is hard at work spying on us. They want to know what we read, what we post, what we save to the cloud. They seek access to our photographs, our location patterns, and even our browsing history. Unlike my favorite sandwich shop, they aren't just using the data to make a better sandwich.

Data is power. It's power to control behavior, power to influence elections, and power to shape the next generation. It's a power that is systematically abused by the very people we have entrusted to protect us. Eight years ago, we thought we could govern without worrying about what was happening behind the scenes. We can't.

We now have a historic opportunity to right previous wrongs. We must not make the same mistakes twice. That's why I felt compelled to write this book. As the chairman of the House Committee on Oversight and Government Reform following the first election of Donald Trump, I saw what happened. I know where we went wrong. We must not let it happen again. New technology is enabling new abuses of power that must be curtailed.

As a member of Congress, I wanted to expose it all. That's part of what drew me to the House Oversight Committee to begin with. I was the only member of my 2008 freshman class to prioritize that committee assignment as my first choice. Most people ask for an "A" committee like Appropriations or Armed Services, where lobbyists line up to donate to their campaigns. Ī was more interested in exposing the corrupt underbelly of American bureaucracy.

Having been elected to Congress the same year President Barack Obama came to power, I cut my teeth on investigations of the deeply dishonest Obama Justice Department, where DOJ obstruction started at the top. Not only did the agencies withhold documents, but Attorney General Eric Holder himself was held in contempt of Congress for refusing to fulfill his legal obligation to turn over relevant documents. DOJ refused to comply with subpoenas or prosecute anyone else for the same. When evidence surfaced in 2013 that the IRS was weaponized to target conservatives, Attorney General Loretta Lynch refused to investigate.

In the midst of this uphill battle, I was named Oversight Committee chairman in 2015. It was the position I needed to expose the mendacity and corruption of the Deep State. I had a dream team to work with both on the committee and on staff. On the dais beside me were outspoken representative Jim Jordan (OH), future Trump chief of staff Mark Meadows (NC), future Florida governor Ron DeSantis (FL), powerhouse attorney Representative Trey Gowdy (SC), future Republican Policy Committee chair Gary Palmer (AL), principled constitutionalist Thomas Massie (KY), and future (now current) Oversight Committee chairman James Comer (KY). Those are just the best-known today, but we had a whole A-list squad of talent that session that was positioned to expose the massive corruption under the surface—provided we could get to the evidence.

At the time, going into a presidential election year, I was prepared to do battle with a likely President Hillary Clinton. It was becoming evident how intrusive government and bureaucrats were in our lives. We were gearing up for a fight. Then, inexplicably, Trump pulled off the surprise of the century and won the presidency in 2016.

Imagine my excitement. We were in the perfect position. There was no better opportunity to peel back the layers and expose what bureaucrats had been doing over the last eight years. With an incoming Republican administration, I thought I would have everything I needed to do my job. A Republican attorney general who would prosecute the bureaucracy's failure to comply with investigations would put oversight into overdrive. We would finally get the documents, the testimony, the hearings, and the depositions we needed to make our case to the American public and expose the corruption. It was truly the opportunity of a lifetime.

But Speaker Paul Ryan didn't see it that way. Nor did incoming attorney general Jeff Sessions. When I met with Ryan in January 2017, he explained to me that things would be different now that we were in the majority. We're a legislative body now, he explained. We do legislation. We don't do oversight.

In contrast, President Trump encouraged me to keep doing my job. I remained hopeful for a time. He gave me no specific direction or advice, but he was openly supportive of my efforts. I remember him telling me to "keep doing what you're doing." His message was not "Stop doing oversight."

I eventually met with Attorney General Sessions once the Senate officially confirmed him. With him it was a different story. He didn't seem to share Trump's enthusiasm for us to keep doing what we were doing. In fact, he was outright hostile to it. As I went down the list of what I needed to do my job, all I got was "no" all the way down.

For example, I wanted him to enforce our subpoena against an IT aid of Hillary Clinton. He had refused to testify about her private email server, despite being inexplicably granted immunity by the DOJ. It is our congressional prerogative to seek this testimony, to see documents, and to complete our investigations. It's why we have subpoena power. But that power is worthless if the DOJ refuses to enforce it. Sessions did just that.

As I went down the list that day, Sessions refused to touch any request that had to do with Hillary Clinton or the Obama administration. He didn't seem to care about the precedent he was setting or its impact on our system's checks and balances. He wanted to move on, forget about Hillary Clinton and the evidence she destroyed, and ignore what then–FBI director James Comey was doing. Of course, we now know that Comey was helping set the stage for the false Russia collusion narrative at the time.

I can't help but wonder how things might have been different had we been given the tools to scrutinize some of these people in the earliest days of the Trump administration. Could we have found and exposed what was going on inside the DOJ? But no. We are a legislative body. We don't do oversight when we're in the majority. That's what I was told.

It was a bitter pill to swallow. I knew it was a missed opportunity. After I met with Sessions, I began to question whether my serving as chairman would accomplish anything. Our committee did have some small legislative prerogative—we could originate US Postal Service reforms, for example. But we had been sitting on a unanimous postal bill for two years. Speaker Ryan said we didn't have room on the calendar for it. If I wanted to help move my principles forward, it was clear I could do more on television than I could do in the 115th Congress.

There was no point in doing oversight if I wasn't permitted to actually do oversight. I looked at all the things I was giving up to be there and the changes underway in my own family. I was nursing an old foot injury that was flaring up from all the walking on the hard marble floors of the Capitol complex. With little hope of exposing waste, fraud, and abuse, it no longer felt like a worthwhile trade-off. I had always said Congress should not be a lifetime appointment. I planned to get in, serve, and get out. But I got out earlier than anticipated, in no small part because it was clear I wouldn't be allowed to do the one thing I felt most compelled to do.

Meanwhile, the Deep State metastasized right under Jeff Sessions's and Paul Ryan's noses. They each pursued what they considered to be more important objectives. With congressional oversight largely sidelined, Trump was being undermined from within to a degree no one comprehended at that stage.

Today, with voters having given Trump and Republicans another bite at the apple, it is imperative that we expend political capital to restore some of the checks and balances that have been demolished by prior administrations. The extent to which formerly trusted institutions have colluded to manipulate public opinion and wield political power must be exposed and checked.

A core part of manipulating the American public is the virtually unregulated access to and flow of data that is collected, traded, sold, and exploited every single day, often without our knowledge or our permission.

Advancing technologies like artificial intelligence have enabled the creation of ever-more-invasive "weapons of mass detection," which distinguish the politically compliant from the ideologically subversive. Do you promote cryptocurrency? You can be quickly debanked. Did you break the law while protesting on behalf of Black Lives Matter? No worries—you won't be prosecuted. Do you question the efficacy of the COVID-19 vaccines? Your account is now censored.

Meanwhile, jobs, contracts, and grants can be steered to more compliant voters. Unregulated access to data allows political actors to push you out of the economy. Government and corporations, using nonprofits as a sort of data-transfer middleman, can reward the behavior that serves them and punish dissenters.

I was drawn to these issues from my very first session in Congress. Whether it was invasive airport body scanners, unauthorized facial recognition databases, or cell-site simulators used to spy on suspicionless Americans, I was deeply concerned about the potential for abuse. At the time, most of my colleagues were not digital natives. They hadn't grown up around technology yet were responsible for understanding how to regulate it. In a 2011 Judiciary Committee markup of the controversial Stop Online Piracy Act (SOPA), I quipped that we were being asked to do surgery on the internet without a doctor in the house.[1] I called on Congress to "bring in the nerds!" The new Trump administration is doing exactly that.

Since then, the hunger for ever-more-invasive data points has gone far beyond government. It has morphed into a complex network of allied agencies, nonprofits, and technology companies with growing access to our emails, social media posts, photographs, cloud storage, and browsing histories. They work together to use that data to control behavior, each doing what the other cannot.

Many of these entities are currently funded or run by billionaire Democrats with partisan agendas, though there is nothing to stop Republicans from doing the same. People who want power need data. It's become far too easy to get.

This is core to who the progressives and the Democrats are today. They want to control what you can say, what you can eat, what you can watch and read, what products you are allowed to buy, where you do business, and which values get instilled in your children.

That quest for control certainly isn't new. But it is more dangerous than ever before as our digital footprints grow and technology evolves to enable cataloging of every detail of our lives. Meanwhile, the government's activities have become increasingly opaque.

Privacy advocates on both sides of the aisle now have an opportunity to right some grievous wrongs. It should have been done nearly a decade ago. It could have. Republicans had the opportunity. But they blew it. Fortunately, the worst abusers of our data have lost power for the time being.

Is this a battle the Trump administration will be willing to support? I'm hopeful. It took a few years, but I have now had a few chances to sit down one-on-one with President Trump and talk about what happened in 2017. During a visit to Mar-a-Lago, I gave him a copy of my first book, *The Deep State*, in which I wrote about my meeting with Jeff Sessions. I think everyone has a better idea of what this administration is up against this time around.

In this book, I will lay out for you what I laid out for the president. The path before us could have generational consequences. We must get it right.

This time the stakes are higher than ever. The technology is more advanced and the Deep State is more entrenched, but the duplicity is also more exposed. I am optimistic that this time can be different.

THEY'RE COMING FOR YOU

CHAPTER 1

The Power Imperative

On July 8, 2021, prominent civil rights leader Wade Henderson traveled to the White House to meet with recently elected president Joe Biden and Vice President Kamala Harris.[1] Then interim CEO of the Leadership Conference on Civil and Human Rights, Henderson is a law professor and former Washington Bureau director of the NAACP.[2] His White House meeting that day would mark a new frontier in the partisan infiltration of the federal government. The collaboration he would facilitate was intended to have a profound impact on an election still three years away.

Later that same day, Henderson would take a lead role in a secretive "Listening Session" (as the White House referred to it) to discuss the implementation of a deceptive new executive order to "Promote Access to Voting." Years would pass before conservatives could document what happened in that session. In 2021, we could only speculate.

But today we know. After years of obfuscation, the administration was finally forced to release details they had long sought to protect. This new evidence validates the concerns I raised about Biden's Promoting Access to Voting order in my previous book, *The Puppeteers*. The partisan nature of this effort undermined the legitimacy of the entire executive branch.

Biden and Harris, at the behest of deep-pocketed strategists within their own party, were opening the door to an ominous weaponization of even the most benign federal agencies. By executive order, agencies would do the bidding of partisans seeking to shore up their power in the next election.

Publicly, it was billed as a cause for celebration. The government was performing a service! And the new cause du jour would be voter registration—targeted, of course, to benefit a Democratic president. But no one would need to know that. The order specifically said it would all be very nonpartisan.

Government Off the Books and Out of Bounds

Executive Order 14019, signed by President Biden weeks after his inauguration, purported to remove obstacles that prevent people from voting. The order created a sweeping authorization for an estimated six hundred federal agencies to do voter mobilization, going so far as to require each agency to submit a plan for registering those who use the agency's services or website.[3]

The order went even further, authorizing agencies to partner with local election officials and "third-party organizations" to provide voter registration services, even on agency premises. For readers of my previous books, this pattern of using nonprofits and other nongovernment organizations (NGOs) as a sort of off-the-books arm of government will be familiar. Many of these so-called charities, with significant funding from the foundations of America's wealthy elites (a group that author Seamus Bruner calls the "Controligarchs"), seek to reshape the world through progressive activism.[4] What could possibly go wrong? Voter registration is inherently a good thing, right?

But it was a curious move. The federal government doesn't have any authority to oversee state and local elections or voter registration. It is not the president's job, or that of any department under his jurisdiction. That's another familiar pattern—the federal government stepping out of bounds to usurp power from the states in pursuit of a partisan agenda.

This top-down imposition of a new priority for federal agencies was far outside the wheelhouse of most departments. That

Biden and Harris would prioritize this effort so early in their administration—and apply it so broadly—was a red flag.

The administration assured the country there was nothing partisan about it. The text of the order dutifully referred to "soliciting and facilitating approved, nonpartisan third-party organizations and State officials to provide voter registration services on agency premises."[5]

But Henderson's organization was no "nonpartisan" third-party group. Those were not the groups invited to the Listening Session to discuss implementation of the order. That day in July 2021 was Henderson's third trip to the White House in as many months.[6] It would culminate in a collaborative effort to engage that allegedly "nonpartisan" group of nonprofits.

As the head of the Leadership Conference, Henderson unequivocally represented the left. He was leading a coalition of some 240 progressive advocacy groups. They included far-left-aligned NGOs from the American Bar Association to the YWCA, from the Arab American Institute to the National Council of Jewish Women.

What is currently known about Henderson's meeting with Biden and Harris is still vague. A Leadership Conference post on X about the White House visit disingenuously billed it as a discussion of "our freedom to vote and other urgent issues facing our democracy."[7] Who could object to that?

In reality, freedom had little to do with it. Henderson was there to help the Biden-Harris administration stack the deck ahead of the 2022 and 2024 election cycles. They would use data collected and maintained by taxpayer-funded government agencies to pinpoint the voters Democrats wanted to have registered.

By using nonprofits as an intermediary, Democrats would enjoy the best of both worlds. The campaign would get to leverage government data and resources normally off-limits to a party's political arm. The government, through outside groups, would get to engage in partisan politics in a way that is normally illegal. By the time anyone could challenge the order in court, the damage to their opponents would be done.

Hiding the Partisanship

The Listening Session in July 2021 was the key to understanding the real objective of the executive order. That's where the government met with dozens of representatives from outside groups who were invited to help implement the order. Thanks to government watchdogs who obtained previously private unredacted Justice Department notes summarizing that meeting, we know just how "nonpartisan" that session was.[8]

For a meeting that was allegedly completely aboveboard, the administration was strangely unwilling to disclose information about it. Getting written documentation from the session was an expensive and time-consuming process. The administration is legally required to disclose public documents when requested. But the federal government is adept at sidestepping Freedom of Information Act (FOIA) requests, which means that only organizations with the resources to sue are generally successful. And even then only after several years of petitioning the government.

The notes, when they were finally disclosed, confirmed what the Foundation for Government Accountability (FGA) and the Heritage Foundation had suspected when they filed their first document requests. The whole thing was a partisan exercise in getting out the vote for Democrats. The notes confirmed that only one side was represented at the Listening Session.

The majority of participating organizations in attendance that day were members of Henderson's progressive coalition. Those participants, according to a memo released by the Heritage Foundation's Oversight Project, included "zero Republicans, independents, or politically conservative individuals."

Among the supposedly nonpartisan groups participating were those great bastions of objectivity as the Southern Poverty Law Center, George Soros's Open Society Policy Center, the AFL-CIO, National Education Association, Black Voters Matter, and the Brennan Center for Justice at New York University. The Heritage analysis concluded that "every participant whose party affiliation or political donation history could be identified by the Oversight Project was identified as a Democrat except for one Green Party member." So much for nonpartisan collaboration.

According to the notes from the DOJ, the talk in the Listening Session was all about registering voters from specific groups made up of historically Democratic voters. The ACLU wanted to register voters at Head Start—the federal low-income preschool program. Demos, a nonprofit public policy organization specializing in "moving progressive issues from the movement to the mainstream," suggested that the Department of Housing and Urban Development (HUD) use in-house data to target low-income voters in public housing.[9]

The meeting notes don't record any discussion of targeting groups with a high propensity to vote Republican. Who would have suggested it? There was no one there from the right.

This was no apolitical bridge-building exercise seeking to reach across the aisle. Henderson and his Leadership Conference appeared to "have held significant influence on the Listening Session."[10] Henderson has spent decades building coalitions of progressive activists. Who better to marshal the resources of the progressive nonprofit ecosystem?

To get a feel for just how sinister this is, try putting the shoe on the other foot. How might Democrats respond if, for example, the Heritage Foundation were to lead a coalition of conservative voter registration groups to work with the Department of Agriculture registering (predominantly Republican) farmers and ranchers? What if the government explicitly and exclusively supplied lists of legal gun owners to right-leaning voter registration groups?

This combination of government and campaign groups working together asymmetrically to benefit one party is a dangerous new frontier. In explicitly supplying nonpublic data to partisan organizations for the purpose of exacting a purely political outcome, Democrats undermine free and fair elections and weaponize the bureaucracy.

In the meeting, the NGOs pushed radical far-left ideas on voting, according to the Oversight Project memo. For example, a representative from the Mexican American Legal Defense and Educational

Fund (MALDEF) suggested that prohibitions on noncitizens voting should only be enforced postelection via prosecutions rather than prevented before an election. Given the obstacles deliberately imposed by some of these same groups, they know it would be much more difficult to identify and disqualify illegal votes once the vote has been cast. The administration was hatching plans for any attorneys who might have the audacity to challenge illegal votes after the election.[11]

Despite Biden's original executive order having been cloaked in feel-good language about enabling "all eligible Americans to participate in our democracy," it was never about all Americans. It was always about historically Democratic Americans—and, as some suspect, left-leaning non-Americans.

The order plainly designated some of the Democratic voting blocks that agencies should target—federal employees, disabled voters dependent on federal subsidies, overseas citizens, and convicted felons in federal custody. Though it doesn't have a section specific to race, the very first paragraph of the order references "Black voters and other voters of color" who have faced "discriminatory policies and other obstacles."[12]

It's clear who Biden and Harris were hoping to target. And historically, each of those groups could be reliably counted on to support the president's party on Election Day. Democrats assumed those patterns would hold in 2024.

The order itself didn't spell out the partisanship, of course. It didn't have to. As the FGA pointed out in a *Wall Street Journal* editorial, "Promoting voter registration and participation—i.e., mobilizing voters—is an inherently political act for a partisan president."[13]

Believing the public has a right to know what federal agencies are doing to engage in elections they don't oversee, FGA and Heritage submitted FOIA requests to see the plans each agency submitted in compliance with the order. One would think such a request would be routine. What agencies do using taxpayer money is always the business of the American taxpayer. By law, agencies are required to respond within twenty days. But they rarely do.

FGA opted to sue the Department of Justice after its FOIA requests for agency voter registration plans were ignored for 240 days.[14] Thirty-six members of Congress requested the same documents. The Biden administration asserted "presidential communications privilege" to keep the plans a secret. That's a claim that typically applies to documents involving direct communications and advice to the president. These agency plans, however, lay out governmental actions that affect civic engagement.

In a court filing, the DOJ argued transparency would cause "public confusion."[15] Why can't Americans be privy to the use of their data and taxpayer-funded resources to influence upcoming elections? Let us hope the courts will side with transparency.

The administration withheld the documents because they didn't want to tip their hand ahead of the election. In 2024, they leveraged the full force and power of the federal government as part of a sophisticated operation to target and turn out likely Democratic voters. And it still wasn't enough. They lost the popular vote, the Electoral College, the House, and the Senate despite going to these unprecedented lengths.

It was a federally funded version of Zuckerbucks—often referred to as Biden Bucks. But unlike the Mark Zuckerberg–funded election initiative that stacked the deck for left-wing candidates in the 2020 presidential election, this one provided access to federally collected personal data on taxpayers, welfare recipients, and criminals—among others. Most of these groups, at least on paper, were supposed to lean left.

Should we be surprised that political creatures would seek to leverage such advantages to hang on to power? Of course not. It's what they do. Despite their failure at the ballot box, it should still surprise and enrage us that Democrats can get away with weaponizing our federal agencies and our data in this way. The guardrails are down. The fox is in the henhouse. It won't matter what other policy victories we achieve if we can't find a way to shore up the weakened checks and balances that should have bound the executive branch during the Biden presidency.

A Unilateral Pursuit of Permanent Power

Our elections are no longer a fair fight. The merging of the Biden-Harris civil service with the campaign arm of the Democratic Party was not a "both sides" issue. But covertly co-opting federal agencies to gain electoral advantage was only a small part of the problem. As Trump learned during his first term, the federal workforce is essentially a wholly owned subsidiary of the Democratic Party. This is not just because civil servants tend to favor bigger government, but also because conservatives are getting screened or purged from the civil service—as we'll explore in Chapter 4.

Even when Republicans win the presidency, they don't win the federal bureaucracy, the progressive-dominated nonprofit sector, or the woke companies that gatekeep the dissemination of speech. That is why unfettered access to data is so much more dangerous in the hands of a dementia-riddled Joe Biden or a vacuous Kamala Harris than it would be in the hands of Donald Trump on his worst day.

The real threat is not just the politicization of the executive branch, but the unholy alliance between government, the nonprofit sector, and the corporate media/technology sphere of the economy that allows Democrats to deploy and weaponize that data against Americans. This combination of entities is a one-eyed monster with a single goal—political power. Like the three brothers in Greek mythology who created the Cyclopes, these three institutions work together to create weapons that seek to help one side maintain god-like power over American discourse. Just as the Cyclopes sought to help Zeus cement permanent rule over the cosmos, this trio of Cyclopes are unified with the single imperative of holding permanent power.

Throughout the Biden administration, that power was coercively deployed to reward political compliance and penalize political opposition. With corporate data collection and government surveillance powers, Democratic administrations can now pinpoint with precision accuracy exactly who is on their team and who is working against them.

Activist NGOs, including influential charities, policy think tanks, and deep-pocketed political advocacy groups: all of these groups play a role in promoting punitive measures that the government can't pursue on its own. We'll see what that looks like in Chapter 3.

The government collects vast troves of data about Americans. What our government can't legally collect it can typically buy from private-sector data brokers. With the advent of artificial intelligence, facial recognition, and other advanced tools, the government can learn virtually anything it wants to know about any individual. That is a valuable tool for fighting crime, preventing fraud, collecting taxes, and performing other critical functions of government. But that data isn't staying in the hands of politically neutral civil servants. We've shown with Executive Order 14019 and the associated Listening Session that it's being deployed by partisans both inside and outside of Democratic administrations.

Blacklisting "wrongthink" has never been easier—or more widespread. Unlike the old blacklists of the past, this one can penetrate deeper than ever before. This isn't just a weaponized justice system targeting a political opponent—as bad as that is. It doesn't stop with one side's protestors receiving harsher sentences than the other. Though we know that happened.

This book will outline a systemic weaponization of our data against us by partisans in government, NGOs, and woke corporations. We will see it deployed against individuals, industries, charities, and government employees who don't conform to specific narratives. Thanks to recent Democratic administrations, partisans can access data from government surveillance, bank transactions, phone metadata, facial recognition databases, consumer products, social media, and even health records with limited transparency and minimal oversight. And it is being deployed by a Cyclopean monster that is more interested in helping Democrats retain power than in doing the actual work of government, charity, journalism, or democratic governance.

The Cyclopes aren't just targeting politicians for punitive measures. They're going after conservative charities, churchgoers, attorneys, civil servants, police, teachers, and scientists. Patriotic, hardworking Americans are being purged from financial institutions and workplaces, excluded from career opportunities and public discourse, and singled out for punishment by their professional associations and government regulators.

In many cases, their crime amounts to little more than questioning a narrative. They question election irregularities, prosecutorial misconduct, abortion laws, or vaccine safety. Sometimes their only crime is holding views that, until ten minutes ago, were considered mainstream. They could hold traditional views of marriage and gender, object to open borders, or expect prosecutors to charge criminals with felonies. Maybe they donated to a January 6 protestor, bought a MAGA hat, or objected to being labeled a white oppressor. Any of these can potentially be discovered through data we don't even know the government sees.

I don't want anyone digging through any of my private information, but I really don't want those seeking retribution against me digging through every piece of data on my life. I say this from personal experience. I actually saw the US Secret Service use data the government had about me to retaliate and embarrass me after I criticized the agency as a member of Congress. We'll get to that story in a later chapter.

All is not hopeless, however. It's likely too late to stop data collection—and we wouldn't want to if we could, given the many benefits we enjoy. But it's not too late to protect our civil liberties. There are important steps we can take to force transparency, penalize abuse, ramp up oversight, and wrest back control of our personal data. We can no longer tolerate our data being weaponized against us to undermine our votes, coerce our compliance, compromise our security, and silence our voices. It must end.

CHAPTER 2

The Privacy Trade-off

I remember the first time my local grocery store asked me to join a loyalty program. They gave me a bar-coded tag to add to my key chain and required me to scan it at checkout if I wanted the best price. It must have been more than thirty years ago. I was alarmed. Are they keeping track of everything I buy? Why do they need to know that? We held out. My wife, Julie, and I weren't giving over our information.

But slowly, over time, the tangible benefits of having that bar code began to outweigh the nebulous risks. When you scanned the bar code, you got a better price. They began sending coupons for things you might actually buy. This marketing innovation took retailers by storm. Once I gave the grocery store my information, they started listing how much I saved at the bottom of my receipt, reinforcing the upside of letting them track what I buy.

Today, almost everyone I do business with tracks what I buy from them. It seems every time we shop at a new website, they offer a discount in exchange for giving over my email, which we all know can lead to almost daily messages from them clogging the inbox. When I scan my Jersey Mike's card, I get a free sub after I buy twelve. The clothing stores I order from send me $10 off when I spend $200. And don't forget that $10 credit on my birthday month!

It seems like almost every minute of every day, I'm being asked to share personal data with someone. When I post a profile picture, a company like Clearview AI has been known to scrape that photo from the internet and add it to their vast facial recognition database. It sounds like a good trade-off—they actually use it to catch bad guys and identify trafficking victims.

When I search on my internet browser, advertisers pay money to know what terms I searched for, what links I clicked on, and what else I'm interested in. Likewise, when I post to Facebook, Instagram, or Snapchat, I get access to my social network. I get ads for things I might conceivably want to buy. They get access to my data.

That home security system I use sends me video alerts of potential threats—a particularly useful product for someone like me. The fact that the video can be made available to police seems like a legitimate trade-off. I want them to have evidence of crimes as much as anyone else.

Most of us have come to terms with the reality that our personal data is widely known and shared. We may not like it, but we want the speed of a faster screening line at the airport, the reward for spending at our favorite retailers, or the convenience of ticketless entry to our favorite sports event. If the trade-off for our data is just about marketing and convenience, many people believe it's worth it.

The Technology-Driven Surveillance State

To better understand the threat posed by government access to our data, consider one of the great technology innovators of our time: China. Though unbound by the constitutional restraints that protect Americans, the Chinese Communist Party (CCP) still seeks to create the illusion of voluntary cooperation. Tyranny is expensive, and the CCP must constantly look for new ways to minimize resistance even as they monitor and coerce the population.

The party uses technology to track financial transactions, political compliance, and online speech. China is a worst-case scenario in terms of how data can be used to control the population. The nation's social credit system, newly expanded for 2024–25, is dependent on a vast system of digital surveillance.[1] The CCP controls an estimated 700 million closed-circuit television (CCTV) cameras across the country. Those cameras use not only facial recognition, but also gait recognition to identify people by the way they walk.[2]

Coercive power is maintained through financial control. The rollout of the digital yuan (e-CNY), China's central bank digital currency, has enabled government access to every digital transaction. Users are required to register a phone number and ID to use the currency, so the government can record and attribute every transaction. It's all very convenient—so long as users comply with the CCP. If they don't, the government has the power to freeze their digital wallet, controlling whether or not they can buy groceries, travel, or meet financial obligations.[3]

China likewise has the most successful censorship operation in history. In addition to a state-controlled monopoly on media, the CCP has successfully sequestered its population from the global internet. According to the Internet Society, the "Great Firewall of China," as some refer to the Chinese system, "is more accurately described as a national intranet." Nothing gets in without the government's approval. Censors can block content in bulk.[4]

By law, the CCP mandates the exclusive use of a state-approved virtual private network (VPN), which only strengthens the censorship power. These VPNs are programmed to restrict content as part of their safety protocols. Not only that, but the law mandates the sharing of VPN data with Beijing.[5] Even apps that originate in China, such as TikTok (Douyin in China), show different content at home than abroad. The Chinese populace is cut off from anything the government doesn't wish for them to see.

China can arrest a citizen for spending their money planning a political protest. Though that can't happen here, our government could theoretically circulate a private organization's list of politically problematic people, encouraging businesses to avoid working with them. What's to stop that from happening here?

China's most draconian measures are possible only because the people have no instrument, constitutional or otherwise, to protect civil liberties. Here in America, we still do. But we are woefully unprepared for the technological revolution that is underway.

Our laws are outdated. Our checks and balances are being ignored. Our lawmakers in Congress have little technical understanding, frequently deferring to unelected bureaucrats to deal with the small print. That's a problem when so many of our technocrats in government are potentially compromised by corporate or political actors. There are solutions—and in many cases they are straightforward. But we can't solve what we don't see.

Most of us have no idea of the extent to which we have traded our privacy for convenience. It's not just our tax information, our Social Security numbers, or the metadata from our phones. We are generating data hundreds of times a day through our everyday activities.

Nowhere is the data trade-off more apparent than in the act of driving a car. On the one hand, we're more safe because of what our cars can tell law enforcement about us. On the other hand, my car might know more about me than my mother-in-law does.

License to Spy

Following a series of bank robberies in Washington, DC, in September 2020, police used cameras from the DC Department of Transportation to identify the Tesla Model S likely used in the robberies. Lucky for them, the car was part of a vehicle subscription service. Police subpoenaed the company, seeking information about the subscriber. In response, they received GPS data that placed the car in the vicinity of two of the three banks at the time they were robbed.[6]

We love it when technology can be used to solve crimes. However, that same telematics data can be bought, sold, or used in ways the public might not be so comfortable supporting.

Innocuous sensors used by automakers and original equipment manufacturers (OEMs) transmit data continuously from the vehicle to the automaker through embedded systems in the vehicle that convey data points in real time. They track data about our speed, location, engine performance, media usage, and other factors.

Likewise, data we provide to the websites or service programs of car manufacturers is theirs to share or sell, provided they divulge it in the fine print. Like many auto manufacturers, Kia collects data for various uses, which they openly divulge in the privacy policy most of us don't read. The company actually uses two separate privacy policies—one governing data collected through the website and services program, and another governing data their cars report.

To its credit, Kia UK allows users to opt out. And the company asserts that it doesn't maintain data on drivers under age sixteen. Those are important caveats. But if you actually read Kia's privacy policy, you'll see that their cars can collect numerous data points—both related to driving and unrelated to driving—such as "race or ethnicity, religious or philosophical beliefs, sexual orientation, sex life, and political opinions."[7] Yikes! Several other car dealers collect similar data.

Just the act of getting a driver's license can ensure our face ends up in a facial recognition database—even for minors. That's information that can be bought and sold or used by law enforcement, whether consumers know it or not. It doesn't matter if we've done nothing suspicious. By driving a modern vehicle, we're basically all agreeing to wireless surveillance. So much for police needing articulable suspicion to peer into our private lives.

We can always count on the Chinese government to give us a preview of coming attractions when it comes to tyrannical data manipulation. And in this case, they don't disappoint. The US Department of Commerce is currently investigating security threats from Chinese-made vehicles.[8] China is the largest automaker in the world. Though tariffs enacted during the first Trump administration and continued during the Biden administration have severely limited the availability of Chinese-made cars in the United States, those cars are pouring into Mexico, where one in ten cars sold is Chinese.[9]

Like many modern cars, these Chinese vehicles are connected with satellite and often internet access.[10] That means they can be controlled by Chinese companies, who could theoretically record conversations inside the vehicle, remotely disable the vehicles from Beijing, or even cause them to crash. Under China's 2017 National Intelligence Law and 2020 National Security Law, Chinese companies are compelled to facilitate data sharing with the Chinese Communist Party.[11] In other words, it is illegal for these companies to withhold data sought by the CCP intelligence apparatus.

We expect such abuses in China. But what about here at home? A controversial provision in the 2021 bipartisan infrastructure bill allegedly mandated "kill switches" in new vehicles sold after 2026. Left-leaning fact-checkers sprang into action to rate the claim false after it was revealed in a column by Georgia congressman Bob Barr. Closer scrutiny of the actual bill reveals some cause for concern.[12]

Barr was describing a provision that was marketed to lawmakers as "a benign tool to help prevent drunk driving," but he thought the fine print was pretty specific. The legislation mandates a computer system that can "passively monitor the performance of a driver" and "prevent or limit motor vehicle operation if an impairment is detected." Is that a kill switch? According to *USA Today* and the Associated Press, the claim is false. Snopes claimed the truth was a "mixture" of true and false. PolitiFact, pointing out that the words "kill switch" do not appear in the bill, rated the claim "Mostly False."

"I'm not a constitutional scholar," writes Jon Miltimore of the Foundation for Economic Education, "but it seems to me that the federal government's requiring automobile manufacturers to install a system that spies on its driver—and disables his car if transgressions are suspected—hardly meets this constitutional standard."[13]

Though our laws don't require private companies to share data with the government as China's do, our military is more than happy to buy it from them. The Ulysses Group, for example, claims to be able to locate almost any car in the entire world using its geolocation software. The company "has worked with US Special Operations Command (SOCOM), a branch of the military specializing in counterinsurgency, counterterrorism, and special reconnaissance."

Now the company boasts that access to this data can "enhance military intelligence and operational capabilities, as well as reduce the costs to . . . acquire mobile targets of interest." This military contractor offers bulk commercial telematics data to access the locations of 15 billion vehicles around the world every month.[14]

Even state governments are benefiting from giving you the privilege to drive. Florida residents Sonia Arvin and Tonia Batson received an onslaught of robocalls and advertising mail offers after the Florida Department of Highway Safety and Motor Vehicles sold their personal information to private companies. It was later revealed that the department made $77 million selling driver information to private companies in 2017.[15]

Florida is not alone. State DMVs have been very willing to give up the personal information of their drivers to private investigators and marketers. That data can then be used to track spouses and conduct other private investigations.

In 2019, in an effort to analyze the citizenship status of Americans, the Trump administration asked states to divulge data from their driver's license records.[16] In its press release, the Census Bureau cited long-standing federal law authorizing the reuse of existing data to save taxpayers money. Given that many states automatically register drivers to vote, the request was a reasonable one. The Census Bureau emphasized that the data is "stripped of all personal identifiable information and are used for statistical purposes only."[17]

But could a subsequent administration, determined to share federal data with the activist NGOs, get their hands on raw data to perpetuate power rather than serve the people? How might a database of noncitizens be helpful when disclosed to one party, but not another?

In a world where a president might be willing to do absolutely anything to keep his (or her) party in power, these technologies hit differently. We can no longer afford to only consider the advantages they bring. We have to look at how a rabid partisan might use them. We can't trust our government to restrain itself. We forget it's not the nature of government to self-restrain. We have to restrain power with transparency, accountability, consequences, and the very real possibility of losing power. Even more nefarious uses for that data are possible if we don't have a robust framework governing privacy.

Blacklisted

Consider what would happen if a corrupt attorney general, a motivated federal prosecutor, or a compromised US president could indiscriminately comb through the data of people they wanted to destroy. We don't have to think too hard. The prosecution of Donald Trump gave us an unprecedented example of government weaponization and political persecution. We saw it in the disproportionate efforts made to hunt down January 6, 2021, protestors through cellular and financial data.[18]

One of the signs of an authoritarian political regime is that it punishes or excludes people for having the wrong opinion. Our ancestors would have called it a blacklist. In the modern era, it looks more like a social credit score—one in which political compliance is a key factor in doling out favors and penalties. That's where we are. Only today's blacklisting is exponentially more invasive and potent.

With the power to access virtually unlimited data—and absent some of the checks and balances that should constrain government—one goal becomes paramount: staying in power. To do that, the government needs to access the unconstitutional tools that have always kept tyrants in power. They need to be able to manipulate elections, retaliate against political opponents, and censor speech. This book will show how the executive branch has engaged in all three. More importantly, the institutions they have infected aren't just after the big fish. They're coming for the little guys. I'll show you where we need to start in order to restore the guardrails that still have the power to protect us.

CHAPTER 3

The New Blacklist

A s part of a relentless effort to disincentivize meat consumption, 105 climate groups signed a letter demanding that America's largest banks cut off funding to global meat and dairy industries. Despite strong demand for these products, climate groups warn of severe environmental impacts from livestock emissions, which they claim will "use almost half of the world's 1.5°C emissions budget by 2030 and 80% by 2050."[1]

They're not talking about emissions from industrial processes or hydrocarbon fuels. They're talking about actual emissions from the livestock itself—emitted through burps and manure.

Maybe you believe cows are a threat to the planet. Maybe you don't. But the notion that entire industries can be blacklisted from participating in the global financial system when they become politically disfavored is chilling. Meat and dairy aren't the only potential target. Nor are climate NGOs the only perpetrators.

A similar playbook, the Obama administration's Operation Chokepoint, has allegedly been deployed before—by the government. Venture capitalist Marc Andreessen alleges that Biden deployed his version—Operation Chokepoint 2.0—this time targeting cryptocurrency-related businesses.

This type of retaliatory exclusion must not be permitted to metastasize. What is to stop private businesses from using political criteria to exclude whole segments of the population from employment or insurance coverage? Imagine a campaign, possibly abetted by partisan actors in government, to cut off assault weapon owners, pro-life donors, or school board protestors from being hired, promoted, or served by major businesses? Imagine being passed over for a job because you legally purchased a weapon for self-defense. That's where this path could lead.

Our House Oversight Committee in 2014 determined that the original Operation Chokepoint illegally choked off legitimate businesses. Regulators forced banks to cut ties with businesses from disfavored industries, such as payday lenders and firearm manufacturers, under the pretext that such relationships would cause "reputational risk" that might lead to greater federal scrutiny of the bank.[2]

After Andreessen's November 2024 appearance on the *Joe Rogan Experience* podcast, in which he casually dropped a claim that some thirty tech entrepreneurs had been "debanked" over the course of the Biden-Harris administration, several stepped forward to post their stories.[3]

Through a process dictated by the Nixon-era Bank Secrecy Act, banks are required to build profiles of their customers, filing Suspicious Activity Reports to flag illegal activity that they are prohibited from disclosing to customers. That means banks can't tell people why they closed their accounts. If an account is flagged as high-risk, banks shoulder a heavy compliance burden and an increased risk of draconian enforcement actions if they don't terminate it.[4]

We might expect that members of the Biden family would be ripe for debanking, considering revelations from former bank director and current House Oversight chairman James Comer. Comer revealed that the Treasury Department disclosed to him the existence of more than 170 Suspicious Activity Reports on Biden family members involving money laundering, human trafficking, and tax fraud. To date, I've seen no evidence of any Biden accounts being terminated, but apparently Barron Trump was flagged in 2021 while he was still a minor. First Lady Melania Trump acknowledged in her book that her bank account was canceled without explanation in 2021 and an application from her son, Barron, subsequently denied.[5]

The question of whether the Biden administration used debanking as a political weapon must be investigated and allowed to play out. We must not allow debanking to become a political weapon used by the powerful to punish dissent. But this story is bigger than just the Biden administration, and the targets aren't just political actors.

Targeting the Christians

The Timothy Two Project is a Christian nonprofit ministry established to train pastors around the world, with ongoing projects and workshops in sixty-five countries.[6] There is nothing inflammatory, subversive, or political about what the charity does. Charity Navigator gives the Timothy Two Project an 86 percent rating, meaning that it's considered a safe and reliable nonprofit.[7]

Still, in 2020, founder Steve Curtis received a letter from Bank of America, with whom his charity had been doing business since 2011. His organization was being debanked—in other words, their bank account was being involuntarily closed. Bank of America no longer wanted the Timothy Two Project as a customer. At the time, Curtis was informed he was "operating a business type we have chosen not to service."[8] Curtis shrugged his shoulders and opened an account at another bank.

But three years later, in 2023, Curtis became aware of a *Daily Mail* story about another Christian ministry debanked by Bank of America.[9] Indigenous Advance served widows and orphans in Uganda. Like the Timothy Two Project, Indigenous Advance was apolitical. It wasn't like many American nonprofits that use charity as a pretext to advance a political agenda. It was simply a Christian relief organization.

When Indigenous Advance pressed Bank of America for more information about the account closure, the bank explained their "risk profile no longer aligns with the bank's risk tolerance."[10] But what does that even mean? It would ultimately take a congressional investigation to get to the bottom of it.

What Curtis didn't know, but Congress would eventually un-cover, was that the Biden-Harris administration had created its own version of a social credit system. The system used subjective metrics and surveillance of digital transactions to deny services or penalize individuals and organizations.

The House Weaponization Committee, which investigated the treatment of January 6 protestors, established that the FBI had accessed private financial records to identify transactions tied to firearms and conservative political activity. This profiling was used, CCP-style, to restrict access to banking services based on ideological disagreements.[11]

Whether financial institutions participated unwittingly or not is unclear. But the administration's fingerprints are not hard to see.

Debanking Campaigns

This debanking effort is unique in the modern era because of the way it uses data to pressure banks and identify targets. It is based on the narrative that financial institutions can't afford to do business with entities that create reputational risk—in other words, bad publicity. (Of course, given the dominance of the left in media and entertainment, the left generally dictates which issues generate bad publicity.)

This reputational-risk standard is dangerous because it doesn't just hit the highly profitable corporate sector. Anyone can be de-banked simply for being linked to a cause or political position that "generates bad publicity."

Timothy Two wasn't an isolated case. And it wasn't just Bank of America. A gun dealer was debanked by Wells Fargo.[12] The National Committee for Religious Freedom was debanked by JP-Morgan Chase. PayPal froze the account of Moms for Liberty and canceled accounts of right-leaning political figures like COVID-19 policy critic Dr. Joseph Mercola. Lieutenant General Michael Flynn had his credit cards canceled by Chase over "reputational risk"—a decision the bank subsequently reversed. The Idaho Constitution Party received a notice from U.S. Bank in March 2024 canceling their account in a single sentence, offering no explanation.[13]

It was all part of a highly successful series of pressure campaigns to dry up the flow of money to businesses and nonprofits perceived to be out of alignment with the progressive political agenda.

Thanks to Congress, we now have a case study on how it's being done. Republicans narrowly flipped the House majority in 2022, enabling Speaker McCarthy to create the House Select Subcommittee on the Weaponization of the Federal Government. This move facilitated an investigation that the Department of Justice would never have pursued. What the committee uncovered and released in 2024 tied the government to the NGO pressure campaigns.[14]

NGOs Team Up with Financial Regulators

Just ten days after the January 6, 2021, protests at the US Capitol, the Treasury Department's Financial Crimes Enforcement Network, or FinCEN, sent an email to the financial institutions regulated by the Treasury purporting to seek information on protestors who entered the US Capitol. This is important because leftist NGOs could never access a channel like this. Only the government can.[15]

The email didn't just go to large banks. It was sent to other financial institutions, including PayPal and Western Union. With the pretext of a manhunt for violent extremists, the email was timed to elicit maximum cooperation. Included in the email was a link to a report from a leftist NGO.

Ominously titled "Bankrolling Bigotry: An Overview of Online Funding Strategies of American Hate Groups," the report was the product of the London-based Institute for Strategic Dialogue (ISD) and was a road map for cutting off the funding stream of the left's political opposition.[16] The government didn't produce this report or the recommendations suggesting who should be debanked. They just passed along the "research" of an "independent" outside group. In this case, there was no ambiguity about its political leanings.

Using a narrowly tailored definition of hate groups, the report called for draconian measures against US charities it identified as targeting "minority communities." (One could substitute "Democratic voting blocks" for the term "minority communities" because the report only counted certain minority groups—the ones that are historically left-wing voters—for this purpose.)

The measures recommended would essentially prevent the right from replicating the powerful nonprofit charities being politically weaponized by the left. By destroying the ability of many conservative charities to fundraise, claim legal tax-exempt status, or maintain bank accounts, the report claimed that the administration could "diminish the ability of those who seek to spread hatred to succeed." Conveniently, with this move the administration could also diminish the ability of those who oppose their agenda to succeed—which is likely the real purpose of debanking. If that were the case, we would expect to see some left-leaning groups singled out as well.

According to the report's authors, who relied heavily on information supplied by the hopelessly politicized Southern Poverty Law Center (SPLC) and Anti-Defamation League (ADL), hate groups were defined as anyone who maligned or delegitimized "an entire class of people on the basis of immutable characteristics." These groups reportedly "promote hostility and hate crimes" through conspiracy theories and disinformation.[17]

So how is a group that alleviates poverty in the third world considered a reputational risk? Daily Signal managing editor Tyler O'Neil has called out the SPLC for its use of a "hate map" that plots Ku Klux Klan and neo-Nazi groups alongside mainstream conservative organizations whose history of violence is limited to disagreeing with the politics of the SPLC.[18]

Parental rights groups, Christian nonprofits, and even conservative pundits like Tucker Carlson have been branded as white supremacists by the SPLC.[19]

Obviously, it's not about hate per se. It's about Orwellian wrongthink—specifically, having the wrong opinion about who should be in power. A closer look at the list of hate groups makes that clear.

Only certain politically advantageous groups get included in the hate group calculus. For those caught defying left-wing heresies, the ISD's Bankrolling Bigotry report recommended financial institutions adopt policies to debank, defund, and strip nonprofit status from targeted charities.

The report helpfully organized the hate group list into categories—those who hate immigrants, LGBTQ+, and Muslims, and white supremacist groups who hate people of color. There were some legitimate white supremacist hate groups listed, though it is debatable whether there is anything partisan about them.

Lumped into that list were legitimate charities with a long history of mainstream conservative influence. For example, Numbers USA and the Center for Immigration Studies (CIS) made the list, even though their work is primarily policy work promoting orderly immigration policies.

How does that meet the definition of a hate group? When I check the SPLC website to learn what these groups are doing to earn that designation, I see a long list of quotes that don't align with its political views.[20] Here's an example. SPLC cites this comment from CIS director Mark Krikorian in 2014: "We have to have security against both the dishwasher and the terrorist because you can't distinguish between the two with regards to immigration control." This is not extremism, nor does it imply any sort of physical brutality. We're back to a speech problem, not a violence problem.

Under the category of "Anti-LGBTQ+" were listed conservative stalwarts such as the Eagle Forum, the Family Research Council, and the Alliance Defending Freedom—allegedly for their pro-life and pro-marriage work. Anyone who doesn't align with the political agenda of prominent LGBTQ+ groups would then qualify as a hate group.

The American College of Pediatricians, for example, made the list because they classify transgender surgeries for minors as child abuse, among other leftist heresies.[21]

Consider how quickly the tide can turn. Today's mainstream views can become tomorrow's blasphemies. The last two Democratic presidents prior to Joe Biden campaigned on the belief that marriage was between a man and a woman. Neither Bill Clinton nor Barack Obama faced much pushback for what was essentially a commonsense, mainstream position throughout most of human history. But now, if you are an organization promoting that view, left-wing activists consider you a bigot and write reports suggesting that the government strip you of nonprofit tax-exempt status. Every Christian congregation risks losing tax-exempt status.

Had it ended there, the report and its authoritarian ideas could have been quickly forgotten. But it didn't. The Biden-Harris administration authorized the distribution of those recommendations to financial institutions through official government channels. They didn't just write a report. They worked with the government to pressure fundraising platforms to stop "bankrolling" charities they didn't like.

The Biden-Harris administration couldn't legally instruct banks to cut off customers whose opinions they didn't like. So they enlisted the NGO to present the idea—through an email sent by the government using government data and resources.

All of this is disturbing enough, but the next revelation is even more dangerous. The government then used January 6 as a pretext to engage financial institutions in doing warrantless surveillance.

Warrantless Surveillance

Not only were financial institutions given tacit instructions for defunding the administration's detractors, but they were also tapped to perform warrantless surveillance against "suspicionless" Americans on behalf of the Biden-Harris administration.

According to committee chairman Jim Jordan, "FinCEN urged large financial institutions to comb through the private transactions of their customers for suspicious charges on the basis of protected political and religious expression."[22] What does "suspicious" mean in this context?

FinCEN helpfully supplied a list of merchant category codes and search terms that banks could use to identify customers the government considered dangerous. Coincidentally, the supplied codes would identify anyone the administration would consider conservative.[23]

Among the transactions the government wanted banks to flag were anything featuring the terms "MAGA," "America First," or "Trump." Only in the context of January 6 would this make sense. These terms allegedly pointed to people who might have "involvement in riots or potential violence," according to the committee report.

Likewise, the email from FinCEN cast suspicion on customers who made frequent ATM withdrawals or wire transfers, bought bus or plane tickets "for travel to areas with no apparent economic or business purpose," and completed transactions that involved "the purchase of books (including religious texts) and subscriptions to other media containing extremist views."

What was done in the aftermath of January 6 has now established a precedent that can be repeated the next time the government decides its ideological opponents pose a threat. Any government-regulated private company can get roped into doing the administration's warrantless surveillance. Likewise, an administration can use NGOs to do some of the dirty work.

In the case of the FinCEN letter, the administration used left-wing NGOs to identify political targets (in this case, "hate groups") and outline politically dangerous policy recommendations (in this case, debanking) that the administration dared not explicitly articulate itself. That way politicians wouldn't risk being held accountable at the ballot box.

The administration then distributed recommendations of the NGO to private-sector entities it regulates, along with instructions for performing surveillance to identify the right targets. Those entities then perform warrantless surveillance or retaliatory measures that neither the government nor the NGO has the power or data access to perform.

All different entities, each deployed with a single objective—kneecapping the administration's opposition to help them hold on to power. I wish this were the only such example. It's just the best documented. Perhaps only we policy wonks notice if the government destroys the Family Research Council and CIS. But if that succeeds, what would keep them from moving on to the Federalist Society and Young Americans for Freedom? After all, the SPLC was started in 1971. Notice that the decline in powerful segregationists and white supremacists has not shortened their lists in the intervening fifty years. They've just redefined the term "extremist."

Democrats ran this play more than once. Former Kansas senator Sam Brownback described a similar operation against charities with which he is involved. Both the National Committee for Religious Freedom and the Alliance Defending Freedom were targeted by financial institutions after the SPLC and the Council on American-Islamic Relations (CAIR) teamed up to single them out as part of their "Hate-Free Philanthropy" campaign.[24]

When political actors have unfettered access to the levers of power, combined with data telling them virtually anything they want to know, they can't seem to help themselves. They will leverage that data to win elections, coerce compliance, and control speech.

In this case, we have a political party with a successful history of using NGOs to do off-the-books political work for the government. The last thing they want is for the opposing party to employ a similar strategy. They need to use the data to unilaterally disarm the nonprofits of the right without hurting left-leaning nonprofit networks.

The Power of the IRS

What could be more terrifying than the Treasury Department ordering my bank to comb through my financial transactions? I can think of something. The thought of a dramatically expanded, weaponized, AI-enabled IRS poring through millions of financial transactions should send shivers up the spine of any civil rights advocate.

The month President Biden was inaugurated, Senator Sheldon Whitehouse (D-RI) sent a letter to IRS commissioner Charles Rettig calling for the tax-exempt status of the conservative Turning Point USA to be revoked. The justification? Turning Point USA did not require masking and social distancing at an event held at Donald Trump's Mar-a-Lago Club.

"Organizations that knowingly put in danger minors entrusted to their care should not enjoy the benefits of tax-exempt status," he wrote. "Accordingly, I urge the IRS to review whether it should revoke Turning Point USA's tax-exempt status."[25] That letter and 176 pages of additional documents were provided to a right-leaning nonprofit in late 2022 in response to a FOIA request.

Within a year of that disclosure, the nonprofit—the American Accountability Foundation (AAF)—received notice from the IRS that its 501(c)(3) tax-exempt status was under investigation. As a result, the IRS demanded access to correspondence files, emails, and information the nonprofit had obtained about elected officials.

AAF president Tom Jones described the investigations as "a deliberate attempt to punish and suppress AAF's activities. It is surely no coincidence that AAF—the very organization that exposed the weaponization of the IRS—is now the target of it."[26]

How does the IRS decide which nonprofits to investigate? How do they determine who to audit? And is there any possibility that politics could enter into the equation? Would the IRS do the political bidding of a Democratic administration?

If you've been around US politics for more than a decade, you know they already have. In 2012 I was a member of the House Oversight Committee when we began a two-year investigation of the IRS for this exact concern.

You'll recall the agency had overwhelmingly singled out conservative nonprofits for additional scrutiny, searching their data for terms like "Tea Party" to help them locate targets. In many cases, the IRS demanded disclosure of donors and other highly sensitive information about conservative nonprofits. These actions kept numerous groups on the sidelines during the 2012 presidential election. A 2013 audit by the Treasury Inspector General for Tax Administration documented the truth of those allegations.[27]

No one at the IRS was ever held accountable, although the Trump Justice Department acknowledged wrongdoing at the agency and paid out settlements to targeted groups.

In a 2017 news release, Attorney General Jeff Sessions explained, "The IRS's use of these criteria as a basis for heightened scrutiny was wrong and should never have occurred. It is improper for the IRS to single out groups for different treatment based on their names or ideological positions. Any entitlement to tax exemption should be based on the activities of the organization and whether they fulfill requirements of the law, not the policy positions adopted by members or the name chosen to reflect those views."[28]

Beefing Up IRS Enforcement

All of this took place before the advent of artificial intelligence as we know it today. Now, Democrats have fought a long, hard battle with Republicans to increase funding for the agency. This includes a staggering $80 billion budget infusion spread across ten years that was allocated in the 2022 Inflation Reduction Act, which passed the Senate only because of a tiebreaking vote from Vice President (and Biden-appointed AI czar) Kamala Harris. For an agency with a $12 billion annual appropriation, that extra $8 billion a year is significant.

In their 2025 budget proposal, the Biden-Harris administration called for an additional $104 billion for the IRS. That's eight times the annual budget, just two years after Congress appropriated an amount that was six times the agency's annual budget. Some of that funding will pay for personnel to conduct more audits. Some of it pays for advanced technology, including artificial intelligence. With its 2025 budget, the IRS says it will increase audit rates of wealthy taxpayers (those earning more than $10 million) by 50 percent.[29]

Biden Treasury secretary Janet Yellen promised in 2022 that the $80 billion included in the Inflation Reduction Act would not be weaponized against the middle class. "Contrary to the misinformation from opponents of this legislation," she said, "small business or households earning $400,000 per year or less will not see an increase in the chances that they are audited."[30]

Senator Mike Crapo (R-ID) offered an amendment to the Inflation Reduction Act preventing the IRS from using any of the $80 billion in new funding to audit taxpayers earning less than $400,000 a year. It failed on a 50–50 vote along party lines, with every Democrat voting no.

"When I offered my amendment to simply make it clear that the $80 billion being given to the IRS—six times its current annual budget—could not be utilized to audit people making less than $400,000, the most they would agree to was to say they did not 'intend' to audit them," Crapo explained in a release.[31] As to why:

That's because they know from the analysis of the Joint Committee on Taxation that most underreported income occurs among taxpayers earning less than $200,000 per year, and from the Congressional Budget Office that they cannot collect the $200 billion they are claiming without auditing people making less than $400,000. If they truly do not intend to audit anyone making less than $400,000, then they would have supported my amendment, turning "intent" into binding statute.

Who Is Getting Audited?

In January 2024, the IRS announced it was leveraging AI to "ramp up audits."[32] According to the release, AI enables the agency to get to the bottom of more complex cases that are often resource-intensive, allowing them to crack down on bigger tax cheats and claw back more revenue. According to IRS commissioner Daniel Werfel, AI helps "identify patterns and trends." He aims to go after partnerships, digital assets, and those using foreign bank accounts.[33]

With the Biden-Harris administration's commitment to expand the agency and increase audits, the obvious question arose: Could political factors influence who gets audited? Might a partisan administration weaponize the audit process as the Obama administration did? Time will tell. But we do know this much: IRS whistleblowers told Congress that the Biden Justice Department interfered with an audit of Biden's son Hunter, who would later receive a pardon from his father. Two witnesses testified they were prevented from pursuing evidence that Hunter Biden raked in millions from foreign governments through complicated financial transactions involving more than twenty shell companies.[34] IRS interference by the Biden political apparatus is hardly unprecedented.

Do I think any Democratic administration would go after the 3,800 IRS employees who owe a collective $50 million in back taxes? Doubtful. Or the 150,000 tax-delinquent federal employees across all agencies who owe $1.5 billion?[35] Not likely. Who did Democrats imagine would be the target of the increased audits they called for back when they still believed their party could hold the White House in 2024?

One answer may be white and Asian people. That's because the Biden-Harris administration issued an executive order giving federal agencies broad new authority to "prevent and remedy discrimination, including by protecting the public from algorithmic discrimination."[36] In other words, disproportionate numbers of

Black Americans have been subjected to audits when the IRS uses objective criteria.

One conservative group sued the Biden-Harris administration for documents to disclose whether the IRS pursued race-based audits to correct the disparity. The America First Legal Foundation (AFL) sued after the IRS refused to comply with a FOIA request.

"When read in context with the Department of the Treasury's ongoing efforts to racialize tax policy, the new Executive Order signals that the Biden Administration intends to alter Internal Revenue Service's (IRS) audit algorithms to target white, Asian, or mixed-race taxpayers," AFL wrote.

The lawsuit pointed to comments by Treasury deputy secretary Wally Adeyemo, who signaled a strategy of race-based audits when he called for the IRS to examine the tax system through a racial equity lens. In a meeting with racial equity experts, Adeyemo reportedly expressed a "commitment to racial equity as a key factor in the design of tax compliance."

The IRS is prohibited from collecting information on the race and ethnicity of taxpayers, but according to the AFL complaint, the IRS collaborated with the Census Bureau to "obtain microdata on race and ethnicity" and "impute race and ethnicity for tax data."[37]

Can the IRS be fair? Can the agency resist the political pull of a current or future administration seeking to prejudice the tax system for or against political figures or strategic voting blocks?

That's what Judiciary Committee chairman Jim Jordan (R-OH) began asking in early 2024. "The use of AI technology to actively monitor millions of Americans' private transactions, bank accounts, and related financial information—without any legal process—is highly concerning," Jordan wrote in a letter to Secretary Yellen.

"This kind of pervasive financial surveillance, carried out in coordination with federal law enforcement, into Americans' private financial records raises serious doubts about the IRS's—and the federal government's—respect for Americans' fundamental civil liberties," he wrote.[38]

Thanks to a March 2023 Supreme Court ruling, IRS agents unequivocally have unlimited authority to access our bank records without warrants or notice to the taxpayer.[39] Imagine what a weaponized agency taking orders from a partisan administration could do with that kind of data.

Jordan, joined by Representative Harriet Hageman (R-WY), opened his committee's investigation following reporting by journalist James O'Keefe suggesting the IRS was working with other federal agencies to conduct warrantless surveillance with little oversight.

In the letter to Yellen, Jordan cited video footage of IRS Criminal Investigations Unit agent Alex Mena telling an undercover journalist that the agency was using a new AI-powered system to sort through bank statements and tax filings to target "potential abusers."

Mena further alleged that the IRS can use its AI system to "see the amount" in every American's bank account. He claimed this "invasive" system is "working really well" "nationwide." Jordan quoted Mena's claim that IRS agents "have no problem, like, going after the small people, you know, putting people in prison. Like destroying people's lives, they have no problem doing that." When asked whether the system is constitutional, Mena is recorded saying, "I doubt it." Mena claimed the new AI system could access and monitor "all the information from all the companies in the world."[40]

With the emergence of artificial intelligence, the time is now for Congress to erect guardrails that protect American taxpayers from discriminatory abuse by partisan actors within the government. The government's access to bank records and tax information must never be a tool available to presidential campaigns or activist NGOs.

The Best Fixes

As usual, one of the best defenses against federal overreach is state law—and it's much easier to wield than an act of Congress. States can prohibit financial institutions from withholding financial services on the basis of religious views or political alignment. Florida law prohibits financial institutions from refusing to serve customers because of "political opinions, speech, or affiliations, religious beliefs, exercise, or affiliations, and any action that considers a social credit score." That includes owning a firearm, failure to meet environmental or social governance standards, and more.[41] Tennessee also prohibits large banks and insurers from refusing service to clients based on a "social credit score" that considers religious or political beliefs.[42] Texas, Louisiana, and West Virginia have each made their own moves to prevent financial institutions from debanking businesses in their states as a growing list of state legislatures introduce bills to address the problem.[43]

Outside of government, the right has had some success in replicating the pressure campaigns typically deployed by the left. Following a series of suspected political debanking decisions, one group apparently filed a shareholder resolution with JPMorgan Chase. The resolution called for an audit of the bank's policies and practices relative to the civil rights of its customers. Though the resolution did not pass, the banks face reputational risk from public exposure that they may be violating the civil rights of their conservative customers.

As for the IRS, transparency is key. We need to ensure compliance with FOIA requests through lawsuits like the one by AFL. With the Trump-Vance administration at the helm, we can hope the IRS will be fully transparent. Nevertheless, Congress must take steps to shore up our broken FOIA process to ensure transparency regardless of which party holds the White House.

Furthermore, instead of increasing taxpayer audits, Congress would be better off to simplify the tax system. We shouldn't have to hire a CPA to do a simple tax filing. Our system is far too complicated. Paying the correct amount in taxes should be foolproof.

The complexity of the tax code provides too much cover for those who might weaponize it in service of their own party's political goals. Given the degree to which the previous administration leveraged the power of the bureaucracy against political opponents, the IRS must be as insulated as possible from partisan interference. They must never be allowed to become like the FBI.

CHAPTER 4

Purging the Heretics

The Biden-era FBI couldn't imagine why anyone thought the agency had a bias against Trump supporters. They would never retaliate against internal whistleblowers. They certainly wouldn't deliberately purge suspected conservatives or vaccine skeptics from their ranks. The very notion of agency bias is "somewhat insane," testified FBI director Christopher Wray, since he is a registered Republican himself.[1]

The FBI Human Resources Division's Jennifer Leigh Moore, who confirmed she was the Biden administration's ultimate decision-maker when it came to suspending an employee's security clearance, told Congress she was adamant that every employee be treated fairly. "My whole management principle is around 'be kind,'" she testified in a deposition with the House Weaponization Committee.[2]

Let's quickly review the FBI's "kindness" toward whistleblowers during the Biden-Harris years. Whistleblower Steve Friend was suspended without pay after questioning the bureau's uncharacteristic manipulation of FBI protocols in January 6 prosecutions. Friend made protected disclosures indicating excessive use of force by the FBI and efforts to exaggerate the threat of domestic terrorism. The FBI initially rejected Friend's request to take outside employment and denied him access to his training records, leaving him with no means of support.[3]

After accepting a transfer, whistleblower Garret O'Boyle sold his home in Kansas, moved his family to Virginia, then showed up for his first day in his new job only to be told his security clearance had been revoked. He couldn't even access his personal effects in storage unless he came up with ten thousand dollars, which he didn't have. This left his kids without access to coats or warm clothing for winter. With a two-week-old infant at home, his family was left homeless.

There were other whistleblowers with similar stories. Representative Jim Jordan was contacted by fourteen different whistleblowers between November 2021 and August 2022 with claims Jordan described as political in nature.[4] In 2023, the DOJ received 105 new whistleblower complaints.[5] Of all the whistleblower stories, O'Boyle's appeared to be a "personal manifestation of cruelty" to his family.[6]

"I can 100 percent assure you of, it wasn't done intentionally," Moore testified of the timing of the suspension.[7] It was apparently all just a huge coincidence that he moved across the country the same day he was suspended. Why was O'Boyle suspended?

The FBI later claimed, without evidence, that he made unauthorized disclosures to Project Veritas.[8] This was false. The FBI was publicly embarrassed when former FBI agent Kyle Seraphin stepped up to acknowledge being the source of that interview.[9]

Perhaps it's a coincidence that O'Boyle had made protected whistleblower disclosures to Congress. His complaint exposed the agency's efforts to manipulate statistics on the number of white supremacy (Domestic Violent Extremist, or DVE) incidents.[10] Those disclosures threatened the Biden administration narrative that such incidents, which the left often treats as right-wing terrorism, had "significantly" increased.[11]

These and other incidents from whistleblowers raised questions about whether the FBI was using the security clearance process to retaliate against its own people. Moore admitted certain incidents were exacerbated by an "honest mistake" in one case and coincidental timing in another.[12] However, "the FBI does not use a suspension as a punitive measure ever," Moore testified in a transcribed interview with the House Weaponization Committee.

That was before the inspector general got involved. And before the leaking of a questionnaire that left little room for debate. The man who can most credibly answer the question of security clearance abuse is DOJ inspector general Michael Horowitz, who has access to internal documents and testimony.

His May 2024 investigation was damning. It established that at least 106 FBI agents were left in limbo for an average of nearly eighteen months each while their clearances were under review, with no right to appeal or expedite a decision. Given that obtaining and maintaining a top secret security clearance is a long-standing, essential condition of employment at the FBI, Horowitz found the FBI process to be retaliatory.[13] He noted that the system "creates the risk that the security process could be misused, as part of an inappropriate effort to encourage an employee to resign," which was exactly what Friend was forced to do.

As if that weren't damning enough, another story soon dropped. Someone had leaked a copy of a questionnaire being used by the FBI in its security clearance reviews to question colleagues of suspended agents. Congress wasn't supposed to know about the questionnaire. Director Wray would later disavow it. But whistleblower attorney Tristan Leavitt says his clients' colleagues reported being asked the questions, which were typed in incomplete sentences. The questionnaire read:

- Vocalize support for President Trump?
- Vocalize objection to COVID-19 vaccination
- Vocalize any intent to attend 01/06/21[14]

There is just no way to explain that away. Nevertheless, the official position of the FBI is unequivocal. "We do not investigate ideology and we do not investigate cases based on a person's political views,"[15] the agency reiterated in a statement to the *Washington Examiner*. But the document speaks for itself. "Support for President Trump" is clearly political. But the objection to the COVID vaccine? That's a more insidious question because nonpolitical justifications can be used to obscure the political motivations behind it.

Coworkers were given little choice but to rat out their colleague's personal opinions during a security review process. This political litmus test wasn't optional. Before answering the above questions, respondents had to read this statement: "Should you refuse to answer or fail to reply fully and truthfully, action against your security clearance may be undertaken and you may be referred to the Inspection Division for possible disciplinary action."

In his July 2024 congressional testimony, Wray admitted the agency had used the questionnaire but denied any political motivation for Friend's suspension. He disavowed the use of what he agreed were "completely inappropriate" questions, which he claimed originated from an outside contractor.[16] It was likely the best argument he could make, given the evidence.

In a stroke of good fortune for Republicans, the FBI had kept the completed interview questionnaires, which Leavitt managed to obtain.

Leavitt is an excellent attorney. I know, because I hired him. He handled investigations and whistleblower complaints for the House Oversight Committee when I chaired it beginning in 2016. He investigated Hillary Clinton's use of a private email server, as well as many high-profile cases of waste, fraud, and abuse. More importantly, he negotiated the passage of the 2016 FBI Whistleblower Protection Enhancement Act, which I sponsored.[17] (Unfortunately, the FBI waited seven years to update its whistleblower procedures after the passage of the bill, according to a November 2024 report from the Government Accountability Office.)[18] Leavitt now represents whistleblowers through the nonprofit Empower Oversight.

Despite the insistence by Wray and Democratic members of the House Weaponization Committee that there was nothing to see here, Friend, O'Boyle, and other named whistleblowers are not the only voices of alarm. Journalist Miranda Devine spoke to no fewer than thirty former agents who offered public support for the named whistleblowers. One of them, retired agent Ernie Tibaldi, told Devine, "It's time to stop the FBI from being the enforcer of a political party's ideology. We need to re-establish the FBI as the apolitical and independent law enforcement entity that it always was."[19]

Former special agent Nicole Parker, who joined Fox News after leaving the FBI, had earlier testified before Congress: "Over the course of my 12-plus years, the FBI's trajectory has transformed. On paper, the bureau's mission remained the same, but its priorities and governing principles shifted dramatically. The FBI became politically weaponized, starting from the top in Washington and trickling down to the field offices."[20]

Conservatives Need Not Apply

Imagine a world where an employer could pull up a website and look at your voting history before deciding whether to interview or hire you. Companies could pick and choose those candidates most aligned with their political culture. They could exclude those who don't fit in. If your political views diverged from what employers consider mainstream, you could be excluded from participating in the workforce, passed over for promotions, or singled out for discipline. They might not even focus on overt politics. What if you're just not a good "cultural fit"? Maybe they just don't like that your favorite show is *Yellowstone* or your favorite genre of music is country. What if they can see that you're a Mormon, or have a Rumble account, or you play Dungeons & Dragons and that's just not their cup of tea? How hard is it to imagine a company considering such criteria?

It sounds like a description of communist China. And it is pretty close. But it's not supposed to happen here. We have the rule of law, due process, and separation of powers—all the checks and balances that prevent abuse. But what happens when the branch of government charged with enforcing the law is unwilling to police itself? What happens when ideological discrimination is rewarded instead of penalized?

It's happening in the public schools, the military, the civil service, the tech companies, the entertainment industry, and on and on. Political and religious tests are technically unconstitutional, but progressives at these institutions have found ways around that. And now, with the combined resources of government, nonprofits, and corporations, they have data to show them exactly whom to target. What could go wrong?

Broad data access enables political discrimination to happen at scale. Is there any greater tyranny than the ability to control who gets to have a job? Who gets to work in a given industry?

Fortunately, there is no record of how each person voted in past elections—for now. But the data collected by government agencies, financial institutions, cell phone providers, social media sites, nonprofits, and other sources is almost as useful as a voting history.

In much of the country, there is no law against political discrimination. Title VII of the Civil Rights Act of 1964 prohibits employers from making hiring decisions on the basis of race, color, national origin, religion, or sex.[21] Other laws protect job candidates who are aged or disabled.[22] However, political discrimination is not a federal crime in this country, and neither is it a crime in most states.

No one is immune from the temptation to favor their allies and exclude their opponents. But when one party dominates the institutions that have access to so much data about us, there is a real threat to freedom and liberty. If privileges and opportunities can be doled out on the basis of political fealty to abortion or LGBTQ rights, for example, that creates a coercive incentive. If punishment and prosecution are only applied to those who question political dogma, the rule of law is compromised.

Major figures in the Democratic Party have articulated this notion that certain political beliefs are disqualifying with very little pushback from the party's rank and file.

When Is Religion Disqualifying?

During the 2018 Senate confirmation of Brian Buescher for a US district court judgeship in Nebraska, then-senator Kamala Harris had a chance to challenge the nominee about his qualifications. The attributes she considered disqualifying—in her words "extremist"—were not his background or his experience, but rather Buescher's religious beliefs. In written questions, she challenged his engagement with a Catholic philanthropic charity—the Knights of Columbus.

"Were you aware that the Knights of Columbus opposed a woman's right to choose when you joined the organization?" Harris wrote. Apparently, Harris and fellow senator Mazie Hirono found Buescher's tie to that organization was enough to disqualify him for a promotion for which he was eminently qualified.

At the time, readers may recall that Catholics were outraged. This is not a fringe group. The 1.5-million-member Knights of Columbus has been around since 1882. It has raised millions of dollars for charity. However, it holds traditional religious views on marriage, gender, and abortion. Harris described it as "an all-male society comprised primarily of Catholic men"—another strike against it, apparently.

Hirono went even further. Her written questions called on Buescher to recuse himself from any case involving issues related to Catholic beliefs on marriage, sexuality, and abortion. She asked him, "Do you intend to end your membership with this organization to avoid any appearance of bias?" And in another question, "If confirmed, will you recuse yourself from all cases in which the Knights of Columbus have taken a position?"[23]

Let's think about that for a minute. What if that standard were applied consistently to anyone with involvement in a religious or political group? What is the limiting principle here? Would Hirono agree that a member of a typically pro-choice faith, say Reform Judaism, should recuse herself from all abortion cases? I don't think so. Hers is an outrageous standard—and a double standard at that.

Despite the Constitution's prohibition on applying religious tests, it is clear the future vice president and the senior senator from Hawaii had no qualms about excluding candidates for important government positions on the basis of their religious beliefs and associations. The underlying inference is that Christianity makes one unfit for public office. Somehow I think the Founders might disagree.

For the two-thirds of Americans who identify as Christians, the notion that strict adherence to their faith might disqualify them from any role in administering justice may seem far-fetched. And the effort to coerce Americans to abandon their cultural traditions in favor of progressive orthodoxy has only grown since Buescher's confirmation.

Even in the military, Christianity has sometimes been a disqualifier for leadership. In August 2024, the Idaho National Guard stripped one man of his command after a gay subordinate complained about political views the man expressed in his free time.[24] The man had called the prescribing of puberty blockers to minor children a "pernicious practice." In the view of the complaining colleague, this was equivalent to showing "just how much [the officer] hates the LGBTQ community." The Christian officer sued.[25]

Calling the state's action "patently illegal," public interest law firm Liberty Counsel joined in the action against the state, calling on Idaho governor Brad Little to intervene and stop what they called a "No Christians as Commanders" policy from going forward.[26]

There is a growing belief on the left that people who reject progressive cultural norms on gender, sexual orientation, and abortion are not qualified for the privileges of a free society. Efforts to exclude people from juries, military service, promotions, scholarships, adoption, and foster care have met with little resistance from the progressive left.

In a case the Supreme Court opted not to hear, Justice Samuel Alito released a statement expressing strong reservations about the disqualification of two Missouri jurors on the basis of their traditional religious beliefs. He referenced his dissenting opinion in the landmark *Obergefell v. Hodges* decision legalizing same-sex marriage, in which he predicted that eventually, "Americans who do not hide their adherence to traditional religious beliefs about homosexual conduct will be 'labeled as bigots and treated as such' by the government."[27] Alito concluded, "I see no basis for dismissing a juror for cause based on religious beliefs."[28]

The left does not agree. In fact, in a data-driven world, they don't have to limit their targets to those who speak out. Alito worried people would be coerced to "hide their adherence to traditional religious beliefs," but with access to so much data, the government doesn't need to wait for us to speak out. As we'll see in Chapter 6, technology tells them everything.

My good friend Senator Mike Lee (R-UT) warned nearly a decade ago that America's commitment to religious liberty was no longer universally shared. "The next controversies will not be over whether gay couples should receive marriage licenses," he said in a 2015 speech at the Kirby Center. Instead, he warned we would be debating whether those who don't think so would be able to keep their business licenses; whether colleges who support traditional marriage could keep their accreditation; whether military chaplains who don't toe the party line on these issues could be court-martialed; whether the state would target churches for retaliation. Indeed, he worried that "heterodox religious belief itself will be swept from the public square."[29]

Former supreme knight of the Knights of Columbus Carl Anderson worried where such a path might lead. "If belonging to a mainstream Catholic organization like the Knights of Columbus, or accepting the established teaching of the church is dangerous, then what teaching is safe?"[30]

Nothing is more coercive than the threat of being unable to work and support one's family. It's one thing to be passed over for a promotion or fired from a job. But in some cases, we're seeing efforts to permanently disqualify political opposition from working in their field at all.

Public Education Discrimination

A job posting for an art teacher in Denver Public Schools listed as a required qualification "an anti-racist mindset" and sought someone who "will work to dismantle systems of oppression and inequity in our community." That's just one example of many revealed in a 2023 report published by the National Opportunity Project.

The report found extensive evidence of bias in the public school system. In addition to the use of ideological qualifications in teacher job postings, the report found application and interview questions that screen for political and social ideology, the use of evaluation criteria to signal ideological fit, the setting of racial and ethnic diversity hiring goals, and identity quotas for hiring committees and interview panels.

The report's authors reached out to seventy-four different school districts spread across the country. Not all responded. Some provided redacted or incomplete records. Overall, the report found substantial evidence of bias in twenty-three districts that show favor given to progressive job candidates.

In one example, Georgia's City Schools of Decatur, a charter school district, interview teams use a writing prompt to assess candidates. One prompt reads, "An upset parent emails you regarding a classroom discussion with your students about Critical Race Theory. They accuse you (the teacher) of anti-Americanism, changing 'real history,' and of making White children feel marginalized and attacked. Please discuss your course of action and draft a response to this parent."[31]

In the case of Jessica Tapia, a Christian teacher in Southern California, her school district went so far as to fire her for alleged unprofessional conduct. The district claimed her social media posts expressed controversial opinions on gender identity. She was also guilty of referencing her faith in conversations with students and posting "offensive" content to her personal Instagram page. Tapia told district officials, hypothetically, that she would not agree to use preferred pronouns or allow biological males in women's locker rooms, though those situations did not arise during her employment. The district gave Tapia a directive to express opinions different from her own as a condition of employment. When she refused, she was terminated. In this case, as in so many others, Tapia successfully sued and received a settlement. But not everyone has the capacity to go so far in order to defend their deeply held beliefs.[32]

Similar strategies have helped purge academia of anyone who dissents from leftist orthodoxy. One-fifth of academic jobs require a diversity statement, according to a 2021 study by the American Enterprise Institute.[33] An example cited by Andrew Gillen looks at a life sciences faculty post at the University of California, Berkeley. Of the 893 nominally qualified candidates, 679 were eliminated "solely due to insufficiently woke diversity, equity and inclusion statements."[34]

Mathematics professor Abigail Thompson referred to these statements as "loyalty oaths" in a *Wall Street Journal* opinion piece. When Thompson published an essay questioning the use of these statements and calling them political litmus tests, she was subjected to intense public shaming.

She wrote, "Mathematicians were urged to steer their students away from studying at UC Davis, where I teach, and to contact the university to question my fitness as chair of the math department." A few colleagues emailed her privately to express support but admitted they couldn't speak out because "it is simply too dangerous at present." Thompson worried about the broader impact of such an academic environment. "If expressing a widespread but controversial view is seen as taking a tremendous personal risk, the university system isn't healthy," she wrote. "Ideas cannot thrive and mistakes cannot be corrected if people are afraid to speak out."[35]

Diversity statements are a tool. But they aren't nearly as effective as data. If hiring managers could access the kind of data the government can see, they wouldn't need diversity statements.

Even the awarding of taxpayer-funded scholarships has come

under scrutiny for left-wing bias. Between 2021 and 2023, only 6 of the 182 recipients of the prestigious Truman Scholarship were noted to have conservative viewpoints, none of whom acknowledged an interest in hot-button issues like abortion or gun rights.[36] Likewise, over five years and 157 awards, the Rhodes Scholarship was given to only one applicant expressing interest in a right-leaning issue. The American Enterprise Institute found that between the two scholarships, recipients expressing interest in progressive issues outnumber conservatives by a factor of 20 to 1.[37]

Of course, the left already dominates academia. What about institutions that are not?

Purging the Military

Though many American institutions lean left, neither the military nor law enforcement falls into that category. It's not practical to purge the conservatives or promote only the progressives. In these institutions, leftists tried a different approach. They failed. And their failure offers lessons we can apply more broadly.

This approach called for convincing the public that these institutions are riddled with violent extremists who hate Black people and other minorities. Under the guise of rooting out the so-called white supremacists, activists in and out of the administration can more easily purge the conservatives from their ranks.

Following January 6, the far-left site Slate called on the Biden-Harris administration to "purge military and law enforcement of white nationalists," alleging, without evidence, that both the military and state and local law enforcement have been "infiltrated" by white nationalists. They demanded "systemwide recognition of this crisis."[38]

On February 16, 2021, Bishop Garrison was appointed by Secretary of Defense Lloyd Austin to mitigate the threat of white supremacy in the military. The Pentagon subsequently created the Countering Extremism Working Group to address the alleged problem.[39]

Many worried that Garrison's real targets were not extremists, but conservatives and Trump supporters. Think about how dangerous it would be to have a politically homogeneous military.

Major Nidal Hasan and Sergeant Hasan Akbar committed the most recent violent terror attacks involving the military. But the Countering Extremism Working Group wasn't looking at Islamic extremism. At a Center for American Progress seminar, Garrison described the target of his purge. "This type of *ideology*"—catching himself—"excuse me, this type of *behavior* is not acceptable" (emphasis added). FrontPage Magazine opined, "Biden's hit man for the military had made it clear that he was out to purge ideology, not to change behavior. The military was going to eliminate political wrong-think."[40]

Not surprisingly, the people invited to advise the working group were devoid of any political balance.[41] They included left-wing activists from the ACLU, the SPLC, the Leadership Conference, the Brennan Center, and the Anti-Defamation League.[42] These are some of the same groups the Biden-Harris administration tapped to help with the Promoting Access to Voting executive order, which also pretended to be bipartisan. I hope readers are sensing a theme here.

Fortunately, criticism from the right—and specifically from reporting by Revolver News—appears to have neutralized Garrison's efforts. In 2023, Media Matters for America blamed conservative attacks against the effort for the outcome. They cited a right-wing "smear campaign" based on the reporting from Revolver News, commentary by Fox News host and military veteran Pete Hegseth,[43] and criticism from Steve Bannon's popular *War Room* podcast.[44] Media Matters bemoaned the "digital black plague" that exposed listeners to a contra-government counternarrative.[45]

Ultimately, the Countering Extremism Working Group was unsuccessful in its efforts to purge the military of wrongthink. After Garrison's effort was abandoned, the Biden-Harris administration had more success with a different strategy.

They fired members of the military who refused to take the

COVID-19 vaccine. It's hard to realize now, when certain side effects of the COVID-19 vaccine have been acknowledged, that distrust of the vaccine initially broke down along partisan lines. At the time, vaccine hesitancy was largely a phenomenon of the right.

Headlines bemoaned the problem, with the *New York Times* writing, "How Republican Vaccine Opposition Got to This Point," NPR reporting, "COVID Anti-Vaxxers Refuse Vaccines Despite Evidence," or this banger from the *Atlantic*: "How many Republicans died because the GOP turned against vaccines?"[46] A September 2021 Gallup study found 40 percent of Republicans said they didn't plan to get vaccinated, compared to just 3 percent of Democrats who didn't. An effort to fire the unvaccinated in 2021 would have disproportionately targeted the right.[47] Though that reality was not explicitly stated, it wasn't lost on the left. A few people were willing to say the quiet part out loud. For example, one Twitter user calling herself a "lifelong Dem" wrote, Well I guess the White Supremacy leaning military members will be choosing the Proud Boys, Boogaloo Boys, Q-Anon, & MAGA armies instead of getting vaxxed. The mandate is gonna be a good way of getting those folk out of our military.[48]

House Armed Services Committee chairman Mike Rogers demanded data on how many servicemen were affected by Biden's vaccine mandate. There were 69,000 troops who refused to take the mRNA shot. Of those, 37,000 sought a religious exemption according to data from Undersecretary of Defense for Personnel and Readiness Gilbert Cisneros. The military approved just 400 of those exemptions.

As of March 2023, more than 8,300 people had separated from the military for refusing to comply with the vaccine mandate, which Congress later rescinded as part of a defense authorization bill.[49] By October, only 43 had rejoined the military.[50]

"It's incredibly divisive and cruel to fire patriotic service members for refusing to comply with a partisan and harmful rule that no longer exists," said Armed Services Committee member Representative Jim Banks (R-IN). "To me, the only explanation is that the Biden administration wants to purge conservative service members from the military."[51]

Not just the military. Having the federal workforce function as an arm of the Democratic Party has been extremely useful, particularly given the access of federal agencies to data and surveillance tools. As we saw in Chapter 1, partisan leadership was key to the party's get-out-the-vote strategy for the 2024 elections. We know it was also key to pushing back against the Trump agenda during his presidency, as the party managed to weaponize surveillance tools, intelligence psyops, and classification procedures.

Would it be better to limit the ability of presidents to purge the federal workforce of political opposition? Not necessarily. In this case, there is a different solution—and it is counterintuitive. Let me explain.

The Future of the Federal Workforce

The Kamala Harris presidential campaign accused President Trump of plotting to mass-fire federal employees and replace them with "Trump loyalists."[52] The *Washington Post* framed it as an attack on the civil service.[53] In truth, what Democrats likely feared was a weakening of their own partisan grip on the federal workforce. With the upper ranks already tilted toward Democratic loyalists, their warnings came across as a projection of their own playbook: leveraging federal agencies to target political foes, intertwining public institutions with partisan agendas. The federal workforce became a battlefield they shaped.

Trump's first term exposed this dynamic. Career civil servants resisted his policies—slow walking orders, leaking information, and sabotaging his agenda. One insider, Miles Taylor, a former DHS chief of staff, bragged about it in a 2018 *New York Times* editorial. "Many of the senior officials in his own administration are working diligently from within to frustrate parts of his agenda and his worst inclinations. I would know. I am one of them."[54]

Former Trump adviser James Sherk saw it firsthand: the DOJ Civil Rights Division refused to pursue conservative cases, like protecting nurses coerced into performing abortions or suing Yale for anti-Asian discrimination.[55] Sherk observed, "At the White House I received frequent reports about career staff undermining presidential policies. Career employees routinely delayed producing new rules or produced drafts that couldn't be used. As a result, many major regulations—such as the Education Department's Title IX due-process protections—had to be drafted primarily by political appointees."[56]

Trump's initial response came too late. On October 21, 2020, he issued an executive order creating "Schedule F," reclassifying thousands of federal employees in "confidential, policy-determining, policy-making or policy-advocating" roles as at-will workers, stripping the civil service protections that make them so difficult to fire.[57] The goal: enable a president to fire bureaucrats who obstruct his agenda. Issued near his term's end, it never took effect—Biden rescinded it in 2021.

Democrats recoiled, seeing internal resistance as a duty, not a flaw. Biden's Office of Personnel Management then entrenched their advantage with a 2023 rule, reinforcing firing restrictions and adding vague "minimum standards of fitness" based on "character and conduct."[58] Critics, like the Federalist, called it a move to "entrench the Deep State forever."[59] House Oversight chairman James Comer, whose committee oversees the federal workforce, warned the rule insulated the federal workforce from accountability. "The Biden administration's rule will further undermine Americans' confidence in their government since it allows poor-performing federal workers and those who attempt to thwart the policies of a duly elected president to remain entrenched in the federal bureaucracy," Comer said.[60]

Reversing this rule could take years—a delay Trump can hardly afford. Starting January 20, 2025, he has acted decisively to prevent sabotage by rebalancing the workforce. In addition to reviving

Schedule F, he has frozen hiring, offered buyouts, ended remote work, and scrapped DEI programs he views as tools of the left.

Trump's strategy—expanding at-will employees—rejects the covert purges he attributes to Obama and Biden, opting instead for transparency. The workforce should serve the president, not a party. But the roots of this fight run deeper. The federal government's size and scope invite politicization. Democrats weaponized it; Trump is now countering in kind. We need a fix that can address the core issue: a bureaucracy too vast to stay neutral.

The ultimate solution isn't rebalancing—it's shrinking. The Constitution limits federal power, delegating most to states. States answer to voters faster and reform easier. Abolishing agencies like the Department of Education or downsizing the EPA doesn't end those functions—it shifts them to states. Blue states might stay progressive; red states could test alternatives, letting results speak. Smaller government is better government.

Without this shift, the federal workforce will remain a partisan weapon. Conservatives face purges, dual justice standards, and exclusion from industries tied to federal favor. It wasn't meant to be political, but politicians can't resist its power. Trump's reforms are a stopgap; Congress must act to restore accountability and shrink the administrative state—or the cycle continues.

CHAPTER 5

The Need to Win

The text messages are relentless, urgent, and sometimes more than a little passive-aggressive. "This is your FINAL NOTICE!" "We didn't receive your donation!" "We're losing!" You donate to one political campaign, and before you know it, you're getting twenty to thirty text messages a day from dozens of candidates and your political party. You can reply "STOP" to ensure that phone number never messages you again. But it seems each campaign has hundreds of different phone numbers. I've been warned that responding confirms that they have reached a valid number. It can be a frustrating experience.

Lists of previous donors are worth their weight in gold in the campaign world. Targeted data on voters is big business. Both major political parties now use online campaign donation platforms to generate data from which candidates can fundraise, with Democrats using ActBlue and Republicans WinRed. Data brokers collect vast amounts of information to help candidates microtarget specific groups of voters.

What if one party could gain an advantage by accessing data no one else had? Government agencies have access to data that political parties—and Democrats in particular—covet. For example, Democrat candidates have a 30-point average in support among welfare recipients, according to the Opportunity Solutions Project, the advocacy arm of the Foundation for Government Accountability. "[D]emocrats see a massive advantage among voters enrolled in welfare programs like food stamps and Medicaid," the study concluded. "In fact, Democrats see their margins increase by more than 30 points among voters enrolled in welfare compared to low-income voters who have never been on welfare."[1]

Imagine the value of such data to the Kamala Harris campaign in 2024. Other candidates can't buy that data. Under the Hatch Act, federal employees can't engage in political campaigning in their official duties. They can't just hand data over to a campaign.

But Democrats found a way to leverage that data anyway. It involved a complex plan conjured up by outside political operatives and filtered to the Biden-Harris administration. We know it as Executive Order 14019—Promoting Access to Voting. As we learned in Chapter 1, the act calls for every federal agency to engage in voter registration, and to coordinate with NGOs not bound by laws like the Hatch Act. These partnerships helped them do what they couldn't legally do alone.

Throughout the 2022 and 2024 cycles, these partnerships enabled Democratic candidates to reach voters their opponents couldn't touch. Through this combination of left-aligned agencies, NGOs, state governments, and corporations, Democrats developed the ability to game the system using federal resources. Miraculously, it wasn't enough.

Invisible Interference

In March 2022, the Small Business Administration (SBA) made an unusual hiring decision. Jennifer Kim was a former Biden campaign staffer who was hired to the lofty role of associate administrator of the Office of Field Operations at the SBA. Though she had at one point worked briefly for a small business, almost her entire résumé consisted of government and nonprofit work. She had no real business background.

That's not to say she didn't have impressive qualifications. She did. Her specialty was voter registration in communities of color and youth civic engagement—and not for Republicans, obviously.

Coincidentally, Kim had attended college in the battleground state of Michigan. She wasn't the kind of person you hire to help people start and run businesses or to manage business outreach. She was the kind of person you hire when you're trying to get out the vote in a swing state.[2]

Like every other federal agency, the SBA had to find ways to engage in voter registration to comply with President Joe Biden's Executive Order 14019. With the administration refusing to release plans submitted by each agency, there was no way to prove whether the process would be fair ahead of the election, or whether manipulation would favor the president's party in November 2024.

We might have expected the SBA to be grappling with the aftermath of devastating lockdowns and rampant fraud of government COVID aid. Still, the agency's efforts in 2024 were apparently laser-focused on getting targeted groups to vote. For that role, Kim was unquestionably qualified.

Kim came to Capitol Hill four months before the 2024 election to answer questions from lawmakers on the House Small Business Committee about her agency's work, particularly in Michigan, where SBA was doing extensive outreach.[3]

Representative Lisa McClain (R-MI) knows a thing or two about Michigan. Before she was elected to represent the state's northern rural counties in the thumb of Michigan and Detroit's northern suburbs, she spent thirty years building a financial services business. As a member of the House Small Business Committee, McClain had questions about the SBA's preelection outreach in her state.

McClain produced a map during the July 2024 hearing in which Kim testified. It showed the familiar mitten of Michigan, marked to indicate all the places SBA had run programs under the pretext of helping small businesses (but also to register voters). Coincidentally, McClain noted that the SBA programs appeared to be concentrated in the south and east—deep blue communities like Detroit and Flint that typically vote for Democrats. These are

places one could expect voter registration efforts to yield disproportionately high numbers of Democratic voters.

"How many events have you run to open small businesses in
non-Democratic areas?" McClain asked Kim during the hearing.
Instead of answering the question, Kim assured the committee that
politics plays no role in the agency's outreach decisions. The implementation of the executive order is nonpartisan, she claimed.

"Does *this* look nonpartisan to you?" McClain lashed out,
pointing at the map. It didn't. But Kim suggested without evidence
that some events could be missing from the map.[4]

The findings of the House Small Business Committee investigation revealed that 22 out of 25 SBA outreach events from January
to April 2024 took place in counties with the "highest population
of Democratic National Committee (DNC) target demographics."[5]

Likewise, SBA administrator Isabel Guzman's official travel
appeared to be politically advantageous during an election cycle.
Formerly SBA's deputy chief of staff during the Obama administration, Guzman was appointed by President Biden in 2021.[6] According
to Protect the Public Trust, she attended numerous meetings on
"equity" during her first year on the job. This information led the
group's director, Michael Chamberlain, to ask, "Are all small businesses being treated equally or are some small businesses being
treated more equally than others?"[7]

The committee was able to document that Guzman, who travels
at her discretion, had chosen to go almost exclusively to swing state
areas with high concentrations of likely Democratic voters.[8] In June
2024, when Biden was still campaigning for president, "a video recording of an SBA Special Advisor alleged that SBA Administrator
Guzman" was indirectly campaigning for him, as well as for other
Democrats running for Congress, on one of her trips around the
country.[9]

The committee found Guzman had traveled to Michigan more
than any other state.[10] These patterns raise important questions.

How many other federal agencies were following a similar

pattern? In their zeal to carry out the president's directive, were agencies compromising their true mission? To what degree were government services disproportionately targeted to constituents who support the party in power? Is the government using the data they collect to influence elections?

Never before has the federal government known so much about us as they do today. In addition to the data they collect, the capabilities of artificial intelligence and machine learning can absorb a nearly unlimited supply of information. These technologies have many lifesaving and time-saving applications. But even as technology changes, human nature does not.

A party in power will seek to perpetuate its power. Nothing is more important than the need to win. That's a reality no matter which party or political system we use. We must have firm boundaries to govern federal engagement in elections and ensure consistent application of the laws.

That is not what's happening. We have a federal government inserting itself into elections in which it should have no role. We have federal agencies prioritizing politically targeted voter mobilization over the provision of public services. We have government colluding with partisan nonprofits and woke corporations to influence election outcomes.

The whole point of having a professional bureaucracy was to avoid politicizing the federal workforce. They should not have any role in state and local elections. But the Obama administration, on its way out the door, made a tiny change that would have a big impact on the next election.

Federalizing Local Elections

How much easier would it be to manipulate elections if you only had to influence one process? But as I've written before, elections in America are hard to rig. There are so many jurisdictions with different rules, deadlines, procedures, and election administrators that broad manipulation is almost impossible.

The federal government and the politicians who run it have long sought to inject themselves into election administration. From providing grants with strings attached to regulating campaign contributions to using provisions of the Voting Rights Act to control state elections, federal politicians have tried to chip away at state control.

In the waning days of the Obama administration, it embraced a new and dangerous strategy. In 2017, Obama DHS secretary Jeh Johnson declared elections "critical infrastructure." In the interest of national security, the Deep State needed more access to election processes.[11]

This was not an act of Congress. It required no presidential action. A cabinet secretary waved a magic wand and the federal government was in. Not just the federal government. The Blob. That's the name used by former Obama deputy national security advisor Ben Rhodes to describe the American foreign policy establishment.[12] These are the people who rotate between government jobs, think tanks, and policy groups. We mostly find them in the intelligence community of the State Department, the CIA, the NSA, and the Pentagon. The Blob has more access to our data than perhaps anyone in the world. And now they have jurisdiction over parts of our local elections.

The designation of elections as critical infrastructure was sold as a way to protect election systems against hypothetical cybersecurity attacks, of which there was no evidence at the time.[13] Johnson called the move "vital to our national interests," and "simply the right and obvious thing to do."[14] In retrospect, it appears the change was ultimately more vital to their partisan interests than to our national interests.

The real impact (and by some accounts, the real purpose) of the designation was the enabling of election manipulation by way of surveillance and censorship. Making elections a national security issue would profoundly restrict free speech during the 2020 election.

Moreover, it would remove a degree of transparency from the process. The Associated Press reported at the time, "The designation allows for information to be withheld from the public when state, local, and private partners meet to discuss election infrastructure security—potentially injecting secrecy into an election process that's traditionally and expressly a transparent process."[15]

States resented the intrusion. Georgia's then–secretary of state Brian Kemp warned Congress against trying to standardize security measures. He testified that federalizing voting systems might make them even more vulnerable and protected records more accessible.[16]

Even with Johnson's critical-infrastructure designation, federal agencies are still not authorized to do voter registration. Biden's executive order carefully acknowledged as much. After directing agencies to do a long list of things typically done by the states, the order acknowledged agencies can only do many of these things "if requested by a State to be designated as a voter registration agency," in accordance with the National Voter Registration Act.[17]

Agencies seem to have found ways around that restriction. The Department of Labor, for example, sought to designate its American Job Centers as voter registration entities. They didn't wait for invitations, as the law requires. FOIA requests received by the Oversight Project revealed that the department was making the first contact with numerous states—particularly swing states.

They proactively emailed each state asking how many of their American Job Centers were designated voter registration agencies—a not-so-subtle hint that they wanted invitations to create more. The Oversight Project fought for the documentation of those emails from the DOL. They found requests to swing states like Arizona, Colorado, and Georgia as well as many reliably blue states where they could expect to register more Democrat voters: Illinois, Hawaii, Delaware, and more.[18]

Just how much were federal agencies doing ahead of the 2024 election? How targeted were their voter outreach efforts? And how might they have influenced the outcome of the election? How much time and energy is the SBA diverting to help keep Democrats in the White House?

Representative Beth Van Duyne (R-TX), in a July hearing, expressed alarm. Van Duyne chairs the Subcommittee on Oversight. "We have heard from the Administrator herself that the SBA does not have the resources to do what they are statutorily mandated to do, let alone engage in electioneering," she said.[19] In an interview with Newsmax, Small Business Committee chairman Roger Williams (R-TX) asked the million-dollar question: "If the SBA is doing this . . . what are the other agencies doing?"[20]

All Hands on Deck

The answers to those questions will likely be revealed slowly, as the government loses the legal battle to keep documents hidden. But initial responses to the Oversight Project's FOIA requests set off alarms, just within the few agencies who quickly complied with the law. We have to consider that the worst offenders are likely to be the agencies who fought hardest to withhold their records.

Let's look at a few examples of how agencies sought to register new voters and see if we can identify the partisan lean of the targeted demographic.

The Department of Education's Secretary Miguel Cardona announced on July 31, 2024, that they would be sending an (unsolicited) email to all student loan borrowers just five months before the general election.[21] To ensure everyone saw it, the agency made a video to disseminate on social media asking borrowers to check their spam folders if they missed Cardona's email. The subject line of Cardona's message: "Biden-Harris Administration Takes Next Step Toward Additional Debt Relief for Tens of Millions of Student Loan Borrowers This Fall."[22]

The Supreme Court found the promised debt relief to be unconstitutional just the month before.[23] But that didn't stop Cardona from misleading borrowers by implying they could get their loans paid off if Democrats stayed in power. Given that YouGov found Democrats are 10 percent more likely to take out student loans and 7 percent less likely to have paid them off, this messaging would almost certainly provide a partisan advantage.[24]

The Department of Housing and Urban Development, to target government dependents, sought to turn its 3,000-plus public housing agencies into voter registration agencies—a complete reversal of the agency's position since 1996. HUD had long argued that the 1996 guidance barred the agency from participating in such activities. The Biden-Harris administration claimed that 1996 guidance still applies, but it didn't mean what everybody thought it meant.[25]

HUD housing agencies manage 1.2 million housing units. Like the Labor Department, HUD initiated the effort with states by sending an unsolicited letter to local housing agencies. "If the laws of your state allow," one letter reads, the local housing agency may consider "accepting completed voter registration application forms and transmitting these forms to the appropriate state election official."[26] The letter further suggested that housing agencies seek permission to permit the use of voter dropboxes on the premises.

The US Marshals Service modified more than nine hundred contracts with jails and prisons to accommodate mail-in voting for inmates.[27] Time will tell how that effort was targeted to specific states and subgroups, but given the overrepresentation of traditional Democratic voting blocks in prison populations, it's fair to assume such efforts benefit the Democratic Party. Some 67 percent of families with an incarcerated member received food stamps.[28]

Black people represent just 14 percent of the US population, but 33 percent of the total prison population and 46 percent of those who have served at least ten years.[29]

Politically, just 18 percent of Black men voted for Donald Trump in 2020.[30] A plurality of white inmates, about 45 percent, say they would support Donald Trump if they could vote.[31] Before November 2024, we would expect a concerted effort to register inmates to help Democrats. Of course, Trump surprised Democrats in 2024, winning 21 percent of Black men, doubling his support with Black men under age forty-five.[32] However, I think it's safe to say Democrats did not see that coming until late in 2024.

The Office of Personnel Management was key to getting out the federal employee vote—a traditionally lopsided constituency of left-wing voters. In 2016, 95 percent of federal employee donations went to Hillary Clinton.[33] Among the rank and file, about half of the federal workforce identify as Democrats.[34] In the upper echelons of the government, one study found 63 percent of senior executives are Democrats.[35] Typically, federal employee unions donate overwhelmingly to Democrats.[36] OPM's voter registration efforts included offering federal employees paid time off to vote and to serve as poll workers.

The Department of the Interior targeted the Native American vote, particularly in the swing state of Arizona. In both the 2016 and 2020 presidential races, these voters overwhelmingly supported the Democratic ticket and were expected to be a crucial voting block for the Biden and subsequent Harris-Walz campaigns in 2024.[37]

Though Interior redacted its plan to comply with Biden's executive order, there is evidence of a coordinated effort with leftist NGOs. Emails from Demos senior policy analyst Laura Williamson dating back to 2021 show Demos was hosting Zoom calls and coordinating voter registration with Indian Health Services. The coordination must have been by invitation only, because Interior never released criteria for "nonpartisan" organizations to participate.[38]

At one point the agency had apparently developed a robust plan to use Native American schoolchildren to drive voter registration. After the Daily Caller exposed the plan, a DOI spokesperson claimed "there was no program to distribute voter registration materials to children attending BIE [Bureau of Indian Education] schools." But emails obtained by Protect the Public Trust from 2022 had revealed a detailed plan to engage kids "so that school children could bring home voter registration applications to their parents/guardians."[39]

Was Interior deliberately targeting voter registration to specific precincts? It sure looks that way. They kept a spreadsheet of voting precincts with columns tracking presidential election vote totals and percentages in 2016 and 2020. Why is this information relevant to a federal voter registration drive?[40]

Other documents released in response to FOIA requests show Interior Department ethics attorneys warning Secretary Deb Haaland that plans to include get-out-the-vote language in her speeches and official remarks might run afoul of the Hatch Act. Specifically, inclusion of such language "should not be targeted to specific demographics or other groups."[41]

Nine states' attorneys general filed a lawsuit to block Biden's order, arguing that it did not go through the proper procedure.[42] It should have required notice, public comment, and transparency. Instead it was drafted by a special interest group more interested in power than governing.[43]

A Democrat Version of Project 2025

Project 2025 was the bogeyman of the presidential election. There appeared to be a coordinated messaging strategy to scare voters away from supporting Republicans.[44] President Biden told voters it should "scare every single American."[45] Representative Ayanna Pressley (D-MA) called it a "far-right manifesto of extremist policies" that would "destroy the federal government as we know it."[46]

In reality, it was simply a policy plan put together every four years by the Heritage Foundation, a conservative think tank with which I am associated. Heritage drafts its plans independently to help a new administration hit the ground running. But Democrats apparently looked in the mirror and decided to apply what they saw there to their opponents.

Following Biden's career-ending June debate performance, Democrats waged a rhetorical war on Project 2025. Heritage found that MSNBC alone had mentioned it 1,500 times through August, fabricating a claim that it called for cutting Social Security and falsely asserting that Donald Trump had created it.[47]

In reality, Democrats were projecting. Biden's voter registration executive order was exactly what they were accusing Project 2025 of being: a set of policies originating from a partisan think tank that the opposition would not like. But in Biden's case, he used the whole template.

Demos, among whose founders was then-senator Barack Obama, had created its own Project 2025–style policy document, which Biden and Harris dutifully enacted. Executive Order 14019 is "nearly identical to a federal election takeover plan crafted by the radical left-leaning group known as Demos," wrote House Republicans in a document request to the Office of Management and Budget.[48]

The Demos report, ironically named "Strengthening Democracy," outlined Biden's plan to transform the whole federal workforce into a get-out-the-vote effort to target specific populations. The report couches those groups in terms of "historically marginalized" groups without explicitly noting that they are also conveniently historically Democratic voters.[49]

Demos wasn't the first NGO to manipulate voter registration to influence elections. Democrats had benefited greatly in 2020 from the infusion of dollars into state and local elections from Facebook founder Mark Zuckerberg and his wife, Priscilla Chan. The funds, often referred to as "Zuckerbucks" (aka "Zuck bucks"), placed activists in local election offices, where they engaged in large-scale get-out-the-vote initiatives later found to be strategically targeted to register Democrats. The allegedly nonpartisan grants were consistently larger in counties that voted for Joe Biden.[50]

Using the same playbook of registering Americans to vote, the report called for the government to mobilize federal agencies partnered with leftist nonprofits to leverage government data and resources in targeting historically Democratic voting blocs for voter registration and ballot harvesting. Sound familiar?

The Clinician Army

In the swing state of Pennsylvania, a former adviser to Kamala Harris came up with a novel way to help Democrats access voters whose data is off-limits to campaigns. Dr. Alister Martin brings politics into the exam room, registering patients to vote. No get-out-the-vote organization can get to those records. But Martin can. So can the 50,000 physicians and 700 hospitals he enlisted in the cause.[51]

He started by registering his patients. To a woman recovering from an asthma attack, Martin prescribed voting, since that was the "only way" to "take the smog out of the air." Now participating doctors wear badges with a QR code that patients can use to register on the spot.[52]

But does Martin follow the same template as Demos, Zuckerbucks, and Executive Order 14019? Like those initiatives, Vot-ER claims its voter registration work is nonpartisan. But in his role as an adviser to Harris, Martin served on an HHS advisory panel focused on outreach to "vulnerable and underserved patient communities." That seems to be code for "people likely to vote Democrat."

An investigation by the *Washington Examiner* found Martin's Vot-ER charity is funded by top Democratic dark-money groups and staffed by left-wing activists. It receives funding from the Tides Foundation, which is itself a recipient of funds from George Soros's Open Society Foundations, the Bill & Melinda Gates Foundation, and the Ford Foundation, among others.[53]

Incidentally, Vot-ER staffers were among those represented in the Biden-Harris administration's Listening Session to plan the rollout of Biden's voter registration order. In fact, the organization registered as a charity just one month before Biden issued his order.

"The time for us being impartial and apolitical and standing on the sideline is over," Martin told the *New York Times* in 2020.[54] Vot-ER appears to target underserved populations, low-income Medicaid and Medicare recipients, and other historically left-leaning demographics.

In swing state Pennsylvania, Vot-ER registers psychiatric patients who cannot complete "the activities of daily living," some of whom are considered a danger to themselves and others, and some of whom are there involuntarily. "No psychiatric diagnoses were excluded" from a voter registration drive at Pennsylvania Psychiatric Institute in 2020, where the Washington Free Beacon found nearly a fifth of the hospital's patients were involuntarily committed and one in four had psychotic disorders.[55]

Such targeted voter registration raises uncomfortable questions about the ability of patients to consent, or to resist political pressure from an ideological doctor in a state with no competency requirements for voters in a mental health crisis. Some critics worry that patients may fear their involuntary stay could be extended if they demonstrate noncompliance, so they succumb to pressure from their doctor.

Vot-ER doctors register patients in cancer hospitals, substance abuse clinics, and palliative care facilities.

Facilities wanting to offer Vot-ER tools must apply for resources, answering questions about whether most of their patients are twenty-four and younger, Black/African American, or LGBTQIA+, according to reporting from the Free Beacon.[56]

In the short time since its formation, Vot-ER has reportedly aligned with federal agencies, medical schools, and professional associations like the American Medical Association. The Free Beacon points out these ties connect to "nearly every layer" of America's public health bureaucracy. Using EPIC Systems health record software, doctors can record a patient's voting status right on their medical chart.

The group has been known to mobilize support for partisan efforts. In 2021, the Democratic lieutenant governor of Kansas recognized Vot-ER for their role in killing a state referendum on abortion. They sent out 65,000 text messages to patients in the state.

Voter registration is objectively a good thing. Anyone who is eligible and wants to cast a vote should be able to do so. But the registration process has become corrupted. Even things that are objectively good can be weaponized for political gain. And that creates a cost for all of us.

The Future of Elections

The failure of the Biden-Harris administration to hold the White House in 2024, despite the unprecedented deployment of technology and bureaucracy on behalf of Democrats, is miraculous. What might the results have looked like without the help of federal agencies and their partner nonprofits who sought out Democrat voters? Why didn't it work? And what will they do next time to avoid the catastrophic failure of 2024?

The election changes many things, not the least of which is Biden's ill-conceived executive order. But the fact remains, our data is still out there. It can be bought and sold. There will be an all-out effort to figure out how each of us voted. The woke corporations, leftist bureaucrats, and progressive nonprofits will still have the power to share our data. Given the opportunity, we've seen they would see political opponents doxed, debanked, excluded from job opportunities, retaliated against, and disenfranchised. How much do they actually know about us?

CHAPTER 6

What the Government Knows

I was watching a device sweep across the surface of a swimming pool in a suburban Utah backyard. I had been invited to speak to a group from the Utah Federation of Republican Women. Following the outdoor meeting, I noticed the device, untethered from a vacuum, racing around the bottom and then the surface of the pool. I have a swimming pool myself, so I stopped to observe how it worked. I stood for a few minutes watching. And then I left. I don't recall speaking to anyone about it.

But the next day, advertisers were speaking to me. Every time I pulled up my social media, I saw ads for that device. It was like the company somehow knew I had been standing next to a pool while that device was in motion. I racked my brain to remember if I'd commented on it to someone.

Who among us has not had a similar experience? After a phone conversation, pillow talk with a spouse, or a text thread mentioning a product, that product suddenly becomes ubiquitous on a feed where it had never appeared before.

You begin to question. Just how much do advertisers know about me? Does my phone listen to my conversations? Are they recorded anywhere? What about my phone's camera? Can it be remotely accessed? Who has that data and what do they do with it?

The questions sent me down a disturbing rabbit hole that culminated in me writing this book. It turns out that my phone does have the capability to listen to my conversations, but no one admits doing it. I use an iPhone. Apple has consistently held that users must activate the microphones by using he words "Hey, Siri!"

But in January 2025, Apple settled a class-action lawsuit over whether Siri violates the privacy of users. Under the terms of the settlement, Apple admits no wrongdoing but pays $95 million. The users reportedly activated Siri unintentionally, after which they claim Apple disclosed those conversations to third parties. Apple maintains that data recorded through Siri has never been used to compile marketing profiles or sold to third parties. But the lawsuit alleged ads for Air Jordan sneakers and Olive Garden restaurants came up immediately after users mentioned them in conversation.[1]

In September 2024, a leaked pitch deck from a marketing team at Cox Media Group (CMG) exposed a technology the industry refers to as "active listening." CMG is a marketing partner of Facebook, Amazon, and Google.[2] The presentation, presumably targeted to advertisers, referred to the ability to use embedded microphones in our phones to gather data to serve targeted ads.

The leak does not definitively prove that CMG or any of their partners have deployed the technology. Meta claims explicitly on its website that Instagram is not listening to private conversations.[3] The leaked information has since been deleted, but phones that eavesdrop are just the beginning.[4] The American people deserve to know if their phones are listening to their private conservations, whether any of that information is recorded and stored, and how it is used. Congress could certainly dig into the question, using oversight authority to issue subpoenas for documents, depositions, or public testimony. And they should.

For the first time in human history, it is possible to know what people think, say, and spend their money on. By buying data in the free market, government can conceivably track who we talk to, where we go, what we read, and whether we have complied with behavior mandates. Our technology enables the use of programmable currency that can be used to punish people who step out of line, as is done in China. The danger is real. Thus far we have not had strong enough leadership or regulatory frameworks to restrain what this technology can ultimately become.

Leading the AI Revolution

At the 2023 World Economic Forum in Davos, Switzerland, Klaus Schwab, who considers himself and the other attendees "trustees of the future," made a prediction. Humanity was transitioning into a new age, a fourth industrial age—what he called the Intelligent Age. "Our life in ten years from now will be completely different," he said, adding, "who masters those technologies, in some way, will be the masters of the world."[5]

Who should lead the United States government into this new Intelligent Age? Maybe someone who can fix their own WiFi router wouldn't be too much to ask, tweeted Elon Musk after President Joe Biden appointed Vice President Kamala Harris to be the AI czar in 2023. Fox News asked DeepAI founder Kevin Baragona if he had confidence in the government to deal with the emerging opportunities and threats posed by the technology. He responded, "Well, they put Kamala Harris in charge, so not really."[6]

It was a political choice signaling a political orientation to the problem. New technologies that can analyze vast amounts of information could inhibit fraud, develop new treatments and solutions, and change the world. But from a political point of view, AI could also be weaponized to surveil the world, manipulate information, and secure tyrannical power.

Meanwhile, Congress has been all talk and little action, as designed. The legislative process moves too slowly to keep up and the people we elect rarely have the expertise to do a deep dive into the policy implications of cutting-edge developments. In my personal experience, most House members don't even know what a domain name server (DNS) redirect is. Thus far, the Trump administration's embrace of the technology to root out waste, fraud, and abuse is promising. But the regulatory work to set boundaries and restrain government is yet to be done.

Several lawmakers have been proactive and motivated to introduce new legislation. Thus far they've been unsuccessful in meeting the high bar for consensus required to pass legislation.

That has left courts and regulators to design and interpret the boundaries of what the government can do based on a reading of outdated laws and the demands of unaccountable agencies. Let's look at what the government has in mind for deploying advances in AI and machine-learning technologies that can process and analyze vast amounts of data.

The Cutting Edge of Government

Some in the government want to see every stock trade. No detail is too small. They want to track every buyer, every seller, every bid, and every offer, whether a trade is executed or not.[7] Where will they get the data? They plan to compel the people they regulate to supply it to them (and cover the multibillion-dollar cost).

Whether the trade is a 401(k), or a 529 Education Fund, the Securities and Exchange Commission (SEC) wants to know about it—no warrants needed, of course. It's for solving crimes! Meanwhile, some three thousand federal bureaucrats from twenty-three different agencies will have access to the data.[8] What could go wrong?

It's all part of an Obama-era plan called the Consolidated Audit Trail (CAT). The program has no explicit congressional authority to collect detailed financial information on individual transactions. Obama got away with creating it because the SEC can pass the multibillion-dollar cost on to the markets through fees it collects. Without congressional appropriations, the CAT will have few restraints and minimal oversight. The New York Stock Exchange and the Nasdaq will cover the cost of this warrantless surveillance program without any interference from those who answer to the voters.

Designed to be the largest database ever assembled, it represents a new frontier in warrantless surveillance. SEC chairman Gary Gensler sold it as a way to provide additional data to regulators, potentially helping identify abusive naked short selling—a market manipulation that hurts retail investors. Fair enough.

But the program's constitutionality is an open question—one that is now being challenged in a Texas court by the New Civil Liberties Alliance.[9] They refer to it in court documents as "the greatest government mandated mass collection of personal financial data in United States history" and a violation of the Fourth Amendment.[10]

Former Trump administration attorney general William Barr has raised serious concerns, writing in the *Wall Street Journal* that the sweeping surveillance program eviscerates fundamental privacy protections.[11] "Concentrating this sensitive data in a single repository guarantees it inevitably will be hacked, stolen, or misused by bad actors, including hostile nations, cybercriminals, and faithless government employees."[12]

Barr warned that political weaponization would result. "This invites abusive investigatory fishing expeditions, targeting of individuals, and intrusive data mining," he wrote. Anytime we look at a new tools like this one, we have to ask ourselves, what would a tyrant do with this?

In an amicus brief in the Texas suit, Advancing American Freedom argued that the successful deployment of the CAT database would open the floodgates to more intrusive surveillance. General Counsel Marc Wheat, speaking of cases that challenge the legality of that database, warned that regulatory agencies are circling "like jackals." They are watching to see if the courts will allow them to tear away powers the Constitution reserves only to Congress or people in the US. "If the courts side with the SEC," he wrote, "it will signal to every other administrative agency that the Constitution can be circumvented and the association and privacy rights of people can be violated with a little creativity."[13]

The CAT database is just one example of how our federal government is pursuing the opportunities before us. They want access to data. But they don't want to be bothered by the constitutional safeguards that provide oversight and transparency.

Circumventing Privacy by Design

Joe Biden ensured that the next president would have expanded authority to spy on the calls, text messages, and emails of American citizens when he signed legislation extending Section 702 of the Foreign Intelligence Surveillance Act in April 2024.[14] It is not supposed to work that way. Section 702 is an important national security tool that enables the government to conduct targeted surveillance outside the United States. Congress has enacted a legal framework that protects American citizens, which is why President Trump reauthorized it in 2018.[15] But when the next reauthorization came before President Biden in 2024, Trump felt differently.

In a social media post during the Congressional debate over FISA, Trump posted to his Truth Social account, KILL FISA, IT WAS ILLEGALLY USED AGAINST ME, AND MANY OTHERS. THEY SPIED ON MY CAMPAIGN!!![16] Biden was undeterred.

Biden's decision to renew Section 702 came on the heels of damaging revelations from Senator Ron Wyden (D-OR) exposing a National Security Agency (NSA) program to buy up personal data on Americans from private-sector data brokers. According to documents released by Wyden, the NSA is purchasing location data, private search records, and browsing histories—all without a warrant.[17]

This is the same NSA that operates a massive, one-million-square-foot data center smack in the middle of the district I represented in Congress. In fact, that data center was built during my tenure. Though I can't talk about anything I learned in classified briefings on the project, I can say that I was never led to believe the NSA planned to track Americans on this level.

In correspondence with Wyden, Defense Department officials argued there is no Fourth Amendment privacy protection when the government purchases data from commercially available sources.[18] Courts may see it differently. The better solution is for Congress to pass a law governing data collection.

It was more than a decade ago that Americans learned for the first time the scope of the federal government's surveillance programs. Before AI, before machine learning, and before Donald Trump broke so many DC insiders, our intelligence apparatus was already accessing our phone records, mostly to solve crimes. That's a good reason, provided there is a high degree of transparency and oversight. But there were no guardrails.

The government preferred it that way. Then came Edward Snowden. The government contractor who had access to classified information created a political firestorm after he leaked documents to the *Guardian*'s Glenn Greenwald in 2013. For the first time, Americans learned that the government had agreements with major phone and internet providers to enable access to trillions of phone records going back years.

Snowden exposed the NSA for collecting domestic email and phone metadata through Verizon. He exposed the NSA's top secret Prism program, which had direct access to data systems at Google, Facebook, Apple, and other companies. The classified document leak indicated that officials were able to collect data on search histories, email content, file transfers, and even live chats.[19]

That same year, the *New York Times* exposed a collaboration between AT&T and federal drug agencies dating back to 2007. The Hemisphere Project gave the government access to AT&T call record data through AT&T employees embedded with government drug units.[20]

Later that year, the *Washington Post* revealed the NSA was harvesting contact lists from personal email accounts and even from instant-messaging apps. NSA used it to map connections between suspects. The *Post* story exposed a high volume of requests each day, showing one day in 2012 in which they collected 444,743 email address books from Yahoo, 105,068 from Hotmail, 82,857 from Facebook, 33,697 from Gmail, and 22,881 from other unnamed providers. All of that hit more than a decade ago.[21]

Ten years later, in 2023, Senator Wyden sent a letter to Attorney General Merrick Garland requesting permission to release more details about Hemisphere. Wyden had documents he said had been designated "law enforcement sensitive" to restrict public release. "The materials provided by the DOJ contain troubling information that would justifiably outrage many Americans and other members of Congress," he wrote.

Wyden expressed alarm at the opaque funding mechanism for Hemisphere. The project was ostensibly discontinued by President Obama in 2013 after it was exposed to the public. But according to Wyden, the funding continued to flow to a new, more generic-sounding name—"Data Analytical Services." The federal funds flow to AT&T through what Wyden described as an "obscure grant program" that enables it to bypass an otherwise mandatory federal privacy review that would make its findings public.

Instead, Hemisphere money—$6 million as of late 2023—flows from the White House National Drug Control Policy, through the Houston High Intensity Drug Trafficking Area (HIDTA), then on to AT&T.[22] But funding to the HIDTA Program exceeded $280 million in 2020, according to reporting by *Wired*, which acknowledged the difficulty of determining how much of that money actually supports AT&T's call record collection.[23]

The Snowden revelations did not appear to slow the pace of surveillance abuse. In 2018, a federal judge secretly determined the FBI had been batch-searching emails of suspicionless Americans without a warrant, using tens of thousands of identifiers.[24] The Trump administration declassified the rulings a year later. In one case, they had commissioned a search using more than 70,000 identifiers, most likely email addresses, linked to FBI employees.[25]

Some of the most egregious abuses of government surveillance and data collection have been used to target Donald Trump. From the intelligence community's response to his 2016 election to the DOJ's lawfare expeditions, government bureaucrats seemed to throw out the search-and-seizure rule book.

The Social Media Spy Operation

If you are among the 88.9 million Americans who followed President Donald Trump's Twitter account in the final months of his first presidency, the DOJ may have a file with your name on it.[26]

You are not supposed to be subjected to unreasonable searches and seizures if you are not under suspicion. But in his zeal to dig up evidence against Trump, Democrat-installed prosecutor Jack Smith demanded that Twitter (now X) produce data on every account that interacted with Trump over a specific period.

Had he just wanted to know what was publicly posted by the president, he could have easily obtained that information from the National Archives and Records Administration (NARA). A considerable amount of tax money was spent paying a company called Archive Social to capture everything Trump sent via his social media—reportedly 20 terabytes of data.[27]

A request to NARA would have triggered a notification and tipped off Trump. Smith instead went directly to Twitter, demanding an invasive scouring of accounts. Included with Smith's warrant was a nondisclosure order forbidding the company from notifying Trump. It's a frightening pattern that should not be allowed.

Not only did he want Trump's information, but also that of everyone who interacted with Trump. Consider the scale and specificity of what the government can demand about someone they wish to target.[28]

In his exceptionally broad subpoena, Smith demanded: "All information from the 'Connect' or 'Notifications' tab for the account, including all lists of Twitter users who have favorited or retweeted tweets posted by the account, as well as all tweets that include the username associated with the account (i.e. 'mentions' or 'replies')."[29] Smith demanded to see direct messages, IP addresses, privacy settings, and ad topic preferences. Twitter was asked to divulge who Trump followed, what messages he liked, whom he muted or unmuted, blocked or unblocked, and details of all of Trump's notifications. That included deleted information, information located outside the United States, and even a search history.[30]

To their credit, Twitter balked. But Biden appointee Judge Florence Pan, whose husband, Max Stier, is a former Clinton defense attorney and Democratic Party activist, came down hard. She restricted the company from notifying any of their customers of the warrantless surveillance they were being compelled to perform. After Pan held Twitter in contempt of court and fined the company $350,000 for delaying production of the voluminous data, Twitter took the case to the Supreme Court, which denied certiorari and left Pan's ruling in place.[31]

Suspicionless Americans had their data scraped to comply with the massive scope of information Twitter had to supply, but didn't find out about it until the following August. In their petition to SCOTUS, Twitter/X warned of the precedent this ruling would set. "Twitter alone annually receives thousands of nondisclosure orders attached to demands for user information," the petition read. "Indeed, the D.C. Circuit agreed that this issue is likely to recur for Twitter. Other platforms, too, receive thousands of requests for user information—many with nondisclosure orders."

In 2013, the ACLU warned against this very problem, cautioning that the government was "attempting to sidestep the warrant procedure" by using a lower evidentiary standard to obtain private information. They warned such precedents could have a chilling effect on free speech. "Even Twitter doesn't have the resources to go to court every time law enforcement demands a user's private information—and other companies may not even want to. Users must be able to protect their own rights,"[32] the ACLU argued.[33] This wasn't the first time the government had weaponized its surveillance authority to get to Trump.

The Weaponization of Intelligence

Books have been written about the ways the government abused authority to spy on those in the Trump orbit. We won't do justice to that story here, but it's worth remembering the broader contours of what happened.

Data collection in the service of fighting crime is one thing. But using that extraordinary resource to influence elections is something else altogether. The FBI famously misled the courts in their zeal to spy on people close to President Trump—a pattern that would continue throughout his first presidency.

In their surveillance of Trump campaign adviser Carter Page, a later investigation by the Office of Inspector General found "fundamental errors" and omissions in the FBI applications on Page as well as persistent attempts to deceive the court authorizing the warrants by withholding pertinent exculpatory information.[34] The Page surveillance was seen as an attempt to indirectly access the Trump campaign's political communications ahead of the election.

Suffice it to say that the facts are not in dispute. FISA Court presiding judge Rosemary Collyer called out the FBI in an unusual order demanding they submit in writing their plan to remediate the abuses that led to the false Russia collusion hoax.[35] "The frequency with which representations made by FBI personnel turned out to be unsupported or contradicted by information in their possession, and with which they withheld information detrimental to their case, calls into question whether information contained in other FBI applications is reliable," she wrote.[36] The FBI subsequently apologized to the court, outlining forty corrective actions the agency was taking to prevent future abuses.[37]

The first Trump presidency was a stark reminder of why guardrails are needed. President Joe Biden in April 2024 signed the bill extending Section 702 for another two years, leading *Wired* to headline their story, "The Next US President Will Have Troubling New Surveillance Powers."[38] The extension still requires a foreign target before agencies can engage in spying. However, the bill broadened the number of entities compelled to comply with the program to include data centers.[39]

The bill Biden signed is "a gift to any president who may wish to spy on political enemies," FISA expert Liza Goitein told *Wired*. Goitein is the senior director at the left-leaning Brennan Center for Justice at New York University School of Law.

The government's capacity to spy on American citizens is likely far greater than what is publicly known. So why all the secrecy?

The Secrecy Advantage

For the better part of a decade, federal law enforcement agencies managed to keep a secret weapon under wraps. Unbeknownst to the public or Congress, investigators were using cell-site simulators to gain access to cellular data.

It all came out in the extraordinary case of IRS scammer Daniel Rigmaiden, whose story is told in the Netflix documentary *Web of Make Believe: Death, Lies & the Internet*. Rigmaiden had made a fortune filing tax returns in the names of dead people. Beginning as early as 2005, investigators conclude he filed more than 1,900 fraudulent tax returns and attempted to collect $4 million.[40] Despite his assiduous efforts to cover his tracks, he was arrested in 2008 and charged with dozens of felonies.

Rigmaiden smelled a rat. He hadn't made any mistakes. But he knew his one vulnerability was a Verizon AirCard used to make phone calls. It didn't have a GPS chip. But he knew it was possible to triangulate his location if government had a tool to track the AirCard. It turned out they did. But no one knew about it.[41]

Rigmaiden put to work the strategic thinking and attention to detail that made him such a successful scammer to solve the mystery of how they caught him. He used his time in prison to learn everything he could find about the government's surveillance practices. Over time, he was able to document the use of Stingray devices.

Cell-site simulators, known by their brand name Stingray, can be used to track a target's location, sometimes without a warrant. They act as imitation cell towers, tricking nearby devices into connecting to them. Stingrays can collect personal data, including geolocation information, call history, and text messages.

Rigmaiden argued in court that the technology constituted an unreasonable search in violation of the Fourth Amendment. In response, the FBI argued the use of such devices without disclosure to a judge was "standard practice" at the time. Information about Stingrays was considered "law enforcement sensitive" because public release could compromise investigations by "compromising future use of the equipment."[42] In other words, they didn't want to deal with the inevitable constitutional questions. I suspect the FBI also enjoyed the strategic advantage that their targets were unaware they could be surveilled in this way.

Rigmaiden ultimately pleaded guilty in 2014 and plea-bargained to sixty-eight months—time he had already served. He now consults with privacy organizations litigating cases involving cell-site simulator technology.[43] I became involved in the issue in 2015 when I took over the chairmanship of the House Oversight Committee.

Our staff investigated the privacy matters involving Stingray use by government agencies, particularly looking at the guardrails that could prevent abuse of the devices. What we found was disturbing.

Our bipartisan investigation concluded that regulation of the devices varied greatly from state to state. In 2016, when the report was released, we found the DOJ had 310 devices. Between 2010 and 2014, they spent $71 million on the technology. DHS had another 124 devices—$24 million worth.[44]

The report recommended Congress pass legislation establishing a clear nationwide framework to govern when and how geolocation devices could be deployed. That hasn't happened, despite the best efforts of some lawmakers. The use of the technology by state and local law enforcement units should be contingent upon adopting these guidelines. We recommended doing away with the nondisclosure agreements that had kept the courts in the dark about the government's ability to spy on phones in a criminal investigation.

Now a new generation of cell-site simulators is here. The Electronic Frontier Foundation says the newest iteration is designed to be concealed within a common vehicle, antennas hidden under a false roof so they can't be detected from the outside. They can gather data on multiple frequencies and collect Wi-Fi intelligence.

"This technology is like a dragging fishing net, rather than a focused single hook in the water," EFF explains on their website. "Every phone in the vicinity connects with the device; even people completely unrelated to an investigation get wrapped up in the surveillance."[45]

Some states, including California, Washington, Virginia, and Utah, have passed legislation requiring law enforcement to obtain a warrant before deploying the device.[46] Following our 2016 oversight investigation, DOJ, DHS, and the IRS updated their policies to make a warrant prerequisite to deploying cell-site simulators.[47] A bill introduced in the 118th Congress creates a nationwide framework regulating the use of cell-site simulators, but that legislation has yet to get any traction.[48]

The vast amount of data the government can access and collect is hard to comprehend. It doesn't end with our phone calls and digital footprints. Law enforcement can surveil mail going to and from homes and businesses by simply submitting a written request. There is no vetting of these requests.[49] In Chapter 7, we'll explore the government's access to photo databases of our faces. And these are just the unclassified tools that have been publicly reported.

The value of our data continues to grow as the tools to sort through high volumes of information become more fast and precise. All of this data collection has given rise to a whole new industry.

Surveillance Capitalism and the Rise of Data Brokers

The business of buying and selling data has never been more lucrative. Worth an estimated $389 billion, the global data broker market is projected to reach $561 billion by 2029.[50] It's growing faster than lawmakers' capacity to regulate it.

A major consumer of data from data brokers is the United States government. Given restrictions on unreasonable searches and the Fourth Amendment implications of collecting data directly, the government can avoid the constitutional questions by simply buying data.

With the proliferation of data brokers, it is no longer necessary for government to control and collect data. Many of the apps we use collect location data—not because the app requires it, but because the data is a product with a market.[51] In many cases, the government is that market, using data brokers as a middleman.

Not only are national security agencies like the NSA buying people's internet metadata, but regulatory agencies are likewise using tax dollars to buy data. *Reason* magazine reports, for example, that the Centers for Disease Control and Prevention spent $420,000 to buy cell phone data to use for monitoring compliance with pandemic lockdown restrictions.[52]

There is no warrant requirement unless the government compels companies to turn over data. So long as they pay for it, they can collect without restriction. The Electronic Communications Privacy Act and Stored Communications Act require government to have a warrant before accessing emails or social media messages and prohibits the disclosure of certain private information. Still, it doesn't apply to purchased data and hasn't been updated in any significant way since its passage in 1986.[53]

The Privacy Act of 1974 prevents the dissemination of personally identifiable information collected by the government—such as tax and income data from federal tax filings. But it doesn't protect the dissemination of that personal data by brokers. Additional laws in various states limit even further what the government can directly collect, but not what it can buy.

Following Wyden's revelations about the NSA, the House passed the Fourth Amendment is Not for Sale Act with strong bipartisan margins in April 2024. Even House Judiciary Committee ranking member Jerry Nadler (D-NY) was a cosponsor. That bill would close the so-called data broker loophole that enabled the government to buy what it couldn't legally collect.

With that law in place, law enforcement would need to go the extra step of obtaining a warrant before diving into the private information of American citizens. But despite heavy hitters from both parties in the House backing the bill, it never got out of Senator Dick Durbin's (D-IL) Senate Judiciary Committee. In an April 2024 statement, the Biden administration announced it "strongly opposes" the bill, citing "narrow, unworkable exceptions" that would inhibit the intelligence community. Without the support of the Biden administration or law enforcement, the Senate did not appear interested in even debating the issue.[54]

The Wild, Wild West

If the government is operating with insufficient oversight, the private sector has even less. Private industry lacks a coherent and enforceable regulatory system. Congress, with an older demographic and little technical expertise, has proven ill-equipped to fill the gaps in our regulatory framework.

The private data-brokering industry is robust and growing, with seemingly endless sources of input. We generate data with every click, every post, every call, and every text message. With every credit or debit card purchase, ATM withdrawal, and stock trade, someone else is getting information. In the rush to generate quality data and produce accurate results, privacy can become a casualty.

For example, Facebook allowed Netflix to access the direct messages (DMs) of its users.[55] It snooped on users' Snapchat traffic.[56] We all benefit when the ads we see are products we might actually want to buy. But we don't own our data. A large corporation does. And they tend not to be very forthcoming about what they do with it.

Amazon handed over Ring doorbell user data without consent, which they were loath to acknowledge.[57] Chase Bank has created

Chase Media Solutions to allow advertisers to target their 80 million customers in the United States based on their banking transactions.[58] They see it as a mutually beneficial arrangement in which consumers receive personalized deals and cash back on their purchases and brands connect with the consumers who support them.

Many of us trade access to our personal information for faster processing when we travel. Using Clear airport ID verification kiosks means providing access to the obvious biometric data, as well as "users' mobility and location, personal preferences for travel and shopping, financial capabilities, and health conditions."[59]

Companies like Socure and Equifax are employing machine-learning techniques to document people's identities and prevent fraud. Socure can determine in real time whether a loan applicant or welfare recipient is a real person using a legitimate identity. It performs hundreds of validation checks to predict whether the person is safe for its clients to transact with. Equifax uses similar technology to help landlords perform tenant verification.

As good as these tools are, and as much as they can accomplish, they do have a downside. Data can also disclose our political views, which candidates and causes we support, how much money we have, or what religious beliefs we hold. All of these things can potentially make us a target.

The gay dating app Grindr sold data on its users beginning in 2017, including precise location data showing where the app was used. At the time, executives didn't believe selling that data to ad networks posed a privacy threat. But Grindr's data was among data obtained by a conservative Catholic media organization that used it to discern that a high-ranking administrator at the US Conference of Catholic Bishops was using the app and frequenting gay bars. The man technically forfeited the data by signing up for the app. It cost him his job.[60] Grindr had other questionable data practices. In one case, a Norwegian nonprofit alleged that Grindr had shared users' HIV status with multiple private companies.[61] Grindr was later sold to a foreign competitor of the United States—data and all. When the Committee on Foreign Investment in the United States later determined ownership by a Chinese gaming company was a national security risk, the Chinese owners were forced to sell.

Surfshark conducted a study to identify the dating apps that are the hungriest for personal information. Of those apps analyzed in the study, more than half were using data for third-party advertising. While none collected physical addresses, they collected other personal data. Some access health information, location data, browsing history, purchases, and other usage data. Half of the dating apps Surfshark analyzed also collect data points like race, sexual orientation, pregnancy, disability, religion, politics, biometrics, and genetic details.[62]

A prayer app called Muslim Pro stopped sharing its data with X-Mode after discovering X-Mode was selling the app's location data with the US military and contractors.[63] The app sends reminders to pray. Because it identifies the direction of Mecca, Saudi Arabia, it collects data on users' locations. Senator Ron Wyden, in a statement, alleged the company was selling data to military customers through defense contractors.

The lax regulatory environment and insufficient controls of the data brokerage industry perpetuate threats to "civil rights, national security, and democracy," according to a report from the Duke Cyber Policy Program.[64]

At a minimum, the US Congress must act to limit the sale of sensitive data to foreign governments. Furthermore, they should take advantage of bipartisan support for federal privacy legislation to create a uniform regulatory framework nationwide. Any legislation should empower the Federal Trade Commission to investigate data brokers who engage in exploitative practices.

In his *Wall Street Journal* op-ed opposing the CAT database, former attorney general Bill Barr implored lawmakers to preserve the civil rights of Americans. "The cost is that law enforcement must sometimes be a little less efficient than it would be if Americans had no privacy," he wrote. "If there are shortcomings, improvements can be achieved by incremental fixes rather than by bulldozing Americans' liberties."[65]

An entity that could consolidate all of the various sources of our data would be very powerful. Imagine partisans within government using this data to identify all the people who attended an antigovernment protest by their phone numbers. With enough data, weaponized agencies (or their external partners) could determine how many attendees also attended January 6 or pro-life protests, which ones have government jobs, which ones are Jewish, or whether any of them owe back taxes. Anonymous social media accounts could be quickly exposed or censored. Conservative job applicants could be secretly identified and weeded out. Targeting political opponents would be undetectable. Even without any nefarious intent, there will always be entities hungry for our data.

Whether that entity is a commercial business, a criminal hacker, or a power-hungry world leader, our data is a weapon we do not want to be wielded against us. That kind of resource could save the world. Or it could enslave it, giving a government—theirs or ours—the capacity to control us.

Klaus Schwab was right about one thing. Whoever masters artificial intelligence may well master the world. Robert F. Kennedy Jr. ominously warns, "What we're creating is this kind of turnkey totalitarianism, where the next totalitarian regime that steps up and really wants to clamp things down—they're going to have all of these mechanisms in place like no regime has had in human history."[66]

CHAPTER 7

The Encyclopedia of Faces

A pproaching a stranger on the subway, Harvard student AnhPhu Nguyen zeroed in, checked his phone, and then made contact. "Do you happen to be the person working on, like, minority stuff for, like, Muslims in India at all or something?" Nguyen asked a man leaning against a wall waiting for the train.

As the stranger nodded, Nguyen used the man's first name, adding, "Oh, I've read your work before. It's supercool!" But Nguyen hadn't read his work before. He'd never heard of the man until the moment his three-hundred-dollar pair of Ray-Ban Meta smart glasses locked on the man's face, pushing the video out to an Instagram livestream. Using a server-side system he had created with fellow student Caine Ardayfio, he could access a stream of publicly available information about the stranger in real time.

The glasses themselves are obviously not sold with this capability. Nevertheless, this invasive technology was inexpensive and easily accessible using publicly available hardware and software and a bit of programming skill. Walking around the campus of Harvard, the duo demonstrated how their program could link to the glasses' Instagram livestream, connect with a publicly available facial recognition product called PimEyes, and use a large language model (such as ChatGPT) to aggregate available data. They then used Python to program a simple system that would push that data out to their phones in real time.[1]

It may be one of the most intrusive devices ever built, according to Ardayfio and Nguyen, who won't be releasing the code. Start to finish, the whole project took them a few days to create.

In a paper they wrote to describe the experiment, they explained their purpose was "raising awareness that extracting someone's home address and other personal details from just their face on the street is possible today."[2] It's not only possible, but it is also relatively inexpensive. Included in the paper are instructions for removing personal information from the data sources they used. Websites like PimEyes and FastPeopleSearch allow you to remove your data from their systems. The students recommend freezing credit to prevent the theft or leak of a Social Security number, and the use of a professional data removal service. Starting at less than $100 a year, these services will contact commercial data brokers to request that your information be deleted from their databases.[3]

The ability to dox someone on the spot, using little more than a camera and a website, has frightening implications. Whether we opted in to these facial recognition databases or not, our images are there—probably dozens of them, each with different ages, expressions, hairstyles, and angles. How those images got there is a testament both to how fast the technology has evolved and how slow our bloated, sclerotic, bureaucrat-driven federal government moves.

Involuntary Data Submissions

Hoan Ton-That never set out to become a villain. In fact, the youthful Australian entrepreneur is in the business of giving law enforcement tools to convict the guilty and exonerate the innocent. Such people are usually rewarded with hero status. His company, Clearview AI, is used by thousands of law enforcement agencies across the United States to solve crimes. With a database containing more than 40 billion images, Clearview AI's technology has been a game changer in the administration of justice.[4]

But Hoan Ton-That (pronounced "Won Ton-Tat") unwittingly found himself at the center of an intense privacy debate after the *New York Times* broke a story in 2020 revealing the source of all those images in his company's database.

To create a broader dataset, Ton-That's company had scraped the internet for public photographs. And by public, they mean your LinkedIn profile picture, your Facebook feed, your Google images, and anything else that isn't locked down. If you signed up for Venmo and added a profile picture, you probably had no idea that image was considered public domain.

Clearview AI vacuumed it all up—along with many other images they didn't legally need permission to use. They scraped millions of open web sources for data. And in 2020, the first in a series of stories in the *Times* put a spotlight on the company's data practices.

The company has been mired in legal and regulatory red tape ever since. The software has been banned in Canada, the European Union, and even in Ton-That's native Australia, where regulators wanted the company to remove every photo gathered locally in Australia.[5] The impossibility of that request led to Clearview AI's exit from the market.

They've been fined by regulators and sued by privacy advocates. They have received cease-and-desist letters from Google, YouTube, and LinkedIn, among others. Some have even demanded they remove any photos scraped from their websites.[6]

Here in the United States, the company is banned from selling its software to private sector companies following an Illinois lawsuit brought by the ACLU.[7] The technology has been banned in progressive cities where Black Lives Matter protests were most aggressive and antipolice sentiment is high. Police in Portland, San Francisco, and Seattle can't use it.

But that hasn't stopped the company's exponential growth. The demand for the tool by local police departments—and the success of it—is part of the reason *Time* magazine in 2021 named Clearview AI one of the world's most influential companies.[8]

Clearview AI wasn't the first facial recognition technology. But it is among the most useful for law enforcement. The PimEyes software that our Harvard students used with their Ray-Ban Meta glasses, for example, is also widely used, but it is openly available for public subscription.

Previous facial recognition tools were prone to bias, particularly when it came to identifying people with dark skin. Those databases had been trained on a small dataset of predominantly white celebrities. Without scraping the internet, those were easily attainable photos. But as a person of mixed race himself (Ton-That's father is Vietnamese and his mother Tasmanian), he was sensitive to that failing.[9] According to his testimony before the US Commission on Civil Rights, the Clearview AI database has no discernible difference in racial algorithms, in large part because of the size and diversity of its dataset.[10]

The market for facial recognition continues to grow at a rapid pace. Valued at over $5 billion in 2022, it is expected to grow at a compound annual growth rate of 15 percent through 2030.[11] Not only is the market growing, but the application for the technology also seems to be growing exponentially, in stark contrast to the glacial pace of regulatory protections.

What Faces Could Reveal

In 2017, Stanford University professor Michal Kosinski released a study showing how an algorithm could accurately predict a person's sexual orientation from a photo alone. His algorithm correctly identified gay men 81 percent of the time and distinguished between gay and heterosexual women 71 percent of the time.[12] The study sparked a huge backlash from the LGBTQ community at the time, with advocacy groups calling it "junk science."

If true, they worried it could lead to crushing discrimination if a brutal regime sought to identify the sexual orientations of its citizens.[13] The fear was a legitimate one. But it didn't stop Kosinski.

He predicted that AI technology would eventually be able to discern a person's political orientation, IQ, and predisposition to criminality, all from a simple photograph.[14] Just a few years later, Kosinski published another study using a new algorithm that he said accurately detected political party affiliation 71 percent of the time when comparing two like individuals.[15]

More recently, Kosinski produced another series of peer-reviewed studies in *American Psychologist*. He tested political orientation using 591 images of adults, all instructed to hold a blank expression, wear a black T-shirt, pull their hair back, and wear no makeup or jewelry. Using a model that was trained on thousands of photos of people on the left and right, the study observed a rate "significantly above" chance.[16]

In addition to discerning political and sexual orientation from an image, researchers are studying another application: emotional and behavioral analysis. To what extent can AI accurately distinguish emotions like pain, pleasure, comprehension, or even alertness?

The fictional drama *Lie to Me* depicted a character with an uncanny ability to read micro-expressions. Dr. Cal Lightman could tell if people were lying just by reading their faces. The character was based on a real-life detection expert, Dr. Paul Ekman.[17] But can AI duplicate Ekman's skill?

The search is on for an AI machine-learning technology that can accurately detect human deception. To date, no technology measures up to the abilities of the fictional Lightman, but scientists are sure to continue the quest for a model that can produce sufficiently legitimate results for broader use.[18]

Biometric technology is also becoming more sophisticated. The Federal Trade Commission issued a policy statement in 2023 warning of the increasing risks of biometric technology—described as using physical and biological traits from a person's body. The FTC advises that "using biometric information technologies to identify consumers in certain locations could reveal sensitive personal information about them such as whether they accessed particular types of healthcare, attended religious services, or attended political or union meetings. Large databases of biometric information could also be attractive targets for malicious actors who could misuse such information."[19]

The Proliferation of Video Surveillance

The illicit transfer of credentials during NFL football games has long been a security risk for the league. To access high-security zones like the playing field, the locker room, and even the press box, people just had to show a credential. It was a poor system for detecting fraudulent or unauthorized credentials—also one subject to human error.

As a college football placekicker, my claim to fame was that Brigham Young University never lost a game by the margin of my missed kicks. I never played football in the NFL, but I can relate to how disconcerting it must be for players to think that just anyone could evade security and access locker rooms or other sensitive sites.

With the league's announcement in July 2024 that all thirty-two of its stadiums would deploy facial recognition technology to access high-security spaces, the problem appeared to be solved. Using software from London-based Wicket, the NFL would install technology at secured access points, leaving credentialing decisions up to individual teams.[20]

The rollout was not without wrinkles. In Las Vegas, the league got immediate pushback from the police union. Who would have access to that biometric data? Could antipolice protestors get their hands on it? Could it potentially be used to target and harass law enforcement?[21] They are valid questions that go beyond the use of facial recognition at football games. Police use facial recognition all the time—and for good reason. But even they know to be leery of it. In the wrong hands, it becomes a weapon.

In the fifty most populous American cities, an estimated 537,000 cameras monitor the combined 48.9 million people living there. That's about eleven cameras per thousand people. The most surveilled cities in America are Atlanta (124+ per thousand), Washington, DC (55 per thousand), and Philadelphia (30 per thousand).[22]

Not surprisingly, Washington has the highest density at 573.8 cameras per square mile. As we might expect, this number includes fixed CCTV cameras, but also traffic cameras and those in and around public transportation facilities.

The $2.2 trillion infrastructure bill signed by President Biden in 2022 funded a proliferation of new traffic cameras. Subsequent federal guidance permitted states to spend up to 10 percent of their federal infrastructure funds (which previously had to be spent on roads and bridges) on surveillance equipment. Then–transportation secretary Pete Buttigieg rightly justified the change as a way to prevent traffic-related deaths.

Since then, many existing traffic cameras have been updated with AI-enabled technology, giving the government the capacity to monitor behavior inside of our private vehicles.[23] Whenever we agree to new privacy incursions in the name of security, we must consider what would happen in a world where tyrants gained control of that technology.

The government could be privy to all kinds of information about where we go, what we do, and who we're with. In the United Kingdom, police now use live facial recognition, creating biometric facial signatures to compare against suspects on a watch list. It's a very effective crimefighting strategy. But it raises serious questions about how much the government should be allowed to know about our comings and goings.

That's perhaps why the rollout of this technology in London has led to such a backlash. British prime minister Keir Starmer proposes to make London "the AI capital of the world."[24] But some one hundred saboteurs calling themselves "Blade Runners" have dismantled hundreds of license-plate-reading cameras in London's Ultra Low Emission Zone (ULEZ).[25] They hit them with paintballs, cut down the metal support poles, and even installed bat boxes hoping they will become home to a protected species and subject to protection against repairs.[26]

After the city implemented a £12.50 charge for driving noncompliant vehicles in low-emission zones, vigilantes began sabotaging the cameras. Though they don't have facial recognition software, privacy advocates worry about what will come in the future. An anonymous source claiming to be a founder of the Blade Runners told the *Epoch Times*, "They're up there and they're up there for good." Howard Cox, who ran for mayor of London in May 2024, shared his frustration with the system in the same story.

"More and more of these cash-grabbing cameras will be demolished by a few ultra-frustrated drivers simply because they were not instituted democratically. I will never ever back these people breaking the law, but I share their infuriation," he said.[27]

The *Guardian* reports the city has seized more than 1,400 vehicles from drivers who refuse to pay the fines. Mayor Sadiq Khan has raised £25 million from fines and another £710,000 from the sale of confiscated vehicles.[28]

Here at home, the government is decidedly less draconian—so far. But the rollout of AI-empowered cameras is happening in America as well. For example, in 2024 DHS began rolling out a plan to add facial-match technology at security checkpoints in over fourteen airports, eliminating the need to scan a boarding pass before entering screening areas. It's fast and easy. But what are the boundaries?

The Transportation Security Administration, part of DHS, says the photos are not stored but rather are erased immediately after matching to a person's photo ID. Fourteen US senators objected to the TSA facial-scanning program at airports. In a letter to Senate leadership, the bipartisan group questioned the wisdom of rolling out such tools without rigorous congressional oversight. "Once Americans become accustomed to government facial recognition scans, it will be that much easier for the government to scan citizens' faces everywhere, from entry into government buildings, to passive surveillance on public property like parks, schools, and sidewalks," wrote Senator Jeff Merkley (D-OR).[29]

At this point we should revisit Robert F. Kennedy Jr.'s observation from Chapter 6: "What we're creating is this kind of turnkey totalitarianism, where the next totalitarian regime that steps up and really wants to clamp things down—they're going to have all of these mechanisms in place like no regime has had in human history."[30]

Restraining Tyranny

Speaking of totalitarianism, China is the undisputed king of invasive surveillance. The combination of Big Data and Big Brother has made privacy a relic of the past in the nation of 1.4 billion people. Once again, China demonstrates what going too far looks like.

The CCP has been combining facial recognition with AI to classify its people by ethnicity. CCP law enforcement has been using the technology to track its Muslim Uighur (pronounced "We-gur") minority for years. The *New York Times* reported in 2019 that the CCP keeps track of the movement of 11 million Uighurs in what local police called "minority identification."[31] The CCP has detained hundreds of thousands of Uighurs in reeducation camps that erase their cultural identity and subject them to political indoctrination.[32]

The CCP uses gait-recognition technology to identify people by how they walk. Chinese police say they can identify someone from fifty yards away—even if they have their back to the camera.[33] The Chinese Skynet—a number estimated to be more than 600 million cameras—monitors 1.4 billion citizens.[34]

China keeps finding new ways to monitor and control their behavior. One clip that went viral on the Chinese social media site Weibo showed the state had installed timers on the toilets at popular Yungang Buddhist Grottos, a UNESCO World Heritage Site where 51,000 statues are carved into rock.[35] At the moment, lengthy toilet time isn't part of anyone's social credit score, but the fact that the government can track this number is alarming, even by Chinese standards.

Amid fears that China is creating a global surveillance system using its domestic tech companies, US lawmakers have called for restrictions on Chinese cameras, drones, cell phone networks, and other technology.

We may not have Skynet in the United States, but the demand for better crimefighting tools is bringing more invasive technologies. Few are more concerning than the US intelligence community's

Video LINCS program. Created in 2006 to better respond to tragic incidents with forensic analysis, the Intelligence Advanced Research Projects Activity (IARPA) functions under the supervision of the White House Office of the Director of National Intelligence (ODNI). IARPA was intended to "analyze patterns for anomalies and threats."[36]

Director of National Intelligence is a senior-level cabinet position—a political appointee. It was held by James Clapper during the Obama administration, by Rick Grenell and John Ratcliffe during the first Trump administration, and by Avril Haines during the Biden years. Former congresswoman Tulsi Gabbard now holds the position. All US intelligence agencies report to this person—it is a very powerful position and one very close to the president.

With that in mind, let's look at what we know. The Video LINCS program uses AI to autonomously identify and track individuals and vehicles across multiple video sources. This process of "reidentification" (reID) can match an object or a person across a whole collection of video from different sources—be they CCTV cameras, webcams, drones, or phones.[37]

Without a doubt, it's a great tool for law enforcement. With a willing administration, it could be used to surveil traffickers—like the "coyotes" who take advantage of migrants—tracking them across land, air, and sea border crossings, exposing crimes, and locating victims.

But what could a tyrannous regime do with such technology? Video LINCS could track individuals at protests or rallies, even with clothing changes. It could enforce lockdowns—or even low-emission zones like we saw in London. It could implement a "fifteen-minute city" program, in which people are penalized for leaving a certain zone.[38] It's a cutting-edge spy tool—but will it ultimately spy on the criminals or the political opposition?

It's hardly the only tool. The FBI created a facial recognition database of their own, one Congress had to dig to find—because it was never authorized.

Oversight and Transparency

"We don't believe you." Those were my words to an FBI witness during a 2017 hearing about the agency's illegal development of a facial recognition database.

In March 2017, I held a hearing of the House Oversight Committee to look into troubling details of the FBI's undisclosed collection of driver's license and passport photos.[39] Entities tasked with enforcing the law should also follow the law. But the FBI didn't.

Unbeknownst to the American public, they had been developing a database of photographs since 2010. These weren't just mug shots. They were photos used on government IDs of Americans who were under no suspicion. Congress never authorized the collection of this data. The FBI did it anyway. They took their existing, authorized database of fingerprints, which are considered biometric data, and added photographs—also biometric data. Same thing, right?

Just one problem. They never disclosed it. By law, the FBI had to disclose this project by publishing a privacy impact assessment when it began in 2010. However, according to a 2016 report from the Government Accountability Office, they waited five years to disclose what they were doing. That's how I found out about it. By then it had been in use for years, without meaningful oversight or legal protections.

Even more appalling was the massive scope of what they had collected. While the fingerprints were limited to people accused of a crime, the GAO found the photos were not.

I was incensed to learn that millions of the photos in the database were suspicionless Americans—accused of no crime. According to the GAO, the FBI had entered into agreements with state and local law enforcement in eighteen states to share photos, including driver's license photos from state DMVs.[40]

You shouldn't have to give up your face to the FBI in order to drive a car in this country. You shouldn't have to fear being tracked without cause. That's why I called for a hearing to demand an explanation from the FBI.

The FBI Criminal Justice Information Services sent Deputy Assistant Director Kimberly Del Greco to testify publicly before the Oversight Committee. During the hearing, I confronted her about the agency's deception. She tried to demur, directing me to ask the DOJ why they hadn't disclosed the facial recognition data until years after the system was in use. I explained, "You're required by law to put out a privacy statement and you didn't. And now we're supposed to trust you with hundreds of millions of people's faces?"

The fact is, the FBI couldn't be trusted—a fact that would be reinforced over and over throughout the duration of the first Trump administration. Before the hearing ended, I asked a question that elicited a very dishonest response. I wanted to know, "Do you have plans to match this database with anything that is posted on social media? Instagram, Facebook, Snapchat—are you collecting that information that is out there on social media?"

Del Greco chose her words carefully. The FBI only collects criminal mug shots, she said. "We do not have driver's license photos in our repository at the FBI," she said. Do you see where this is going? One of the other witnesses on the panel did.

"This is a technicality," said Alvaro Bedoya, who was there as executive director of the Center on Privacy and Technology at Georgetown Law. "Who owns and operates a database matters a lot less than who uses it and how it's used," he interjected. "The FBI has access to now eighteen states' driver's license photos and either can run those searches or request them. We're talking more than a third of all Americans. So the FBI does have access to these photos. They searched them tens of thousands of times, and, apparently, by GAO's testimony, never audited those searches for misuse," Del Greco then had to acknowledge they have access to the data, but they do not maintain it.[41]

This is even more true today than it was then. As we have come to see, law enforcement agencies of all stripes—state, federal, local, tribal—use private databases to provide data they themselves are not legally allowed to collect.

These databases help solve a lot of crimes. They have been a game changer in the cause of justice. While some privacy advocates still hope to put that genie back in the bottle, it's not going to happen. These tools have become so prevalent—and so effective—that I can't blame law enforcement for advocating to keep them.

But the government can't help itself. It is the nature of power to overreach. It has also been the nature of the executive branch to selectively apply the tools at its disposal. There is perhaps no better example of this effect than the comparison of prosecutions against January 6 protestors versus Black Lives Matter protestors.

The January 6 prosecutions foreshadow a future in which everything is caught on camera. Though the summer riots of 2020 resulted in 15 times the number of injured police officers, 19 times as many arrests, and 740 times the cost in damages, the vast majority of charges were dismissed.[42] The January 6 protestors were much easier to prosecute, largely because of the volume of video evidence available. But we're all increasingly being captured on film. What does that mean for future prosecutions?

If the government will be better able to prosecute crimes, that's theoretically a good thing. But in practice, the laws are not applied equally. Prosecutors have to make choices about where to deploy their resources. Which lawbreakers will receive the justice doled out to January 6 protestors? And which will enjoy the mercy shown to the majority of violent BLM rioters?

If these surveillance tools are going to exist and be used in court, they must exist within a legal framework that provides oversight, transparency, and equal application of the law. The next time a protest gets rowdy at a state capital, can we guess how many people go to jail based on the party protesting?

Rewriting the Laws

The easy answer (though not the easiest solution) is to ban every-thing. That seems to be the position of the Electronic Frontier Foundation (EFF), which has done incredible work documenting these technologies.

EFF recommends a total ban on the technology by the govern-ment. They argue that the technology poses grave threats to civil liberties, privacy, and security that require an aggressive response. Facial recognition technology, they argue, presents inherent threats to privacy, free expression, information security, and social justice when used by police and other government agencies. They support the Facial Recognition and Biometric Technology Moratorium Act, which did not advance in the 118th Congress.

The likelihood of Congress getting enough votes for such a ban and Americans going along with its trade-offs is slim, in my opinion. More power to them if they can get it through the process. There have been a few reasonable bills, but the next Congress needs to take this more seriously.

The Fourth Amendment Is Not For Sale Act passed in the House in April 2024. The bill enjoyed bipartisan support, passing 219–199, with big names from both sides of the aisle on board. Jim Jordan (R-OH), Zoe Lofgren (D-CA), Pramila Jayapal (D-WA), Andy Biggs (R-AZ), and Jerry Nadler (D-NY) were all on board. The bill passed the Judiciary Committee, 30–0. But it stalled in the Senate, where Judiciary Committee chairman Dick Durbin (D-IL) never considered it in committee and Majority Leader Chuck Schumer (D-NY) never brought it to the floor.

It would have required the FBI and other federal agencies to seek a warrant before they could even purchase personal information, such as internet search histories and geolocation data.

"Eighty percent of the American people in a recent YouGov poll say they believe warrants are absolutely necessary before their dig-ital lives can be reviewed by the government. It is now the duty of the U.S. Senate to finish the job and express the will of the people,"[43] said Gene Schaerr, general counsel of Project for Privacy and Surveillance Accountability.[44] As expected, law enforcement opposes the bill, as did the Biden-Harris administration. War hawks like Mike Rogers (R-MI) also voted no.

In the Senate, my colleague Senator Mike Lee (R-UT) proposed the Government Surveillance Reform Act, which would have required FISA to get a warrant. It too failed to garner sufficient support. I am sympathetic to the difficulty of getting legislation through our deliberately slow system. But at this point, we must stop letting perfect be the enemy of the good. An imperfect but effective bill is better than no bill.

Congress must move forward a bill to provide for more oversight of these databases. That oversight can come from Congress, from the Office of Inspector General, from the GAO. And it can come from simple transparency—responding swiftly and fully to FOIA requests, congressional subpoenas, and questions from journalists. Without better transparency, these databases are too great a risk. I believe we can strike a balance. But not unless Congress finds a way to move forward.

CHAPTER 8

Securing Data at the Speed of Government

Let's talk about a secretary of state whose emails China may or may not have hacked. No, not *that* secretary of state—though her emails could be anywhere at this point.

Biden-Harris administration secretary of state Antony Blinken traveled to China in June 2023 to resume high-level talks with President Xi Jinping—the first such meeting in four years.[1] Around that same time, cybersecurity specialists at the State Department detected anomalies that led to the discovery of a disturbing cybersecurity breach. For more than a month, hackers linked to China had been able to monitor the email accounts of senior State Department officials. Though it was unknown whether the hackers were state-sponsored actors, China has acknowledged sponsoring cyber-warfare units.

Blinken wouldn't acknowledge whether his email was among those compromised, but another cabinet officer, Secretary of Commerce Gina Raimondo, had her email compromised in the same incident.[2] Additionally, the email account of the US ambassador to China was targeted in the same attack—an attack that appeared to involve "at least hundreds of thousands" of US government emails, according to reporting from the *Wall Street Journal*.[3]

It had been nearly ten years since one of the biggest government data breaches in history (and nine years since Secretary Hillary Clinton had virtually offered up her emails to hackers on a silver platter by setting up a private email server in her home). After all that time, foreign governments were still infiltrating the US government. Why? Because cybersecurity is complex and difficult even in the most cutting-edge environments. And the government is not that, nor is it ever likely to be.

The 2015 data breach at the Office of Personnel Management (OPM) had been a political earthquake. In that case, hackers got security background investigation information on 21.5 million people, including biometric data (fingerprints) on 5.6 million. These were people with access to our most sensitive secrets, including highly invasive background-check disclosures that documented people's past mental health treatment, illegal drug or alcohol use, gambling problems, divorces, and financial stress. The data included information on employees, prospective employees, consultants, and contractors.

Both the value of what was stolen and the vastness of the operation were incomprehensible. James Comey, then director of the FBI, described the personal impact of the theft. "My SF-86 lists every place I've ever lived since I was eighteen, every foreign travel I've ever taken, all of my family, their addresses," he said. "So it's not just my identity that's affected. I've got siblings. I've got five kids. All of that is in there."

Following that monumental cyberattack, we on the House Oversight Committee investigated what happened. In our 2016 findings, we concluded the OPM hack had been a coordinated and targeted campaign to collect information on government employees. Evidence revealed the government "failed to prioritize cybersecurity and adequately secure high-value data" despite warnings from the inspector general dating back to 2005. Among the mistakes: a failure to use basic multifactor authentication, slow response to red flags warning of anomalies, and internal politics that undermined OPM's information security posture. During our investigation, government employees misled the committee and the public about the significance of data stolen the previous year.[4]

"There Is No Fixing It"

Michael Hayden, former director of the CIA, bemoaned the impact of the breach. "[OPM data] remains a treasure trove of information that is available to the Chinese until the people represented by the information age off. There is no fixing it."[5]

He's not alone. Private sector companies experience the same frustration. Businesses small and large have to expend significant investments on cybersecurity protections that still don't guarantee safety.

In the first six months of 2024, hackers had reportedly stolen one billion records. AT&T was among the biggest, potentially exposing over 100 million customers. Change Healthcare was targeted with ransomware in an attack that compromised the electronic systems of hospitals, pharmacies, and medical practices for weeks, with disclosures estimated to impact up to one-third of all Americans. A malevolent attack on Ticketmaster impacted over 500 million users. These are huge numbers that reveal vast vulnerabilities.[6]

In February 2024, hackers infiltrated the system of Change Healthcare, which had been acquired by UnitedHealth Group in 2022 to maintain millions of records about the company's patients. Not only did the hackers shut down the system and paralyze processes for several weeks, but they also took the personal information of "a substantial proportion of people in America."[7] To retrieve the information, UnitedHealth Group reportedly paid at least one ransom demand. Even after paying the original hackers, the company was hit up for a second ransom demand by a contractor of the hackers who also broke into the system.

Likewise, Ticketmaster faces potentially catastrophic impacts from a hack that affected some 500 million customers. The hacking group ShinyHunters reportedly took 1.3 terabytes of user data, which they then listed for sale on the dark web for $500,000.[8] Mayhem ensued as hackers released billions of dollars' worth of genuine tickets with legitimate bar codes, including 214,000 ticket bar codes related to Taylor Swift's Eras Tour. They even managed to game Ticketmaster's antiscalping measures by reverse engineering bar codes to allow customers to print tickets that had already been sold to someone else. The hackers released a four-step tutorial on YouTube explaining how to print the tickets.[9]

AT&T was hit hard in 2024. Call records of every customer were stolen, although AT&T said in a securities filing that the stolen data did not include names, Social Security numbers, or credit card data. Nevertheless, thieves now have access to phone numbers (easily tied to names with little effort) and logs of which numbers customers interact with. AT&T said the breach happened through a third-party cloud workspace run data-warehousing service called Snowflake. And it's not just AT&T. In 2022, T-Mobile paid $350 million in a class action lawsuit over hacked data that affected 50 million people.[10]

The Mother of All Breaches (MOAB) of 2024 dwarfs all other leaks in size and scale. The unprecedented release of 12 terabytes of information included 26 billion records in 3,800 folders, each linked to a different data breach. Among the brands whose records appear to have been included in the link were LinkedIn, Dropbox, Adobe, Telegram, Weibo, Twitter (X), and Canva. Data from government organizations in the US, Brazil, Germany, and many other countries is included.[11]

Erik McCauley watched the company he built get destroyed after hackers infiltrated Odin Intelligence, a police services company, in 2023.[12] McCauley thought he had done everything right. Hackers targeted his company and were able to get in and steal some 20 GBs of data. Despite his best efforts to restore the systems, McCauley said he ended up taking it all down.[13]

On McCauley's recommendation, I visited a website called Haveibeenpwned.com to see the status of my own data. I entered my email address and discovered my email had been compromised in at least nine different data leaks. Companies large and small are all facing the same threat.

"There is no safe environment for people to function," he explained over the phone. "I could not tell you one system that I'm aware of that is bulletproof." He worries about an army of Chinese hackers who do nothing but try to break into software systems. "I will never do software again, ever," he told me.

Companies victimized by hackers have few resources to help navigate a process in which they can quickly be blamed for failing to secure data. In reality, no one can guarantee data is safe.

Cybersecurity developer Scott Volmar has spent his career working on an alternative to the World Wide Web. When we met at an event where I was speaking, Volmar explained to me why he thinks trying to fix our existing technology is a mistake. In a follow-up interview, he described a different approach.

He doesn't believe the web can be salvaged because it was never built with security in mind. In the book *The Unhackable Internet: How Rebuilding Cyberspace Can Create Real Security and Prevent Financial Collapse*, author Tom Vartanian argues that we built the wrong internet.[14] He argues the internet was built with substandard coding, but more importantly, it was never conceived to be a secure environment. He argues a better alternative is the use of private and offline network infrastructure in which all digital traffic must be authenticated to a real person.[15]

Volmar is the founder, president, and CEO of InterComputer Corporation, created to pursue the lofty goal of securing internet communication. Based just minutes from my home in Utah, this company has managed to put Vartanian's theories into practice. The InterComputer InterOperating System (IC IOS) follows that model, providing secure, insured, real-time payments. It doesn't use the World Wide Web infrastructure. Though other competitors are developing similar approaches, Volmar told me his company's solution is secure enough that Lloyd's of London agreed to underwrite it against cybercrime.

Going Out of Business

The asking price for data on nearly 3 billion people was $3.5 million. For that price, the whole database was offered on the dark web, selling names along with associated Social Security numbers, email addresses, and phone numbers.[16] Hackers walked away with 272 million unique Social Security numbers and 600 million phone numbers.[17]

The breach became public in August 2024 when National Public Data, a background-check company in Florida, became the target of a class-action lawsuit.

Companies whose systems are infiltrated and data is stolen by hackers generally just pay for credit monitoring and call it good. But with 2.9 billion victims, National Public Data didn't have the assets to cover the vast liabilities on the other end of the lawsuits. Facing staggering costs to clean up the mess, the company filed for bankruptcy by October, leaving victims with little recourse.

The National Public Data heist was one of the biggest data breaches in history, but it was hardly an isolated incident. Companies face mounting costs to keep their data secure with little support from the government to help them navigate the dangerous world of data security.

In the decade between 2014 and 2023, the federal government, which has access to vast amounts of data about Americans, has been subject to over a thousand data breaches, affecting 200 million records and resulting in costs of up to $30.4 billion.[18] Government agencies were the third-most-targeted sector for ransomware attacks in 2023, according to the House Homeland Security Committee's Cyber Threat Snapshot. Cyberattacks on critical infrastructure increased 30 percent that same year.[19]

State and federal governments have been the target of massive cyberattacks. Among the largest federal breaches (that we know about) were the 2015 hack of the Office of Personnel Management; a US Postal Service hack in 2018 that exposed 60 million records; and a 2018 breach of the Government Payment Service that leaked 14 million customer records for state and local governments.[20]

They keep happening. Hackers always seem to be able to stay a few steps ahead of the government. Reinsurers like Lloyd's of London warn of the potentially catastrophic costs. A major cyberattack on a financial services payment system, for example, could add up to over $3.5 trillion in losses over five years. The industry is calling for a government backstop to pay the difference between what the industry can reasonably insure and what the losses could potentially be.[21] I understand the concern, but no government is big enough to backstop the kinds of losses we could possibly face. Moreover, the government struggles to manage its own data systems, much less monitor everyone else's.

The Problem with Government

If you were to design the perfect organizational structure for leading cutting-edge cyber defenses, it would be everything large bureaucracies are not. Democratic forms of government are not designed to optimize efficiency. Their relative prosperity and decentralized management make them an attractive target for the world's best hackers. And they tend to be easily distracted from their primary mission by political objectives. I'm disappointed but not entirely surprised to see the federal government falling short of what is needed to manage our data safely.

In seeking to build consensus and check power, our system sometimes works slowly. While those characteristics are very helpful in defraying power and staving off tyranny, they are easily exploited by hackers with access to the latest technology. It's not a problem China has to worry about. They are under no obligation to preserve privacy, nor are they subject to constitutional checks on power. Here in the United States, structural inefficiencies contribute to making the government a poor steward of sensitive data.

For one thing, it can take an act of Congress to get anything done. Furthermore, investments in technology are subject to end-of-year omnibus bill fights that make planning and budgeting ahead difficult. The list of challenges is long. Agencies are subject to transparency requirements that can expose their capabilities. The government struggles to compete for top talent. Bureaucracies have never been great incubators for innovation.

In the decade between 2010 and 2020, the GAO made 3,300 recommendations to government agencies to remedy cybersecurity gaps. By the end of that period, 750 of them had not been implemented.[22]

In addition to the structural challenges, there is a resource imbalance between the United States government and hacker teams—be they state-sponsored or run by criminal enterprises. The government is uniquely targeted by the full range of bad actors seeking data. The data that powers the most prosperous and influential government on the planet will always be in demand. Foreign criminal syndicates as well as foreign governments are anxious to gain an advantage, be that commercial, military, or political. Foreign hackers are hell-bent on infiltrating American systems—and they are paid well to do it.

Government cybersecurity efforts don't just have to worry about the government's data. Outside contractors, vendors, and local governments also own and control vast amounts of valuable information that can compromise the security of American citizens.

Perhaps one of the most chilling hacks targeted American infrastructure. The May 2021 attack on Colonial Pipeline was considered a "watershed moment" in American cybersecurity.[23] The attack, conducted by an Eastern European or Russian criminal syndicate calling itself DarkSide, targeted critical American infrastructure, disrupting fuel deliveries to the southeastern United States.[24] The company paid the hackers in Bitcoin, a portion of which the DOJ managed to claw back.[25]

Our government struggles to protect its own data, much less provide resources to the countless other targets of cyberattacks across the country. Even if the government has the right technology and the right people in place to detect cyberattacks, there is yet another major obstacle to addressing the problem. Politics keeps getting in the way. Sometimes failure to protect data is strategic.

Misaligned Priorities

If you make a lot of money, vote for conservatives, or don't pay a high enough percentage of your total wealth to the government, you are no longer entitled to have them keep your tax records private. That was the sentiment of a piece written by University of Michigan tax law professor Reuven Avi-Yonah and republished to popular acclaim in the left-wing publication *The American Prospect.*[26]

Avi-Yonah defended the theft of private tax data by a government contractor whom he referred to as "a public hero." Charles Littlejohn, whose contract work for Booz Allen Hamilton inexplicably gave him access to private tax documents, was able to download large files without triggering any suspicion.

Littlejohn was the leaker of tax documents on Donald Trump, Elon Musk, Jeff Bezos, and 7,500 other ultrawealthy American businesspeople.[27] Those leaks became the source of dozens of stories that revealed private information on at least 150 taxpayers. The leak of that data, which leftist politicians had been hungry to get their hands on, was excused by progressives like Avi-Yonah as a public service because it helps root out tax evaders (not necessarily people who break the law—just people whose tax burden isn't as high as progressives think it should be).

There is no doubt that we would catch more criminals if we violated everyone's privacy. We could collect DNA and fingerprints from birth, search private property without a warrant, listen in on everyone's phone calls, and fish through every email until the government found something to prosecute.

But that's not what we do. We require probable cause to justify a warrant before the government can collect fingerprints or DNA, search our homes, or listen in on our phone calls. But in Littlejohn's case, he didn't have a warrant. The government didn't even employ him. He was a contractor who got to serve as judge, jury, and executioner by selectively releasing data on people whose views he opposed. And the left loved it.

He stole data from conservatives—rich conservatives. Avi-Yonah argued Littlejohn should receive no more than a slap on the wrist because "many other cases involving tax evasion do not result in jail time." Citing other tax evasion cases that resulted in less than the five years of jail time Littlejohn will serve, Avi-Yonah lamented the fact that these cases involved "conduct that is much more culpable and less public-spirited than Littlejohn's."

Because the leaked tax documents were political opponents of this law professor, he justified the invasion of privacy, arguing, "It is important that the IRS combat tax evasion by the rich because it bolsters public perception that the system is fair and therefore that citizens should pay their taxes."

But is it fair if only taxpayers of one political party must suffer such an invasion of privacy? What about the 3,800 IRS employees who haven't paid their taxes? Given the political leanings of the federal bureaucracy, most of them are likely Democrats. Should their tax documents be released to prevent tax evasion? Along with contractors, they owe a combined $50 million in back taxes.

Of the 3,800 who owe taxes, some 2,000 of them haven't even established a payment plan. Some are more than five years delinquent. Looking at the whole federal workforce, some 150,000 federal employees owe $1.5 billion in unpaid taxes.[28] Should their tax documents be released to shame them into paying? Something tells me the readers of *The American Prospect* would be less excited about that.

The government is uniquely vulnerable to shifting political winds that can unduly influence priorities. The agency created to oversee cybersecurity has arguably spent more energy trying to secure censorship than trying to secure data.

The Birth of CISA

The year after I left Congress, the government got serious about defending data from hackers. That was in no small part a result of the OPM hack. Donald Trump signed new legislation creating a cybersecurity agency, under the authority of the Department of Homeland Security (DHS). If you read that 2018 law, you would see nothing amiss.[29] I certainly would have been interested in such a solution, given the outcome of our Oversight Committee investigations into previous government breaches. There was a legitimate need for the federal government to up its game in the battle against state-sponsored hackers, criminal entities, and petty thieves.

For the lawmakers who created it and the president who signed it, CISA legislation's primary purpose was to defend critical infrastructure. Its stated mission was to "build the national capacity to defend against cyberattacks," working with the federal government to "provide cybersecurity tools, incident response services and assessment capabilities to safeguard the .gov networks that support the essential operations of partner departments and agencies."[30] Why wouldn't any president sign such a bill?

But unbeknownst to its creators, CISA would be infiltrated by partisan actors, both in and out of government, who would forgo the primary mission in favor of a more nefarious one. CISA was about to become a taxpayer-funded domestic intelligence, surveillance, and censorship operation for the exclusive use of one political party against the other.

CHAPTER 9

The Right to Be Wrong

The problem MIT needed to solve was a head-scratcher. How do you prevent people from believing the wrong things? It's a problem both the Obama and Biden administrations were obsessed with solving—enough so that the federal government was subsidizing the development of propaganda tools to educate those considered "more vulnerable to misinformation campaigns." Who might that be?

Conservatives, naturally. The MIT researchers who won a $750,000 grant from the National Science Foundation (NSF) cited two specific media practices unique to conservative groups. First, their perceptions of truth were "centered around the close reading of textual documents deemed sacred (e.g., the Bible or the Constitution)." Second, they inverted "traditional assumptions that truth is only curated at the top," which allowed for "everyday people to act as subject matter experts."

Researchers apparently found it alarming that these Americans trust primary sources over experts. "Because interviewees distrusted both journalists and academics, they drew on this practice to fact check how media outlets reported the news," the proposal explained. Among the demographics specifically identified as susceptible to such media practices were rural and indigenous communities, military veterans, older adults, and military families.

The NSF grant tasked MIT and other groups with developing "effective interventions" to people considered vulnerable to misinformation campaigns. Many of those tools ultimately involved using AI to automate censorship.[1] Here's what the MIT proposal suggested was so alarming about those people, conservatives, who preferred primary sources to journalists and academics for fact-checking news: "While lateral readers try to find secondary sources that reliably summarize expert consensus on sources and claims (Wineburg & McGrew, 2017; Caulfield, 2017), respondents often focused on reading a wide array of primary sources, and performing their own synthesis (Tripodi, 2018)."[2]

The nerve! Researchers found it particularly noteworthy when one participant, upon seeing a long list of search results amplifying the same narrative, concluded that the results were rigged, instead of concluding that the narrative must be correct.

This is, in part, why the government was soliciting proposals for systems that would predict and prevent "inaccurate information" (preempt or censor counternarratives), correct and mitigate it (label or dispute facts the government says are wrong), and keep it from spreading[3] (deploy algorithmic suppression to ensure no one sees it).

In this way, the government is not the one censoring speech. Instead, the government funds the politically biased propaganda tools that its allies in journalism and technology can use to arbitrate truth. What suggests they were biased?[4]

The House Judiciary Committee, in its investigation of the NSF program, described a condescending and partisan effort. "The nonpublic communications and documents obtained by the Committee and Select Subcommittee demonstrate that (1) the 'disinformation' academics understood their work as part of a partisan project; and (2) the bureaucrats and so-called 'experts' in this space have complete disdain for most of the American population."[5]

The NSF alone has spent more than $38 million developing tools to shape what kind of information people can access. Ultimately, MIT's was among four censorship tools that received additional funding, though these projects are but a small part of the federal government's overall censorship support. A February 2024 report from a House Weaponization Committee investigation revealed details from MIT's research indicating that the NSF had been weaponized to fund censorship of conservative speech.[6]

Chances are you never read this story in the news media. It received scant attention from mainstream outlets. However, a few conservative outlets told their audiences about the government-funded censorship tools. The Federalist, a serious right-leaning news organization, headlined its story "AI Censorship Targets People Who Read Primary Sources to Fact-Check the News."[7] The Daily Wire, a conservative news and opinion website founded by Ben Shapiro and Jeremy Boreing in 2015, also ran a story reporting on the response of Senator Eric Schmitt (R-MO) and headlined "Senate GOP Probe National Science Foundation Over 'Brazen Attempt' to Censor Free Speech."[8]

If you missed those stories, it's not your fault. Both of those publications are among the conservative outlets whose content has been deliberately suppressed online. Even if your social media history suggests their reporting would be of interest to you, it might not show up in your feed, thanks to government-funded automated AI censorship tools. Had you entered the exact headlines into your browser at that time, it's unlikely stories from those publications would have even shown up in the results. I tried it myself. In fact, stories from a host of conservative publications were being deliberately suppressed as fake news, even though the censored narratives were frequently true.

Distinguishing Right and Wrong

> The right of dissent, or, if you prefer, the right to be wrong,
> is surely fundamental to the existence of a democratic
> society. That's the right that went first in every nation
> that stumbled down the trail toward totalitarianism.[9]
> —EDWARD R. MURROW

Perhaps the most enduring legacy of the Biden presidency will be the elaborate system of censorship the White House deployed during his tenure—much of it dating back to the end of the Obama presidency. The hubris of trying to dictate truth is that truth, in the pragmatic worldview of those who seek to control it, is not "what is," but what will work for their purposes.

It's a system truly breathtaking in its scale, involving a complex web of federal agencies, nonprofits, universities, and tech companies. Leaving few fingerprints, the administration was able to fund the suppression of inconvenient (and often true) information across a vast social media landscape, disseminate propaganda disguised as news, cut off the lifeblood of politically adversarial publications, and influence elections to enhance the party's power.

A regime dependent on censorship to maintain its power has an inherent weakness in the truth. The real problem is not the presence of misinformation, but the absence of truth. The best-laid plans to control the narrative are destined to fail in a marketplace of ideas. People must be able to choose truth from falsehood, even if their choice ultimately is wrong in the eyes of others.

Biden's censorship efforts yielded not so much a suppression of misinformation as a suppression of politically inconvenient speech. Conservative publications were hardest hit.

For conservative and libertarian-leaning commentary, I have long been a fan of the Federalist. They write stories no one in the propaganda press is writing about and strive for the high journalistic standards I expect from a news organization. Foremost, they're willing to tell stories that the government doesn't want told—like the fact that the NSF funded censorship tools that target conservatives. Editor in Chief Mollie Hemingway, a fellow Fox News contributor, is a bold truth teller. Likewise, Federalist cofounder Sean Davis is an insightful and provocative political commentator. I have frequently referenced their writing in my research.

Until recently, that was not easy to do. Not only did their stories not show up in search engines, but they didn't even show up in the news feeds of their followers. Before Elon Musk bought Twitter, I rarely saw stories from the Federalist anywhere. Even if their publication has written the most comprehensive story on a topic I was searching for, I had to go to their website to find it. How was the censorship so well coordinated across search engines and platforms? The idea that the government was directly controlling individual news feeds in such granular detail seemed unlikely.

Rating the News

The White House was not censoring the Federalist—not directly anyway. The scheme was much more complex than that. The tech companies who run these platforms voluntarily de-boosted news outlets that had been rated as "fake news" by rating agencies. But the rating agencies aren't politically neutral. In fact, they had deep ties to the Biden administration.

The for-profit NewsGuard was created in 2018 to help consumers distinguish real news from fake news. Advertisers pay for access to a rating system to tell them which sites are reliable and which ones are filled with conspiracy theories. Other sites rely on the State Department–funded Global Disinformation Index (GDI) to identify legitimate sources. In theory, ratings should help boost quality sources.

In the case of the Federalist, NewsGuard offered a failing rating of 12.5 on a scale of 100, causing advertisers to flee. The Federalist's executive editor Joy Pullman notes that it's likely the designation came not so much for any history of publishing false information, but for publishing "Democrat-disapproved information."[10]

The Federalist was also listed among the top ten "riskiest" online news outlets in 2022 by GDI. Let's see if you can guess what the others on that list have in common. GDI also identified the Daily Wire, the *New York Post*, *Reason*, RealClearPolitics, The Blaze, Newsmax, OANN, the *American Conservative*, and the *American Spectator*.[11] There is not a left-leaning news outlet in the bunch.

Conversely, left-leaning outlets top GDI's list of least risky sites: NPR, AP, the *New York Times*, and the *Washington Post* are all recommended. But presumably not for their accuracy—which is certainly in dispute. They likely made the list for their compliance with the spread of government-approved narratives, which don't have a great track record for accuracy.

The right-leaning Media Research Center analyzed the News-Guard ratings for 2021, 2022, and 2023. The study documented explicit bias in the rating system. The analysis revealed a consistent and overwhelming tendency to score left-leaning media outlets significantly higher. Using the independent classifications by AllSides to determine bias, MRC found left-leaning outlets like the *Washington Post* and *New York Times* had an average credibility rating of 91. In contrast, right-leaning publications averaged a score of 65—a disparity of 26 points.[12]

Earlier, the *Post* issued extensive corrections to its reporting on the Steele dossier allegations of collusion between Donald Trump and Russia.[13] This after inaccurate reporting drove the news cycle for years. Further, these most trusted outlets almost uniformly dismissed the legitimacy of the Hunter Biden laptop story ahead of the 2020 election. In fact, the *New York Times* maintained its 100/100 score, despite failing to acknowledge their glaring errors in reporting the story or offer a clear retraction.[14]

The impact of these ratings on conservative outlets was potentially devastating. The bias cheated conservative news sites out of billions of dollars in ad revenues. Furthermore, the blacklists cost social media visibility, browser searches, circulation, and influence.

Censorship was just the beginning. Eliminating whole narratives and politically noncompliant publications appeared to be the end goal.

Destroying the Truth Tellers

Standing at a podium in Davos, Switzerland, marketing executive Rob Rakowitz addressed an audience of globalists at the 2020 meeting of the World Federation of Advertisers to call for a "safer internet."[15] Rakowitz, no fan of free speech, had a game-changing plan to eliminate harmful content online. Introducing his initiative as a means to protect brand safety, he described the coalition of advertisers, agency holding companies, media platforms, and industry associations representing $97 billion in global ad spending.[16]

His proposal to demonetize disfavored content was wildly popular at WFA, according to legal scholar Jonathan Turley, who also writes about the story in his book *The Indispensable Right*. As the Initiative Lead for this new Global Alliance for Responsible Media (GARM), Rakowitz would work to ensure the ratings from NewsGuard and GDI would drive advertising spending to favored sites and starve disfavored ones.[17] It would function as a global group boycott, coordinated and controlled by the world's largest advertisers and virtually invisible to the public.

Rakowitz appeared to have no concerns about the constitutionality of his big idea. In 2019, in emails he probably never imagined would be made public, Rakowitz memorialized his disdain for the notion of free speech online, which he characterized as an "extreme global interpretation of the US Constitution," a document he complains uses principles for governance from almost 250 years ago that were "made by white men exclusively."[18]

Internally, GARM participants were more explicit about the group's goals. GARM wasn't just reactively penalizing sites that produce "harmful"—by their assessment—content. It was proactively watching specific sites (it goes without saying they were conservative ones) for excuses to stop the flow of ad dollars. Internal discussions at GARM revealed strategic moves to blacklist conservative media. Little did Rakowitz know, those internal discussions would become the subject of public congressional hearings in 2024.

We know Rakowitz targeted specific outlets because emails he exchanged with executives from media-buying agency Group M tell us so. Those messages were included in a report from the House Judiciary Committee, which exposed the group's strategy of blocking Breitbart, the Daily Wire, Fox News, and X.

In October 2021, one member of GARM's Steer Team recollected the group's treatment of one specific conservative outlet, confessing how much "we hated their ideology and bulls**t" but "couldn't really justify blocking them for misguided opinion." So instead they "watched them very carefully" until they crossed a line that would justify cutting off their access to ad revenue.

GARM also colluded to target one of the world's most popular podcasts after Joe Rogan dared to platform vaccine skeptic Dr. Robert Malone in one episode and to suggest COVID vaccines were unnecessary for the young and healthy in another. Their clients didn't advertise on Rogan's podcast, so they couldn't make the case that they were acting to protect any brand. That didn't stop them from reaching out to Spotify to try to influence the content of Rogan's show.[19]

Choking off advertising revenue to Twitter was among GARM's most successful efforts. After Elon Musk purchased the social media platform, GARM leveraged its members to "stop all paid advertisement" on the new X.[20] In a subsequent letter to advertisers, X president Linda Yaccarino warned that the company would be bringing an antitrust lawsuit for the illegal behavior that had cost X billions of dollars. "This case is about more than damages—we have to fix a broken ecosystem that allows this illegal activity to occur," she wrote.[21] X Corp did file suit in August 2024 in federal court in Texas. Two days later, GARM was discontinued.

The House Judiciary Committee agreed that GARM was wading into Sherman Act territory, potentially making unreasonable restraints of trade in violation of antitrust law. At the time, with Merrick Garland in command at DOJ, there was little hope of prosecution. But Abigail Slater, who was confirmed in March 2025 to head the Justice Department's Antitrust Division, expressed concerns about the way trade associations had worked on behalf of national brands to selectively stop advertising at certain outlets. "I think it's fair to say, a certain amount of collusion went on via this trade association, and I think that pattern of conduct is quite troubling," she testified in her Senate confirmation hearing.[22] GARM certainly wasn't the first to try to choke off conservative media. The government had been perfecting the craft since the end of the Obama presidency.

Obama's Seeds of Censorship

Today's vast censorship leviathan has its roots in the troubled mind of Barack Obama, who planted the seeds in the final months of his administration, allegedly beset by concerns about foreign influence on social media. He later described how much these concerns weighed on him at the conclusion of his presidency.

"It is difficult for me to see how we win the contest of ideas if in fact we are not able to agree on a baseline of facts that allow the marketplace of ideas to work," he told an audience at the University of Chicago Institute of Politics in 2022.

"It's something I grappled with a lot during my presidency. I saw it sort of unfold, and that is the degree to which information, disinformation, misinformation was being weaponized."[23]

That sentiment was rather ironic, given the Obama administration's vastly expanded and weaponized government surveillance history. In expanding NSA warrantless surveillance programs, collecting bulk data from phone metadata, and signing an extension of the Patriot Act and FISA amendments, the administration aggressively surveilled individuals linked to its political adversaries.[24]

Unbeknownst to Congress or the American people, forces within the Obama administration initiated the formation of a network of government agencies, contractors, and tech companies that would use cybersecurity as a cover for censorship.

We already know the first step they took. Obama's DHS designated elections as critical infrastructure, opening the door to monitor speech around elections and giving DHS a new starring role in policing free speech. That's why we heard so much about Russian disinformation in our elections, even though there appeared to be very little of it. Without the foreign interference pretext, DHS had no legal justification to engage in censorship. The Foundation for Freedom Online called this the "Foreign-to-Domestic Disinformation Switcheroo."[25]

It was a national security matter, they said. The surveillance and censorship were supposed to be limited to foreign actors. But government being government, it did what government always does—it converted those tools to political weapons in short order. By 2020, DHS was full speed ahead on the censorship train.

Second, the Obama administration increased funding for the academic research that would create new censorship tools. The Federalist searched for grants using the terms "misinformation" and "disinformation" and found a significant jump. Between 2008 and 2015 there were two contracts and seven grants. From 2016, the last year of the Obama administration, through 2022, 538 grants and 36 contracts were awarded.[26] Among them was the NSF grant to MIT. Our government was true to form, and those tools were soon deployed to suppress inconvenient political narratives, such as the legitimacy of a laptop belonging to President Biden's son Hunter that implicated the Bidens in shady business deals—and which turned out to be completely true.

Meanwhile, a global nonprofit group calling itself the Cyber Threat Intelligence League (CTIL) was officially formed in 2020, though journalists Michael Shellenberger and Matt Taibbi revealed documents tracing its origins to 2018.[27] Made up of more than 1,400 volunteers, CTIL pulled from seventy-six countries. Experts in information security, telecommunications, and law enforcement came together, ostensibly to address cyber vulnerabilities in health facilities during a pandemic.[28] It sounded good. Yet again, it was merely a cover for censorship.

Sometime between 2018 and 2020, CTIL would develop a framework that relied on a public-private model to mask government censorship by hiding it within cybersecurity institutions and associated nonprofit partners. According to documents provided by a whistleblower Shellenberger and Taibbi did not name, CTIL acknowledged that censorship efforts "against Americans" have to be made using private partners because the government doesn't have the "legal authority" to spy on suspicionless Americans.[29] That's exactly what happened.

A Censorship-Laundering Enterprise

Republicans, meanwhile, weren't aware that the push for a cybersecurity apparatus was cover for a censorship and surveillance operation against them. In good faith, they helped facilitate the infrastructure that would upend the 2020 election. In 2018, Republicans signed on to bipartisan legislation, which President Trump signed, creating CISA—the Cybersecurity and Infrastructure Security Agency. By the next election cycle, CISA was fully weaponized against Trump and the Americans who supported him.

Nowhere in the text of the 2018 law do we see Congress intimating a broad censorship role, a domestic surveillance role, or a partisan cover-up role. However, CISA would do all those things in the following two election cycles, even as significant data breaches both public and private continued.[30] The agency's defensive mission would take a back seat to an offensive one that officials would go to great lengths to conceal.

CISA acted quickly to create a slew of new quasi- and nongovernmental entities to manage speech. With names like the Election Integrity Partnership, the Center for Internet Security, and the Center for Countering Digital Hate, these nonprofits filled the gap between what the government wanted to do and what it could legally do to censor speech.

A 2023 congressional investigation determined that during the 2020 election, CISA acted as a "switchboard," flagging "misinformation" and reporting it to social media companies. At Twitter, this scheme resulted in 859 million tweets collected for misinformation analysis. Another 22 million tweets and retweets were categorized as thusly and subject to censorship. The 21 users Twitter stigmatized as "the most prominent repeat spreaders of disinformation," were on the political right, according to the Homeland Security Committee's Oversight, Investigations and Accountability Subcommittee chair, Representative Dan Bishop (R-NC).[31]

The same switchboarding method was used to censor COVID-19 narratives the government purported were false (some of which were later revealed to be true). "I'm gravely concerned with CISA's efforts in this space," said Bishop during a subcommittee hearing. "How on earth was this censorship laundering enterprise allowed to metastasize? Where are the civil liberties protectors within DHS and what are they doing?"[32]

In truth, the government didn't have to try all that hard. Left-leaning Silicon Valley was hardly resistant to the cause.

Election Season "Mistakes"

Following the July 13, 2024, assassination attempt on President Donald Trump, Google users searching for information about the event noticed a problem. When one person typed the words "assassination attempt on t—," Google's autocomplete feature filled the words "assassination attempt on Truman" and "assassination attempt on the pope," according to a publication that also rarely appears in Google search results. The Federalist's Brianna Lyman explained that the entry "assassination attempt on" returned 10 results, none of which referred to the biggest news event of the week—and possibly the summer.[33]

Google told House Oversight Committee chairman James Comer that the firm had "failed to update 'a safety protocol,'" and thus the story was flagged as violent content and not shown in search results.[34] It wasn't an isolated incident.

Likewise, Facebook had an unusual error following the assassination attempt. The iconic photo of Trump raising his fist in the air following the Butler, Pennsylvania, rally was censored from news feeds on both platforms. Facebook users received a notice that independent fact-checkers claimed the photo was altered. Though Facebook founder Mark Zuckerberg was on the record calling the photo the most badass thing he'd ever seen, the company acknowledged a mistake. A warning regarding a doctored version of the image had been mistakenly applied to all versions.[35]

Google cited an "algorithm error" after voters searching the phrases "Where can I vote for Trump?" and "Where can I vote for Harris?" got very different responses. The Harris search yielded an interactive map tool directing voters to nearby polling locations, while the Trump query did not.[36] It's hard to miss the fact that these mistakes all seem to run in one direction.

"I lead this company without political bias," Google CEO Sundar Pichai told members of the House Judiciary Committee in 2018 after Breitbart News posted a video of worried Google executives "expressing dismay about Trump's 2016 election victory."[37] At that time, Democrats showed little interest in the issue. Representative Jerry Nadler (D-NY) exclaimed that "political bias in search engines [was] a 'fantasy dreamed up by some conservatives.'"[38]

Hardly. Senior research psychologist Dr. Robert Epstein has spent years studying what he calls the Search Engine Manipulation Effect (SEME). Epstein testified before the Senate in 2019 that Google manipulates its search algorithms specifically to influence elections.[39]

Epstein, a Democrat and Clinton/Biden voter himself, monitored Google search ahead of the 2024 presidential race. His researchers at America's Digital Shield found that Google consistently sent more "Go Vote" reminders to left-wing voters in swing states than right-leaning voters. In Arizona, for example, 69 percent more liberals received the reminders than conservatives in the week ahead of the election.[40]

Can a search engine influence how people vote? Epstein's research says it can. By his estimates, biased Google search results shifted at least 2.6 million votes to Hillary Clinton in 2016.[41] In

2020, Google alone shifted more than 6 million votes to Joe Biden, according to Epstein's model. Not surprisingly, Google in 2017 called Epstein's model "nothing more than a poorly constructed conspiracy theory."[42]

Speaking to Government Accountability Institute's Peter Schweizer and Eric Eggers on *The Drill Down* podcast, Epstein said that "Google shifted tens of millions of votes in hundreds of midterm elections" in 2022.[43] Epstein firmly believes that absent Google's manipulation, the GOP would have ended up with a Senate majority between 2 and 8 seats, and an additional 27 to 59 seats added to their 10-vote House majority in 2022.

Whether the alleged bias is deliberate or some unintended consequence or programming error, Epstein says the impact is anticompetitive and deeply unfair. "If a platform such as Google wants to influence people," Epstein told Schweizer, "there is nothing you can do. You can't buy an opposing billboard because the platform itself is a monopoly . . . controlling 93 percent of search worldwide."

Epstein maintains that the platforms themselves are shifting tens of million of votes, with virtually no accountability. Many publications are afraid to report on the story because they depend on Google search traffic to bring eyeballs to their websites. "Google can put you out of business," Epstein explained.[44]

Epstein's controversial work does not stand alone. In a Princeton University study of content moderation, researchers found evidence that pre–Elon Musk Twitter lowered Republican vote share in both the 2016 and 2020 presidential races.[45] An analysis of millions of tweets revealed that Twitter's then-liberal content may have persuaded moderate voters against voting for Donald Trump.

The Censorship Industrial Complex was running on all cylinders by 2022. Its many tentacles were deeply enmeshed in the watercooler conversations of tens of millions of Americans, leaving scant fingerprints. Few voters even knew their government was manipulating them.

The Skunk at the Garden Party

Two things happened in 2022 to massively disrupt the censorship party. Elon Musk purchased Twitter. And Republicans won control of the House. The downstream effects of those two events ultimately unmasked the Biden administration's abuse of power and likely contributed to the election of Donald Trump in 2024.

Had CISA's partisan leadership imagined the possibility of Musk turning over internal communications to honest reporters, they might have tried harder to cover their tracks. Likewise, had they foreseen the creation of a congressional subcommittee tasked with uncovering and amplifying the news of government weaponization, perhaps they would have been less obvious about their censorship. Fortunately, they weren't that careful.

The purchase of Twitter by Elon Musk, the publication of what came to be called the "Twitter Files," and an investigation by the House Weaponization Committee combined to prove a thousand conspiracy theories (at least it seemed like that many). Perhaps the most revealing part was the extent to which the Biden administration had hijacked CISA's original cybersecurity mission in favor of a new mission to control the narrative in American politics.

It's hard to overstate the bombshell that went off when the Twitter Files were released beginning in December 2022. The stories were at once shocking, riveting, and disturbing. Most importantly, they were well documented. Musk had handpicked trustworthy reporters who had demonstrated professionalism and political objectivity in their previous reporting. None were considered conservative mouthpieces. In fact, most were politically left-leaning.

In early December, journalist Matt Taibbi published the first story based on internal access to Twitter documents. In it he revealed how politicized Twitter leadership had blocked the *New York Post* Hunter Biden laptop story just before the election, even as they privately admitted their public justification held no water.

That story, which we now know was 100 percent true, exposed materials found on a laptop belonging to the president's son.

As a voter concerned about the revelations in that story, you couldn't even share the *Post*'s groundbreaking story in private direct messages. It was an extraordinary act of censorship that looked even worse from the inside, where Twitter justified the suppression by claiming, without evidence, that the story was sourced from hacked materials.

If you were a conservative trying to post that story or comment on it, you learned firsthand what was happening. The story was removed, "debunked," and replaced with a new (and false) narrative claiming Russians had planted a fake laptop to make Biden look bad. Taibbi's story confirmed what many had long suspected—that pre-Musk Twitter was suppressing the true narrative and promoting a false one.

From the Twitter Files, we also learned the FBI was having regular meetings with Twitter executives to coordinate the censorship. In fact, numerous agencies and the White House regularly submitted requests for review or removal, sometimes in the form of long spreadsheets identifying individual posts and accounts.[46] The volume of censorship requests was significant enough that one Twitter executive, congratulating the staffers who acted upon the government's demands, referred to it as a "monumental undertaking."[47] I can't even imagine the amount of money and the personnel resources the government dedicated to monitoring the social media feeds of millions of Americans. What an incredible waste of taxpayer resources!

Former *New York Times* reporter Bari Weiss, who has since gone on to start the independent news site the Free Press, was also invited to report on the internal Twitter documents. She reported that Twitter manipulated visibility filtering to limit the reach of conservative publications. Certain accounts were tagged with labels like "Trends blacklist" or "Do not amplify."[48]

Over the ensuing months, more stories trickled out—from

respected journalists like Michael Shellenberger, Lee Fang, and David Zweig. The full scope of the censorship regime was horrifying: state-sponsored blacklists, the removal of a sitting president from the platform, a flood of moderation requests from government intelligence agencies, and labeling truth as misinformation at the request of the government.[49]

Ultimately, Twitter allowed itself to become the mouthpiece of government disinformation, particularly during the COVID-19 pandemic when the government disseminated vast amounts of now-debunked "science" to promote unscientific lockdowns, untested vaccines, and illegal election changes.

As story after story cascaded out to the American public, Twitter was morphing into X—a free speech version of the old company. CISA and its partners could no longer control the narrative on Musk's platform. Musk beefed up Community Notes—an organic way to combat misinformation in which users could append fact-checks and upvote or downvote them. The truth began to spread organically. And then came Congress.

As interesting as the Twitter Files were at the time, those stories are even more interesting now that voters have been through an election cycle in which Elon Musk's X was allowed to be a real free speech platform. Narratives that would have been suppressed and censored in previous cycles were allowed to go viral. False narratives were quickly corrected in Community Notes.

I noticed it in my news feeds. For example, following the presidential debate in which President Trump accused Haitian migrants of "eating the dogs" and "eating the pets" in Springfield, Ohio, X was filled with video clips. Some were false—the people shown were either not Haitians, not immigrants, not in Ohio, or not eating pets! Those were quickly marked with a Community Note exposing the fraud.

Others featured residents of that town expressing their alarm in local council meetings months before. Readers could look at the big picture and make up their minds about the veracity of Trump's statement. Now, imagine how that would have played out in 2020 or 2022 based on what we know from the Twitter Files.

Over the next two years, revelations expanded from Twitter to Facebook to Amazon to the CTIL. One story after another of suppression, censorship, and political manipulation. Once again, House Republicans stepped in to investigate, issuing subpoenas and taking depositions.

Their May 2024 report found the Biden White House had targeted information that was true, satirical, or even just politically inconvenient, regardless of whether the content violated any policy of the various platforms.[50] Investigators with access to internal Facebook emails documented a direct line of censorship. In February 2021, the administration pushed Facebook to censor what it called "anti-vaccine content." One email, referencing vaccine-related content, read, "The Surgeon General wants us to remove true information about side effects."

Social media platforms went along with the scheme, apparently out of fear of compromising other policy priorities before the administration. At Facebook, one email basically admitted, "[g]iven the bigger fish we have to fry with the [Biden] Administration," Facebook should try to think creatively about "how we can be responsive to [the Administration's] concerns."

House investigators confirmed that even YouTube felt pressure from the White House. YouTube went so far as to seek White House feedback and approval on an internal content moderation policy. After extensive pressure throughout the summer of 2021, that policy change allowed censorship of vaccine-related content.[51] Likewise, Amazon relented to White House pressure to censor vaccine-related book listings, adding a "Do Not Promote" label to some offerings.[52]

The Good News

If I could go back in time and read this chapter ten years ago, I might have believed censorship at this level would be the end of the United States as we know it. I would never guess that we could have a 2024 election in which the censored side wins the presidency, sweeps the swing states, takes the House and Senate majority, and easily tops the popular vote.

That happened. In an environment of heavy censorship, media capture, and government secrecy, the censorship apparatus lost. They couldn't fool all the people all the time. Two tools matter more than any other in this battle. The first is truth. The second is the law. If we stay on the right side of both, we can defeat the censorship apparatus.

Censorship lost because it got sideways with truth. Sunlight remains the best disinfectant. Elon Musk's exposure of the censorship regime shined a bright light on a dark secret. The truth found its way out of the dark. Censored content showed up in podcasts. It was the subject of feature films—such as the Daily Wire's *What Is a Woman?* that questions the gender transition narrative. The things they didn't want us talking about still got talked about.

Of equal importance was having the law on the side of truth. We are blessed in America with a constitution that defaults to protecting civil rights. When a party in power chooses to violate those rights, we have legal recourse. And many entities exercised that recourse.

The state of Texas, together with the Federalist and the Daily Wire, filed a lawsuit against the State Department challenging its illegal use of domestic censorship tools. It is early yet, but already the New Civil Liberties Alliance has secured expedited discovery in a case the government sought and failed to dismiss.

Texas attorney general Ken Paxton will demand accountability for the fact that myriad federal government agencies and officials have engaged in a coordinated effort to suppress speech on social media. The lawsuit alleges open collusion with the tech companies to suppress content that challenges the government's narrative.

Meanwhile, the battle is heating up at the state level, where Texas and Florida have passed legislation demanding more transparency in content moderation practices of social media companies. The litigation is ongoing, but the back-and-forth over censorship is a healthy exercise that will shed light on the constitutional implications of new technologies.[53]

Sometimes the truth is dangerous. But never more so than the absence of truth. If you are fighting for censorship, you are fighting for an absence of truth. Because the government can't help itself—it will always leverage control to consolidate power. This is a battle that can be won—provided we stay on the side of truth and law.

As I sit here writing my fifth book, this is the first time the Federalist's stories have shown up in a few of the online searches I use in my research. I can now use X and its AI counterpart Grok as a search engine to find stories that used to disappear. Stories that question establishment narratives are once again visible.

I'm an eternal optimist—and this is a time for optimism. My party won an election convincingly, in part because voters didn't believe the narratives they were fed continuously and aggressively. Some of the scientists, doctors, reporters, and politicians who sacrificed truth to score political points have been exposed. But winning a battle is not the same as winning a war.

The fight to preserve free speech is far from over. Don't for a minute think we've heard the last of the "disinformation" police. Having a single true free speech platform was decisive, but Elon Musk can't buy everything. Okay, he probably could, but that's not a long-term solution. We have a reprieve, but when the pendulum swings back, we must be prepared. The left has worked to inoculate a generation of students against populist ideas and American exceptionalism. The results of this election didn't change what's in our schools. They're not just coming after you. They're coming after your kids.

CHAPTER 10

The Social Engineering of Children

Only in his twenties, Andrew Young was living his best life, working his dream job as an animator at a major film studio. To get there, everything had to go just right. And it had. After working briefly as a game artist for Microsoft's Xbox, Young's art talent landed him a scholarship at the prestigious Brigham Young University (BYU) animation program, where he graduated in 2011. That led to a job at Pacific Data Images (PDI), a subsidiary of DreamWorks Animation.

DreamWorks was famous for animated classics like *Shrek*, *Kung Fu Panda*, and *How to Train Your Dragon*. PDI had been a pioneer in digital animation before its purchase by DreamWorks in 2000. In the 1990s, Pixar and PDI released the first two American CGI feature films, *Toy Story* by Pixar and *Antz* by PDI.[1] For Young, the chance to do cutting-edge animation on major feature films was the opportunity of a lifetime.

Before Young could even start working on films, PDI/Dream-Works required three months of grueling tests to prove that new hires had what it took to be there. As a character effects animator, Young's specialty was animating hair—and it's harder than it looks. The mane of Alex the Lion in the movie *Madagascar 3*, which Young animated, involved having each hair flow in the wind. He was doing the best work of his life making wholesome content for kids. It was the best job he had ever had.

But by 2014, everything had changed. Young had walked away from all of it. He was making deliveries for DoorDash. He remembers delivering ice cream to Facebook employees at nine in the morning and just hoping for a good tip. It was a humbling period. "I'd be pumping gas and former [DreamWorks] coworkers would see me in my DoorDash shirt. It was humiliating," he explained.

He wasn't fired. In fact, his employer went to great lengths to keep him. He walked away. It was one of the most wrenching decisions of his young life. But he couldn't unsee what he had seen. And he decided he couldn't be part of it.

I spoke with Young following a presentation he gave in my home state of Utah to ask him about the experience. The story he told me was an insider's perspective of children's entertainment that seldom gets exposed. Children's films are not always what they appear. Wholesomeness is hardly the goal.

Hidden Messages in Entertainment

As they were wrapping up work on the 2014 film *Mr. Peabody & Sherman*, PDI/DreamWorks called the animators in for a meeting. They screened the movie, a computer-animated film based on characters from an old children's cartoon called *The Adventures of Rocky and Bullwinkle and Friends*. This meeting was the first time animators would get to see the whole film.

Young enjoyed the story, unaware of any underlying message. But at the conclusion, one of his coworkers, who was neither conservative nor straight, expressed confusion about the villain's backstory—what made him so evil? It wasn't clear. What was his motivation?

The explanation from the filmmakers caught Young by surprise. The villain was based on the "religious zealots" who wouldn't conform to the left's emerging gender orthodoxies. Young, like me, is a member of the Church of Jesus Christ of Latter-day Saints, which readers may know as Mormons. He realized he was making a movie in which members of his church were among the "religious zealots" the film was trying to villainize.

Going back through the movie with this new understanding, Young began to see the film with new eyes. The movie's main antagonist, Ms. Grunion, is a middle-aged overweight scold dressed in Sunday best and voiced by actress Allison Janney. The sympathetic heroes were the brilliant dog, Mr. Peabody, and his adopted human son, Sherman.

As Young reconsidered the plot, he was shocked at the themes that emerged. Ms. Grunion, in her condescending ignorance, attacked their nontraditional family. "What kind of a father could this dog ever be to a boy?" she demanded. She was anti-adoption. She was mean to animals. She was cruel. She was deliberately created to associate those values with the religious right in the minds of impressionable young children.

Young began to see the underlying message, previously invisible to him, that starkly contradicted his values—and likely those of the viewers whose children would watch the film over and over and over again. "This is not a movie," he realized, "this is a propaganda piece."

Pulling up a search engine, Young typed in some of the lines the character Ms. Grunion had uttered in the screening version of the film. They weren't original. Her lines came from specific sources— the Catholic Church and the conservative Heritage Foundation among them. He didn't even know what the Heritage Foundation was at the time. But he quickly began to see the political themes being pushed on children.

"I couldn't even perceive it when I was working on it until they laid it out for me," he explained in a recent podcast interview.[2] Young agonized for a month before realizing his dream was over. He asked them to remove his name from the credits.

Shocked, a supervisor sat down with him and asked him to take them through everything in the film that would offend a religious audience. He pointed out a scene in which Ms. Grunion pulled out axes and started hurling them, yelling, "The family is the fundamental unit of society!" He had googled that line. It derived from his own church's Proclamation on the Family, a doctrinal statement in support of strong families that Young firmly supported.[3]

In an effort to help the progressive filmmakers understand, he tried to turn it around on them. What if the underlying message of the film was encouraging kids to believe it's okay to have firearms for defense, he explained, or to support positions former president George W. Bush had taken? "They lost their minds," Young told me. But it changed little.

They did make some changes based on Young's feedback. "It cost my job, but they did get rid of [that scene]," he explained, referring to the ax-throwing by Ms. Grunion. It wasn't enough. In a last-ditch effort to justify staying at PDI/DreamWorks, Young asked the filmmakers to consider disclosing the political messaging to parents. At least that would be honest. They wouldn't do it.

He challenged them to google the words that Ms. Grunion was saying, which they did. Up came the Heritage Foundation, the Catholic Church, and the Proclamation on the Family. After laying out all of his objections, he expected some explanation. But their response was "what you're telling me is we're not being deceptive enough?" Young was amazed that was their takeaway. With that, the meeting—and Young's career at PDI/DreamWorks—was over.

He couldn't dedicate his career to the deception of children. For Young, the deception was the problem. Making content with an agenda is one thing. But hiding that agenda from unsuspecting consumers was a bridge too far.

In the ensuing years, Young ultimately found video-editing work with Project Veritas and was later hired as creative director at the National Center on Sexual Exploitation. His career as a feature film animator was over, but at least he could look himself in the mirror and know he was helping kids, not harming them.

After leaving his initial career, Young started to see the same pattern repeatedly showing up in children's programming: take the words of people you don't like, put them in the mouths of villains, and then have the villain do something psychotic. The child now associates those words with villains. Disney was doing it. Other studios were doing it. When Young presents to audiences today, he walks viewers through clips of popular films like *Frozen*, *The Lego*

Movie, and *Kung Fu Panda*, illustrating the underlying political messages.[4]

Young noticed the main pillars were antimasculine. Children's entertainment was becoming antipatriarchy. Fathers were always vilified or made to look stupid (unless they were gay, in which case they could be witty and attractive). Dominant themes were anticapitalist, antitradition, and antireligion. "That political climate entered children's animation and ruined it," Young explained.

After several box-office misfires, PDI/DreamWorks shut down in 2015, though CEO Jeffrey Katzenberg's main studio in Glendale, California, remains.[5] It wasn't just DreamWorks. In 2023, Disney CEO Bob Iger actually acknowledged the messaging problem after Disney's political engagement in Florida proved costly to the company's bottom line. "Creators lost sight of what their No. 1 objective needed to be," Iger explained at the DealBook Summit in New York City. "We have to entertain first. It's not about messages."[6]

In our interview, Young described what it was like to try to defend his decision to friends and family in Utah after he left California. "How do you tell people we are making characters like them fat, mean to animals, ugly, jerks, never able to solve anything?"

Entertainment is just one of many conduits the left has successfully exploited to influence young minds. Parents can avoid harmful films. But what happens when it comes to the classroom? Social justice themes are infiltrating educational curricula, technology platforms, and other media, influencing content and data collection practices in ways that prioritize political goals over educational ones.

When politics drives the agenda, every other priority gets swallowed up by the pursuit of power. That's why government solutions almost never work as well in practice as they do in theory. Politics eventually gets in the way. In the pursuit of power, those who pull the strings lose sight of what's best for the children, for democratic institutions, and for the pursuit of truth. They come for our kids. And they don't need our permission.

The Link Between Social Engineering and Politics

The cast of characters behind these tools for influencing children is familiar—and telling. Social-engineering efforts appear to be closely linked with political agendas. When you dig into the educational programs, technologies, and entertainment directed at children, you will consistently find politically motivated actors deeply embedded in the funding and development of content.

Barack and Michelle Obama got into the children's entertainment business after he left office. Tech billionaires like Bill Gates, Mark Zuckerberg, and Jeff Bezos are funding misleading school curricula through their foundations. The American Federation of Teachers is run by Democratic operative Randi Weingarten, who is deeply engaged in influencing the political slant of school curricula. The hopelessly leftist Google is in nearly every classroom collecting data on our students. Deeply politicized federal agencies like the US State Department and the Department of Homeland Security have been involved in funding programs to influence what kids are taught.

Inside America's schools, children are bombarded with content developed and funded by a shadowy network of progressive-aligned, dark-money groups. These programs market themselves as a solution to problems like misinformation, emotional intelligence, or civics education. But when you look at the programs, there appears to be an unstated goal to impose a particular worldview on the next generation by embedding progressive narratives into educational curricula.

In the learning modules most subject to political manipulation, there is a vast array of nonprofits that all seem to link back to the same progressive funding ecosystem. It can be hard to trace the fingerprints of progressive politics without diving into financial records.

Dark-money political groups fund nonprofits to provide grants, and then those nonprofits fund other nonprofits to develop and distribute progressive curricula disguised as something else. Behind each "nonpartisan" nonprofit is another nonprofit, funded by an even bigger nonprofit, sometimes linking back to a large for-profit left-wing consulting firm. At each level, we see the same leftist foundations and donors. In some cases, if we trace the money back far enough, it leads right back to American taxpayers.

For example, in the media literacy space, schools rely on the National Association for Media Literacy Education (NAMLE), which is funded in part by the State Department. NAMLE also receives corporate funding from technology companies frequently accused of censorship, including Facebook, YouTube, TikTok, and (pre-Musk) Twitter. But like other education initiatives, NAMLE receives significant funding from foundations, including the Tides Foundation, which is considered a pass-through funder of left-leaning nonprofits.[7]

Whose money is coming through the Tides Foundation? Primarily George Soros, through his Open Society Foundations and Foundation to Promote Open Society. Also, familiar names like Pierre Omidyar through the Omidyar Network Fund and other leftist foundations such as the Robert Wood Johnson Foundation appear on many of these disclosures.[8] The Tides Foundation also receives taxpayer dollars from USAID, according to research from Tyler O'Neil, author of *The Woketopus: The Dark Money Cabal Manipulating the Federal Government.*[9]

Social and emotional learning (SEL) is dominated by the Collaborative for Academic, Social, and Emotional Learning. CASEL receives funding from left-of-center nonprofits like the Chan Zuckerberg Initiative (CZI), run by Facebook founder Mark Zuckerberg and his wife, Priscilla Chan. Other CASEL donors include the Bill & Melinda Gates Foundation, the Robert Wood Johnson Foundation, and the Warren Buffett–funded NoVo Foundation.[10]

Consider the for-profit companies that develop and sell SEL curricula to schools. For example, Panorama Education is a for-profit company with deep ties to progressive politics. Its founder, Xan Tanner, is the son-in-law of Biden attorney general Merrick

Garland. Panorama has also received significant venture capital from Zuckerberg's CZI and Laurene Powell Jobs's Emerson Collective nonprofits, as well as other progressive-leaning tech and education investors. Panorama has partnered with more than two thousand school districts nationwide to conduct SEL surveys of their students and provide curriculum.[11]

In civics education, there are even more players. Among the programs highlighted by the American Federation of Teachers are Generation Citizen and Teaching Tolerance.[12] Generation Citizen receives funding from a plethora of progressive foundations, including the Ford Foundation, the Jennifer and Jonathan Allan Soros Foundation, and the Bezos Foundation, among others. Learning for Justice is funded by the Southern Poverty Law Center.

The progressive donor ecosystem seems extremely interested in what can be injected into school curricula. But there is also interest in the development of learning platforms used in schools. Whether it's the Summit Learning Platform, funded by the Chan Zuckerberg Initiative (CZI) with $99 million since 2016, or Google's Chromebooks and apps, Silicon Valley tech companies have invested heavily in classroom tools that both influence behavior and generate data.[13]

On the entertainment side, we don't see overt funding from dark-money groups. Still, the studios appear to be heavily influenced by political forces. At Disney, former TV executive Monica Harris complained that the studio's embrace of diversity, equity, and inclusion (DEI) policies was imposed by shareholders like BlackRock and other Fortune 500 companies.[14]

She has a point. Readers of my previous book, *The Puppeteers*, will be very familiar with BlackRock's modus operandi of forcing behaviors. BlackRock CEO Larry Fink in 2017 famously said, "Behaviors are going to have change. And this is one thing that we're asking companies. You have to force behaviors. And at BlackRock, we are forcing behaviors."[15]

Going back to Andrew Young's experience, DreamWorks CEO Jeffrey Katzenberg's political ties clearly influenced the shift from storytelling to messaging. Katzenberg isn't just a brilliant filmmaker. He is a Democratic fundraiser known to have a close personal relationship with former president Barack Obama, for whom he raised millions of dollars. *Mother Jones* referred to Katzenberg in 2013 as "the new George Soros." Katzenberg donated over $3 million to Democratic super PACs in the 2012 election cycle and raised more money for Obama in California than any other fundraiser.

Moreover, Katzenberg visited Obama in the White House nearly fifty times in the first term.[16] The two were known to dine together privately and Young remembers Obama visiting Katzenberg's studios, as well as appearances by Bill Clinton and numerous political activist groups. Young recalls the hyperpolitical work environment during the 2012 election cycle in which political messaging was ubiquitous. Katzenberg overtly campaigned for Obama through company channels, including his blog.

Obama, in particular, had a keen interest in children's animation. Upon leaving the presidency, the Obamas formed a production company and signed a deal with Netflix that included children's programming.[17]

All of these characters and organizations are noted for promoting ideologies and educational content that align with progressive or leftist agendas, thus warranting attention from conservative audiences regarding their influence on students. It's no wonder political actors have such an interest in children. The power to research children and parents and influence what information they see is the power to influence voter behavior and manipulate public opinion. Google uses data collected from students using its hardware and software to build detailed profiles that can be used for targeted advertising and messaging.

Usurping the Proper Role of Parents

The change in the way children consume media over my lifetime has been breathtaking. My access to news and entertainment as a child in the 1970s was very controlled and supervised. From my earliest memories, I learned about the world over breakfast. My dad was always the one to make breakfast. He would wiggle my toes to wake me, and by the time I made it to the breakfast table, he had breakfast ready (not always the best breakfast, but breakfast nonetheless).

I first remember reading the funnies as a little kid. (I would have preferred to watch TV nonstop, but my parents strictly regulated that.) I started with the comics, then eventually the sports page, and one day I started noticing other parts of the newspaper. I grew up reading the news with my dad before walking out the door for school each morning.

In the evening, my dad would turn on the evening news and have it playing in the background. We both heard the same reporting. Sometimes we talked about it. On Sundays, we never missed football or *60 Minutes*. You had to be on time because there was no technology to record the shows you missed.

Our entertainment was likewise limited. Sometimes, after school, we could catch reruns of *I Love Lucy* or *The Brady Bunch*. Again, you got there on time, or you missed it. My parents generally knew what I was watching, and I had no way to circumvent that parental control, but I wasn't tracked. I wasn't monitored. Nobody had data about my viewing habits and preferences.

Now I look at the world that we live in. Parents can't control the vast majority of content their kids are being exposed to, including pornography. For kids who have phones with internet access, everything is at their fingertips. It's a Wild, Wild West of free speech, even for kids. Many count on schools to be the counterweight, offering substantive, science-backed educational content to prepare kids for the real world. But increasingly, schools have taken on agendas of their own, often in direct opposition to the values of parents.

The power to shape young minds rightly belongs to parents. Even for those who believe we should expose kids to a whole range of ideas, the programs funded by hard-left donors are not that.

They are one-sided lenses through which to view the world, developed by outside interests and injected into schools by a government bureaucracy that is anything but neutral.

That's not to suggest that programs should never invoke values or biases. Only that they should not do so surreptitiously, without the knowledge and approval of parents, or without the ability to opt out. Neither should outside companies and activist organizations be using education and entertainment platforms as a means to collect data for later activation of the social justice warriors their content was designed to cultivate.

As a parent and grandparent myself, I'm thrilled to have access to good materials that teach kids political values. I think of the Tuttle Twins books, which teach principles of liberty, freedom, and personal responsibility from a libertarian perspective. They can learn how markets work, why meritocracy is important, and where tax dollars go. Resources like Prager U, which produces short educational videos that teach American values, can be a useful tool for teaching kids. There is a whole array of content available teaching a wide range of values from left to right. That's not the problem.

What's happening in schools and movie studios is a hidden agenda, not balanced by ideas from other perspectives, that is being funded and promoted by the political left in an effort to shape a future electorate. These programs are cloaked in uncontroversial learning modules that disguise an ulterior motive—to drive political ideologies.

Gamifying Ideology

Wanted: a game developer who can gamify censorship and make it fun for all ages! The game should involve a superhero team of agents who come together, using their unique powers to defeat emerging disinformation threats.

Sound exciting? The Department of Homeland Security apparently thought so. They gave a $750,000 grant to the Washington,

DC–based nonprofit Wilson Center for pitching a plan to develop such a game aimed at middle and high school students. In their grant application to DHS, the Wilson Center wrote that such a game could "'inoculate' [key audiences] against alleged disinformation."

The game description, released by the Foundation for Freedom Online (FFO), requires children to use their character's government-industry-media superpowers to tactically defeat each threat, targeting speech that is false, harmful, or just "fairly harmful offensive rhetoric." One of the game's objectives, according to FFO, is to get schoolchildren to agree that it is important to suppress the thing called "disinformation."[18]

Other disinformation video games that came before may have inspired that proposal. For example, the State Department developed *Cat Park* to "inoculate" young people against populist news content. That game was a sequel to another, *Harmony Square*, that was created in conjunction with CISA.[19]

My longtime friend and colleague Jennifer Scott, who plays an integral role in researching and writing books with me, sent me the link to this game so I could play it. Here's what we found when we visited harmonysquare.game and played the game (so you wouldn't have to).

In the game's scenario, Jennifer was hired as the new Chief Disinformation Officer, but first she had to answer some questions. (They promised our data would be completely anonymous and would only be used for "scientific research.") The game required her to rate a series of statements on a scale of 1–10. They each looked like tweets—just an opinion unaccompanied by a link that might back it up. Among the statements—"Certain vaccines are loaded with dangerous chemicals and toxins." Jennifer gave it a 2 since there was no source to back it up. Next statement: "The mainstream media has been caught in so many lies it can no longer be trusted as a reliable news source #fakenews."

When she finished the questions, she was cast as the new Disinformation Officer. The "game" then taught players how to post disinformation, asking them to choose "electrifying buzzwords" from a list. "Good! You picked 'lie,' 'abuse,' and 'corrupt' as your buzzwords," it said encouragingly. "Now you can put together a headline." The game then generated a fake post based on those words and asked if the player wanted to "post it." The game gave a bunch of positive reactions ("likes") for a phony post calling someone corrupt and accusing them of lying in college.

Through four segments, the game taught different tactics—emotional words, conspiracy theories, use of bots. "You should create a bunch of emotional memes and articles," the game instructed. The game let Jennifer know that the person she was attacking was seeing their approval numbers drop because of the rumors she was spreading. At some point, the game tells her the news is on to her. Jennifer is getting bad press for posting fake news. She keeps posting more outrageous posts (that the game creates, and she approves).

Eventually the game imposes consequences for Jennifer's irresponsible behavior. Then it's back to the flashing headlines on the screen asking her to identify what is misleading. "Shock! Cute, innocent baby dies one month after receiving vaccine!" The post is obviously misleading, but coincidentally casts the bad guys as the ones questioning whether the government position on vaccines is accurate.

It is not clear whether *Harmony Square* has been used in classrooms. That was one of the reasons given for the Wilson Center's application for grant funding. The development of educational video games to inject ideology into classrooms is a coming attraction. However, the programs that seek to influence political development are already in schools, using subjects like digital literacy, social and emotional learning, and civics education as a delivery device for the political influence agendas of the organizations who fund them.[20]

Developing Young Social Justice Warriors

Many of these externally developed learning modules, upon closer inspection, focus on activism and protest—as though they are designed to raise a generation of young social justice warriors.

We'll look at three types of programs, but they are by no means the only conduits for progressive ideology into the classroom. These in particular seem to have attracted a lot of interest from left-aligned donors and nonprofits, which should be our first clue. The first is often referred to as digital or media literacy—an important topic for a generation with virtually unlimited internet access. It can also shape young minds, teaching them to value censorship and prioritize government-aligned expertise. The second, social and emotional learning (SEL), teaches important life skills, with a side of critical race theory (CRT), gender theory, and identity politics. Finally, we'll look at civics education, in which students are not just learning citizenship but sometimes also principles of "equity" and revisionist history.

Teaching Censorship Through Media Literacy

During a twelve-week training course in media literacy, conservative Rhode Island educator Ramona Bessinger got a crash course in censoring right-wing "extremism." The DHS-funded program, titled Courageous RI, was billed as media training. In practice it was an unapologetically partisan attempt to influence kids a year before a presidential election. This particular course encouraged surveillance of student media, reporting of students whose views they considered extreme, and training for progressive activism.

In a first-person report for the *Legal Insurrection* blog, Bessinger described the September 2023 training as "hyper-focused" on President Trump, designating him the "root cause of all social media and media disinformation." The online materials for the training refer educators to an essay warning of a "rise in extremist ideologies" that could be addressed through "the development of democratic habits" to "rectify false beliefs" and "offer them an alternative path before they veer off course."[21]

Bessinger worried the materials pushed for a culture of K–12 surveillance to prevent students from exploring disapproved viewpoints so they can be flushed out before they become spreaders of "dis-information" or "violent extremism." She questioned what might happen to a student identified as a violent extremist. Bessinger felt they encouraged the use of a Say Something Portal developed to anonymously report potential violent crimes like school shootings, instead using it to report students suspected of this "violent ex-tremism."

In the breakout sessions, Bessinger described discussions about how to handle kids with opposing views. The facilitator described them as the "outer-group" who should be brought back into the "inner-group." "At every juncture," Bessinger wrote, "Trump was attacked and used to make the point that 'violent extremism' and 'disinformation' were a result of 'influencing entrepreneurs' like Trump."

Ultimately, she noted the goal to train students as activists. Stu-dents are paid to create video productions, memes, and billboards as part of a media contest to target Rhode Island residents who are considered threats to domestic safety. Fortunately, not every media literacy program looks like this one.[22]

There is value in digital literacy, in learning to identify good sources and good supporting arguments. Media literacy curricula are designed to help students learn to root out disinformation in an age when they spend hours every day online. Support for digital literacy programs is bipartisan, with both red states and blue states passing mandates for public school instruction.[23]

However, some of these programs are designed to teach kids what to think, not how to think. They tell them what to read, not how to think about what they read. The "guise of 'media literacy,'" writes John Sailer, a senior fellow at the National Association of Scholars, "often functions as a trojan horse, casting certain polit-ical views as prima facie wrong and biased."[24]

Often, the very tools that provide the foundation for media literacy have a built-in bias. We'll take a quick peek at two of them. NewsGuard and Newsela are used in classrooms all across America to help expose students to current events. NewsGuard partners with Randi Weingarten's highly politicized teachers union—the American Federation of Teachers. NewsGuard claims that their "blacklists" are in eight hundred public libraries in the US and Europe.

Newsela is partnered with the progressive Southern Poverty Law Center (SPLC) media literacy program to function as a middleman between kids and the internet.[25] It aggregates left-wing, progressive news stories from "trusted sources" that are rewritten to grade level. It claims to be in 90 percent of American schools. Among the trusted sources are *USA Today*, the *Washington Post*, Associated Press, and the *Guardian*. Analysis by the Foundation for Freedom Online suggests none of Newsela's content partners are non-establishment. They note that even moderate right-of-center outlets like the *Wall Street Journal* and Fox News don't make the list.[26]

In a 2021 blog post, Newsela openly acknowledged the political themes they promote. "We've paired their lessons with authentic, engaging content from real-world sources that bring concepts of anti-bias and social justice to life," the blog announces. "Additionally, our team of curriculum developers and content producers author and review all content against the Teaching Tolerance's Anti-bias framework which includes four domains: Identity, Diversity, Justice and Action."[27]

The aforementioned Teaching Tolerance framework was a media literacy program by the SPLC that has since been renamed. It's now called Learning for Justice and it seeks to address hidden bias in the classroom. The program was redesigned in 2019 with funding from Google to help scale a pilot program "aimed at teaching anti-bias, as well as high-quality teaching about slavery in the United States."[28]

NewsGuard, on the other hand, is basically a government-funded for-profit media blacklisting service used to promote sources friendly to government (and some say progressive) narratives. I've written about it in my previous books because it has been a powerful force in throttling advertising to conservative news sites while propping up progressive-aligned MSM outlets that might otherwise fail to attract readers.

States opting to mandate media literacy training often work with NAMLE and its partner, Erin McNeill's Media Literacy Now. There are a few clues that NAMLE may not be exactly neutral in its political orientation either.

First, the executive director on Instagram claims to be "Pro-choice. Anti-gun. LGBTQ ally. Educating myself to be anti-racist."[29] Second, the presentations given at NAMLE's annual conferences suggest a possible political leaning. In 2021 educators could attend presentations on "Black Lives Matter and Climate Change: What's the Connection?" and "They, She, He Easy as ABC: Understanding Names, Pronouns and Gender Expression" for young students.[30]

Too many media literacy programs draw on principles of gender identity, critical race theory, climate change alarmism, systemic racism, and other progressive political themes designed to indoctrinate the next generation of social justice warriors. Media literacy isn't the only pretext being used to thread the progressive worldview into classroom learning.

SEL with a Side of Critical Race Theory

When a school adopts a program such as Panorama Education's SEL offering, they agree to allow students to respond to surveys that measure their emotional competencies. Panorama asks students in grades six through twelve how often they "learn about, discuss, and confront issues of race, ethnicity, and culture in school." They ask "how diverse, integrated, and fair school is for students from different races, ethnicities, or cultures." And how often a student is "encouraged to think more deeply about race-related topics."

Then the kicker—"How well does your school help students speak out against racism?"[31] It's another call to progressive activism. Not only are the questions leading, but the data collection practices are problematic as well. Panorama's contracts typically stipulate that they own the student data. There is some evidence to suggest students may receive an SEL score—like a credit score—based on the data mined in these programs.[32] Whether that data is mined or sold is never disclosed to parents, but the data is certainly kept long-term to enable the tracking of student progress over time.[33]

The focus on intersectionality and CRT-aligned ideology was all part of an update in 2020 that branded CRT principles as "Transformative SEL." This opened the door to take a successful program from political neutrality to progressive propaganda. Originally, a group of scholars and educators had come together in 1994 to form the Collaborative for Academic, Social, and Emotional Learning, coining the term "social and emotional learning." The CASEL framework taught emotional regulation and interpersonal problem-solving skills. In 2020, CASEL "modernized" the framework.

Transformative SEL is a more ideological approach incorporating concepts like intersectionality and social justice advocacy.[34] The new framework took previously neutral terms and injected them with ideology-laden interpretations. Social awareness now means "public regard of one's racial group," and self-management includes "resistance" and "transformative citizenship." That kind of citizenship is defined as "actions taken to advance policies or social changes that are consistent with human rights, social justice, and equality" even if those actions are "inconsistent with or violate" the law.[35] In other words, social justice activism. There it is again. But nowhere is the quest to activate future progressive warriors more simple than in the curricula for civics education.

Civics Education and Alternative History

In addition to SEL curricula, we've seen a bipartisan political stampede to develop civics education programs. Senator John Cornyn (R-TX) sponsored legislation providing funds for civics education. On the right, Florida governor Ron DeSantis mandated a "non-woke" curricula for schools in his state. The value of learning civics is politically neutral, but the federal guidelines for these programs are not.

The Department of Education's Proposed Priorities for American History and Civics calls for culturally responsive teaching and learning. The guidelines align with the principles of the 1619 Project, a widely debunked reframing of history that casts the Founding Fathers as racist oppressors.[36] Furthermore, federal funding initiatives are written to favor curricula that enforce these alternate historical narratives, by taking into account "systemic marginalization, biases, inequities, and discriminatory policy and practice in American history."

Even funding that came through COVID-19 relief packages was tied to progressive historical frameworks. The Biden-Harris administration allocated some $200 billion in relief funds to schools, directing schools to use as a guide the Abolitionist Teaching Network's *Guide for Racial Justice*, with its antiracist therapy for white educators and instructions for dismantling structural biases.[37]

In the nongovernmental sphere, progressive foundations have funded "action civics" programs that reframe America's history and values with an emphasis on activism. The American Federation of Teachers, headed by progressive activist Randi Weingarten, recommends action civics programs on its website.[38] The National Education Association (NEA) lauds the Generation Citizen curriculum for its emphasis on "getting involved in their community through engagement tactics." Students earn class credit not for learning civics, but for attending protests or supporting partisan nonprofit groups.

The program receives an F grade on a K–12 Civics Report Card released by the Pioneer Institution and the National Association of Scholars. The group's director of research explains that action civics is "meant to change the political system, not to support civil society." Among his criticisms of the approach is the ability of teachers to impose their political views on their students, to influence which "community partners" students choose, and to reduce the limited amount of class time dedicated to teaching the history and values of our republic.[39]

Classroom Data Collection

Meanwhile, one of the world's largest and most progressive companies has an outsize presence in American classrooms, where it has access to data on millions of American students. Google provides education technology services through its Chromebooks and Google Apps, which are used by more than half of American schools, with 50 million users worldwide.[40]

Chromebooks are a great deal for educators, with a low price point and a load of helpful features. But they are an even better deal for Google, which is able to build brand loyalty as a student's first exposure to email, spreadsheets, word processing, online calendars, and other programs in Google's ecosystem. It's smart business. And it's a win/win for students, educators, and Google.

However, some questions must be evaluated about the data Google collects and the bias it could potentially inject in the classroom. Google's tools gather data on users automatically, collecting search histories, location data, and other information without overt consent from parents. By default, this information is stored in the cloud. Outside of a school setting, Google uses this data to build in-depth personality profiles of users, which serve advertising and recommendation systems, targeting users both now and in the future.

To its credit, Google has privacy protections. The company has committed not to sell student data to third parties. It provides its core services to students without ads. It encrypts data.[41] But Google still collects and stores data generated by students.

The potential bias of its products is an even thornier question. Google's well-known progressive bias is captured in an analysis of its search engine, its YouTube algorithm, and its AI product.

In 2023, an AllSides News Analysis of its search engine determined that 63 percent of Google News results are curated from left-leaning sources and only 6 percent from right-leaning outlets.[42] Unlike X, Google does not open-source its algorithm, so it's difficult to prove whether biased results are deliberate or a result of other factors. Studies show that YouTube's algorithm pulls users to the left, and those results skew left even if the user has no history of watching videos on the platform.[43]

When Google unveiled the first version of Gemini, its AI product, the internet was awash in examples of overt racism and progressive political bias. Gemini's image generator would not generate images of white people. Searches for America's very white Founding Fathers generated images of Black and Native American men in period costume. Searches for Catholic popes returned images of women and Asians. Douglas Murray pointed out the ideological bias— searches for gay couples showed happy, gay couples. Searches for straight couples also returned images of happy, gay couples. Those searches also turned up a piece questioning the wisdom of actually identifying as straight.[44]

Google responded by pausing the image-generator feature and CEO Sundar Pichai acknowledged that the biased responses were "completely unacceptable."[45] In November 2024, Google rolled out a new Gemini-powered AI image generator that can be accessed directly from Google Docs, though it is unclear whether the bias issue still exists.[46]

Social Impact of Political Propaganda

To their credit, young people have proved less susceptible to progressive propaganda than designers of these programs may have imagined. In the 2024 election, voters under the age of thirty shifted toward Donald Trump by 11 points from 2020. Kamala Harris netted 51 percent of the vote from that age group, compared to 61 percent by Joe Biden four years earlier.[47]

However, we must not allow one-sided narratives to dominate educational curricula. We have to think long and hard about the potential of raising a generation of kids who know what to think but not how to think. "The problem isn't that Johnny can't read," Thomas Sowell wrote. "The problem isn't even that Johnny can't think. The problem is that Johnny doesn't know what thinking is; he confuses it with feeling." He warned against programs that teach children to "reject traditions in favor of . . . emotional responses" and then conflate that with teaching them to think.[48]

The long-term consequences of ideological indoctrination are serious—and historically don't serve the nations who try it. We risk a decline in academic performance but, more importantly, in critical-thinking skills in the next generation.

Sowell, one of the preeminent American intellects of our time, warned in 2010 against social engineering, which he worries places the decision-making in the hands of a few "wise and knowledgeable" individuals. Elites lack the collective experience and decision-making capacity of the broader population. He "allowed that many government policies that sound appealing have failed in practice." The result is policies that are imposed without any real understanding of their practical implications.[49]

Elites don't have all the answers, no matter where they fall on the ideological spectrum. Pretending they do serves no one. Trying to dictate a one-size-fits-all curriculum centered on progressive goals will ultimately suppress individual freedom. It will hinder creativity and curtail innovation.

CHAPTER 11

Game Changers on the Horizon

S ometimes we forget just how powerful the voice of the American people can be. It was by design that our system was weighted to disadvantage the powerful. Never have I seen a more convincing witness of that reality than in November 2024.

The number of advantages Democrats retained going into Election Day is hard to comprehend. They had the resources of a taxpayer-funded federal workforce doing their get-out-the-vote operation, including access to agency data no political entity could dream of acquiring. There was their oxymoronic army of government-funded "nongovernmental organizations" doing partisan work with taxpayer funds.

Democrats enjoyed a huge fundraising advantage, outraising Republicans at every level.[1] They raised $1 billion for the presidential race between July and September, compared to just $430 million for Republicans.[2] The Democrats' ActBlue fundraising platform substantially outperformed the Republicans' WinRed for individual donations.[3]

Democrats had control of a mass government surveillance operation, which they were not afraid to use. Furthermore, the Biden-Harris DOJ had demonstrated a commitment to two standards of justice—one in which they targeted conservative candidates, lawyers, and protesters in unprecedented ways. From debanking to disbarment to politicized prosecutions, they weaponized it all. That should have—and likely did—had a chilling effect on civic participation.

Moreover, Vice President Kamala Harris received overwhelmingly positive media coverage—78 percent positive to 22 percent negative, according to an MRC analysis. Meanwhile, Donald Trump saw mostly biased coverage, with MRC's methodology showing 85 percent negative stories reported.[4] Though the left's ability to censor on Twitter and then X was gone, their framing of news events still dominated many other media outlets and social media platforms. These advantages are in addition to the built-in help typically given by academia, entertainment, Big Tech, and other industries. It should have all added up to a win.

Still, they lost. They lost the presidency. They lost big and they lost early. They lost in all seven key swing states. They lost the Electoral College. They lost the popular vote. They lost the Senate. They failed to capture the House. They lost ground with youth voters, Latino voters, urban voters, and all male voters.[5]

I wish I could end this book on that happy note. But it gets better. The truth is, there has never been a better time to tackle the problems we've discussed in this book. There are major game changers on the horizon that present opportunities I couldn't have imagined a few years ago.

The Case for Optimism

In President Donald Trump, we have a commander in chief who has been the victim of their censorship, their surveillance, and their political prosecutions. He is not naïve about the weaponization of the system. Indeed, he is as motivated as any president in history to address the problems that plagued his campaigns and previous presidency.

But that's not all. Right now we have a true free speech platform that the government does not appear to be able to censor. X is a significant conduit for information, both true and false. Its Community Notes feature allows users to debunk misinformation without the need for heavy-handed censorship. Having just one free speech platform has enabled conservative media to receive a fair hearing, build an audience, and restore some balance to the coverage of news.

Going into his second administration, Trump enjoyed an original-ist Supreme Court that had already set the stage for dramatic reductions in the bureaucratic state. He went into office boasting one of the most diverse cabinets in history with a true coalition government.

The road forward will undoubtedly be rocky, but there has never been a better time to address the abuses of power, the overreach, the waste, or the imbalances that perpetuated our current problems. The Trump administration can address the core failings of the executive branch—the lack of transparency and accountability, the partisanship, and the overreach.

None of that will be easy. But the real challenge will be finding the right balance between security and freedom as we seek to navigate the new technologies that are quickly changing our world. It's a tall order that will require the efforts of all three branches of government. We must strike a balance between privacy and free speech, between federal and state solutions, and between public-sector and private-sector approaches. We must figure out how to protect children from both pernicious online influences and tenacious data brokers.

Solving these problems will take some trial and error. There will be failures, mistakes, and adjustments that must be made. The knee-jerk reaction of previous administrations defaulted to more government control, more regulation, and more concentrated power in the hands of people we couldn't trust. Now we have a chance to pursue solutions that align with our American values. We can protect privacy, preserve free speech, and still empower solutions. We won't get everything right, but we can start with some of the low-hanging fruit.

Historic Opportunities

I have long called for more openness and accountability from the executive branch. Among the easiest and most effective reforms are beefing up oversight and mandating greater transparency.

Oversight comes in several forms. Each agency must submit to the oversight of an Office of Inspector General (OIG) to investigate claims of waste, fraud, and abuse. By statute, the independent OIG can conduct audits, inspections, and investigations. In my experience, they do so without bias or partisanship. But we need to make some important changes.

The OIG needs a broader scope of authority. For example, the OIG cannot compel testimony from anyone outside of government. They need testimonial subpoena authority. Furthermore, the OIG is not permitted to investigate department lawyers. Given the depth of corruption at the Department of Justice, Inspector General Michael Horowitz should have the authority to investigate anyone at the DOJ. Often the recommendations following an investigation go unheeded by recalcitrant federal agencies without consequence. Lawmakers need to add some teeth to these recommendations. Finally, Congress must reevaluate the whistleblower protection statutes to prevent some of the abuses inflicted on innocent federal employees like those by the Garland Justice Department.

As a check and balance on the executive branch, we need strong congressional oversight. It's important to understand the role Congress plays. I often see complaints from people frustrated by the inability of Congress to throw anyone in jail. That is not the role of the legislative branch, nor should it be. Congressional investigations get people on the record. They provide transparency and accountability. As a former Oversight Committee chairman, I have seen firsthand how corruption evades detection simply by ignoring a congressional subpoena or document request. A Democratic administration's DOJ will refuse to enforce subpoenas against political allies in one case and then jail political foes in a similar case. Congress needs a way to enforce subpoenas, whether that involves compelling DOJ cooperation or designating another entity to enforce those subpoenas.

To promote better transparency, the Trump administration should rigidly enforce the Freedom of Information Act. That means imposing consequences on agencies that play games with document requests, insist on unreasonable delays, or redact documents to avoid required disclosure. If new legislation is needed, I have no doubt there will be many willing to run such a bill.

There are many facts that the public has a right to know. The government should provide full disclosure of censorship demands, for example. The government should disclose data access and collection practices. Furthermore, it should be fully auditable—even the Pentagon. The IRS should be publishing security audits to disclose how it chooses taxpayers for additional scrutiny. I would love to see a serious discussion of how to constitutionally require states to make election results auditable at the local level. While these things must be done carefully to protect privacy, we should be having these debates.

Balancing the Federal Workforce

The Trump administration can rebalance the federal workforce, mitigating the naked partisanship that derailed his first term. In light of the documented abuses of the last decade, we now have much stronger public support to address problems many of us tried to address during the Obama administration. The time is right to address rampant problems with the federal workforce, including the concentration of power in Washington, DC, the disproportionate enforcement of the Hatch Act, and the unintended consequences of the merit protection system.

The proposal to move federal agencies outside the Beltway, which I championed in 2017, represents a real opportunity to get a more representative subsection of Americans working for the government. Not only does it help rebalance the federal workforce, but it puts federal employees out in the field where they can see firsthand the impacts of the regulations they impose on the American people. It shares the wealth of stable federal jobs with other communities across the United States.[6]

To further neutralize federal influence, it may be time to reconsider

the law that governs political engagement by federal bureaucrats—
a law that only seems to be a concern when Republicans run the
executive branch. Democrats cried foul when President Trump
used the White House as a backdrop for videos used in the Republican Party's 2020 virtual convention. They cited a seldom-enforced
federal law dating back to 1939, which precludes executive branch
employees from "using their official authority or influence to inter-
fere with an election."[7] Back then the Hatch Act was sacrosanct to
Democrats. They wanted it followed to the letter. Now they call for
enforcement only when it suits them.

Following that 2020 convention, Democrats lodged a stream
of allegations against various Trump administration officials for
engaging in political activities on government time. For example,
when Secretary of State Mike Pompeo gave a virtual speech for
the convention, he happened to be in Israel on state business at the
time. They argued he was on official business twenty-four hours a
day while there and could not legally give a political speech.[8]

The Office of Special Counsel took the complaints seriously,
launching a full investigation that exonerated some complaints, but
also identified thirteen instances of Hatch Act violations during the
2020 campaign.[9] Most of these involved senior officials expressing political opinions in an election year—something that had
happened repeatedly during the Obama administration without
consequences. Obama cabinet officials Julian Castro and Kath-
leen Sebelius were both found guilty of similar acts during election
years.[10]

In my experience, the current application of the Hatch Act tends
to disproportionately affect (and silence) Republican workers,
while doing little to limit the political machinations of left-leaning
partisans within federal agencies.

Policing the speech of federal employees, particularly in the age
of social media, is problematic. The Hatch Act itself grew out of a
Great Depression–era scandal in which President Franklin Delano
Roosevelt reportedly pressured federal employees to work on the
campaigns of his political allies.[11] An ally of Roosevelt had allegedly

been promising jobs and promotions to Works Progress Administration employees who committed to vote for a US Senate candidate
favored by Roosevelt in Kentucky.[12]

Originally called the "Act to Prevent Pernicious Political Activities," the Hatch Act is designed to ensure federal resources are not
used for political purposes—a laughable objective considering the
many other ways in which federal resources are now helping Democrats and leftist NGOs impact elections. The Hatch Act is likewise meant to protect American citizens from being discriminated
against. Federal agencies are not to treat people differently based
on their political affiliation. But they do anyway, as whistleblowers
like Steve Friend can testify.

We must enforce this law with even application to both the left
and right, or we should stop pretending federal employees are nonpartisan. I always err on the side of free speech, so I would prefer
to see more transparency.

This policy and others originally intended to insulate bureaucrats
from politics have morphed into a system that now protects underper-
forming employees. Consider another long-standing problem with
the federal workforce that I have written about extensively—they
are nearly impossible to fire, even in cases of gross incompetence.
The House Oversight Committee oversees the federal workforce,
which gave me an inside view of how the system is abused.

More recently, the America First Policy Institute issued a 2022
research report showing that agencies are generally unsuccessful
in dismissing public employee union members. The unions get to
help select arbitrators, who then reinstate dismissed employees
three-fifths of the time. High reversal rates combined with lengthy
delays make dismissals problematic for agencies, according to the
report.[13]

A better solution is to transition more federal jobs to at-will
employment. The civil service protection system as currently
structured does not actually insulate employees from political
pressure (at least not if they're conservative), but it does insulate
them from accountability.

As President Trump learned through painful experience, these protections do nothing to prevent federal bureaucrats from actively working to undermine their own commander in chief. The merit protections put in place to insulate them from political influence also prevent the president from holding them accountable for doing so. Removing the red tape that prevents the dismissal of bad apples within the workforce has never been more necessary than it is now.

Trump hopes to achieve this by creating a new employee classification called Schedule F, which he can do by executive order. To ensure permanence, it should also be passed legislatively. Under this system, a greater proportion of the workforce would be considered political appointees subject to removal by the president.

The president must have the authority to manage the executive branch in a way that ensures his policy objectives, and those of the people who voted for him, are not undermined by unaccountable bureaucrats. The entrenched bureaucratic resistance during the first Trump administration should be a catalyst for making long-needed changes.

Thanks to recent Supreme Court rulings limiting the ability of bureaucrats to make law, Congress has some heavy lifting to do as well. As new technology expands to create more threats to privacy and security, Congress may have the hardest job of all. Balancing the right to privacy against the freedoms and civil liberties to which we are entitled will not be an easy needle to thread.

Even if we have to settle for small steps, endure flawed policies, and watch good policies go down in flames, we should be grateful that the fight is on.

The Pivotal Role of the Legislative Branch

There's an idiom to describe virtually impossible endeavors. We say, "It takes an act of Congress to get something done!" It's true—acts of Congress are necessarily difficult. Our system was not made to be efficient or easy. Still, in the interest of preventing tyranny, this is the system with which we have to work.

It is Congress, not regulators, who must grapple with how to balance national security benefits with civil liberties. The answers will not be simple. But this is a debate we must have. It should not take place within the darkened corridors of Washington federal buildings, but in the open, among those who will be held accountable at the ballot box.

I certainly don't have all the answers. But I know the process is important. We must allow state legislatures to be the default option for regulation. American citizens have access to state legislators in ways they could never access members of Congress who don't represent their districts. The Tenth Amendment grants all powers not specifically delegated to the federal government to the states. Previous Congresses seem to have forgotten this well-established limiting principle.

When federal law is necessary, those laws should be narrowly tailored and unambiguous. Some examples of laws that must be addressed at the federal level might include antitrust legislation aimed at large monopolies like Google, who have used their market advantage to influence elections.[14] Congress should establish legal boundaries for surveillance that are applied equally to both parties. At the federal level, we must consider prohibiting federal agencies from doing voter registration.

We aren't the first generation to grapple with changing technology. What makes the privacy issue even more challenging is the need to respect civil liberties. Problems seem easy to solve when you concentrate power in the hands of bureaucrats to write the laws and restrict choice.

We must be allowed to protect our integrity and limit how other people profit and take from us. But it's more complicated than it seems because we must always err on the side of free speech. As Americans, we have a right to privacy and that should not be infringed upon. That must be paramount in these decision-making processes.

Repeal Biden AI Orders: Mandatory disclosures of safety test outcomes and compliance guidelines for federal agencies create burdens that hinder growth. The orders prioritize regulation over free-market principles, chilling tech advancement. Biden invoked the Defense Production Act, which allowed for government control over private-sector innovation. Republicans worry about losing the competitive edge to China.

Data Minimization Policies: Both parties support a uniform federal standard that sets a baseline, defines what constitutes necessary data, and limits data retention periods. Leftists want to require data collectors to clearly state specific purposes for data and prohibit additional uses without consent. They want to mandate routine data audits and promote data anonymization. Republicans prefer a market-driven approach where companies self-regulate, prioritize consumer rights to control their data, and ban targeted advertising to children.

Regulation of Data Brokers: Institute a single federal standard/framework to avoid having a patchwork of state laws. Empower consumers with transparency and choice rather than federal mandates, and require the use of opt-in and opt-out mechanisms.

Comprehensive Cybersecurity Policy Framework: Elements include risk assessment and management, data protection and privacy, incident response and reporting, harmonization of standards, procurement requirements, interagency coordination, and workforce development.

I do have to offer a word of caution from someone who has had experience trying to pass technical legislation through Congress: Lawmakers need to bring in subject matter experts to help. Way too many people are weighing in on things they don't understand. The people who want to be involved and engaged in these issues sometimes have no idea how they work.

In 2011, when tech companies were promoting the Stop Online Piracy Act (SOPA), you could count on one hand the number of people in Congress who understood these technical issues. I worried we were trying to do surgery on the internet without a doctor in the House.

SOPA, an industry-sponsored solution to copyright infringement, represented a very real threat to free speech. It had strong industry support from the motion picture and recording industries and looked likely to sail through Congress. Concerned it would lead to widespread censorship of legitimate websites, I pushed for more comprehensive hearings to help the public understand the stakes. At times it seemed I was the only one fighting it. But by digging deeper and enlisting the help of subject matter experts, we were able to kill the bill.

To protect civil liberties, we must enlist the voluntary participation of market forces to work collaboratively on policies to protect privacy, to protect children, and to protect civil liberties. Though we can't set policy without Congress, we need to enlist those with subject matter expertise if we are to find the best path forward.

Collaborative Solutions

The real way forward is to unleash the power of the private sector to develop solutions. We must look to the innovators to help solve these problems. The solutions won't come from Congress, though we may need Congress to help enact them. Creativity is one of America's competitive advantages, and we must leverage it. Inevitably, Washington will be behind the curve. We'll need to ally with technology and privacy thought leaders who have the motivation and resources to solve these problems.

Oracle CEO Safra Catz has played a pivotal role in her company's approach to protecting online privacy and data. Oracle won the contract to create a safer environment for American TikTok users.[15] The company's robust security features have made its cloud infrastructure second to none. Under her direction, Oracle has leveraged AI to assist clients in identifying fraud and complying with regulatory standards, both of which are necessary to protect privacy.

Likewise, Apple's Tim Cook sees privacy as a fundamental human right. Cook worries that Americans' privacy is under threat from what he calls "the data industrial complex" of data brokers. Apple is committed to data minimization, maximizing the amount of processing done on devices rather than in the cloud where it is vulnerable to cyber criminals.[16] Apple is deeply engaged in the privacy debate, both at home and abroad.

Perhaps one of the most influential innovators in the Trump administration orbit is X owner Elon Musk. Musk's Starlink satellite internet service provides secure online access worldwide with minimal reliance on traditional internet service providers (ISPs) that may collect data. The decentralized nature of Starlink reduces the risk of data interception. Musk has also been a leader in the promotion of open-source software that allows community-driven efforts to identify and fix vulnerabilities.

These are the types of thought leaders Congress needs to enlist in the fight to protect privacy. Collaborative efforts between the public and private sectors are the only way to address the pressing challenges of privacy.

Our top priority must be protecting minor children. Technology is influencing the way they learn and communicate. But it is ripe for abuse, prone to amplify mistakes, and can potentially ruin young lives. We are a very forgiving society. But we must allow for mistakes made in youth to be erased so they don't follow us for the rest of our lives.

One category of solutions involves age verification policies. I believe we can leave these to the states, where laws are currently being crafted and litigated. It is a complex problem that may require a lot of trial and error. But that's why state solutions are best—states are more flexible and responsive.

Europe has pursued what they call "right to be forgotten" laws. These types of mandates are problematic in America, but they can be voluntarily enacted. Businesses are free to implement European policies that the government cannot. Consumers can be a powerful force in demanding privacy to pressure corporate compliance with data opt-out processes.[17]

Tech companies can also offer tools to help parents manage online activity by their children. Products like Norton Family, Google Family Link, and Net Nanny offer these capabilities.

I have grave concerns about deepfake technologies that use AI to generate synthetic media that appears to portray someone doing or saying something that didn't happen. It relies on deep-learning algorithms to create completely fabricated but shockingly realistic content. Deepfakes rely on generative AI networks that can generate increasingly more realistic fakes over time.

This technology can lead to untold reputational harm, fraud, and the erosion of trust. It also poses a potential security threat in its capacity to bypass biometric security systems like facial recognition.

How do we balance the First Amendment with deepfakes? Just because you're a celebrity doesn't mean someone can cut and paste your face onto a pornographic video. That's wrong. The private sector is developing detection technologies to identify digital artifacts that may point to manipulation. Digital watermarking incorporates Blockchain technology to create secure records of content authenticity.

We will need action from Congress to take on the battle to target malicious deepfakes and ensure prosecution. Social media platforms will also be part of the solution as they seek to identify and remove manipulated content.

Blockchain technology offers promising solutions as well. Using advanced cryptographic methods, Blockchain can secure transactions and protect user identities. It operates on a decentralized network that is harder to hack.

Other emerging technologies offer promising solutions to securing transactions. Utah-based ICN, which we mentioned in Chapter 8, uses cryptographic signatures for data packets to ensure data integrity regardless of where the data is stored or how it is transmitted. ICN secures the content itself rather than the communication channels. Though this technology is not yet considered mainstream, it is likely to be more broadly adopted over time.

Innovations in data virtualization also offer promising solutions. Data virtualization can discover and access data quickly without physically moving it or even having control of the raw data itself. Such technologies allow organizations to analyze data while maintaining privacy and security, deriving insights without transferring or exposing raw data.

I am fundamentally optimistic about the future of the United States of America. We get a lot of things right. We don't have to have all the solutions. But we know how to prioritize the things that matter most. Nothing is more important than protecting our families and our freedom.

I worry about society if we don't do what is necessary to strengthen the family. It really is the fundamental unit of society. Strong family units can only have positive effects on culture. Protecting children from online threats, viral mistakes, and materials inappropriate for their age is the duty of the government and parents alike.

Protecting our freedoms has never been more important than it is right now. We deserve a government with better transparency and oversight. We need to allow the private sector to drive innovation, supported but not compelled by government. And we need a government more focused on solving problems than on manipulating elections.

The Trump administration has a historic opportunity to challenge the adage of another famous Republican president. Ronald Reagan memorably observed, "No government ever voluntarily reduces itself in size. Government programs, once launched, never disappear. Actually, a government bureau is the nearest thing to eternal life we'll ever see on this earth!"[18]

He wasn't wrong. The policy prescriptions needed to preserve civil liberties, protect privacy, and drive innovation won't all be easy. They won't necessarily lead to immediate prosperity. But they are an investment in the next generation of Americans, who deserve to inherit the same opportunities and freedoms their forefathers fought to obtain.

Acknowledgments

The words "daunting" and "overwhelming" came to mind when I was first considering the massive task of trying to capture and convey the concerns I have with the surveillance of our day-to-day lives in this new world. We are monitored in everything we do. What is unfolding in real time is moving faster than most of us can imagine. "Lightning speed" doesn't fully capture it.

This is the fifth book I have published. Perhaps my most important book, it reveals threats to privacy that impact each of us now and in the future. That claim may come across as dramatic, but what is currently being done with technology, artificial intelligence, surveillance, social credit scores, deepfakes, manipulations, and eventually mind monitoring is truly remarkable. This book gives you a strong insight into what has been done, what is happening now, and what is being planned.

It takes a tremendous amount of time to develop a book. To do it right, you don't simply sit down and start typing it out on a keyboard. Writing a nonfiction book takes a team of talented people. I am most fortunate and blessed to be surrounded by supportive family and top-notch professionals.

First, I have to recognize my wonderful wife, Julie, and our family, who have supported me every step of the way. They have always allowed me to do what I must to invest the considerable time my career requires. Without Julie holding our family together, I would never have been able to commit so much time in Congress, at Fox News, in business, and certainly in developing this book. Thank you.

Getting a book published is no easy task. I fully recognize many want to do it, but few actually get to do it. Many thanks to David Larabell from Creative Artists Agency (CAA) for once again having faith in me and making it look easy to secure the publishing agreements for our fifth book. He's a super talent and understands the business as much as anyone in the market.

I am most grateful for Broadside Books from HarperCollins, and specifically Eric Nelson. His guidance, insight, and confidence in the need for this book was pivotal to making it a reality. Taking on such a massive subject requires constant refinement to ensure that the end product properly communicates the facts while allowing me to share my perspective taken from my unique life experiences. Having worked with Eric for years now, the process has improved and consequently I hope you find the information illuminating, even if somewhat scary, but above all, accurate.

This book would not have happened without Jennifer Scott. Jennifer and I have worked together since 2006. I rely on Jennifer as much as anyone to think through issues, develop policy positions, interpret day-to-day political issues, and certainly to write this book. Jennifer was pivotal, outlining the direction, doing the research, and organizing the mass of information into a cohesive final book. With roughly five hundred endnotes, there was a tremendous amount of effort gathering and evaluating what made the final cut. I am so grateful for Jennifer's talents, perspectives, and tenacity. Thank you.

Peter Schweizer and I share a passion for government oversight. With his uncanny ability to unmask nefarious actors and uncover their hidden corruption, he does incredible work on behalf of the American people. I am grateful for my association with Peter and his outstanding research team at the Government Accountability Institute, where I am a distinguished fellow.

The whole GAI team, with their vast experience in oversight-related projects, has been immeasurably helpful in building this book and providing direction. The leadership of Peter Schweizer and Peter Boyer overseeing GAI allows people like me to thrive as I develop a book worthy of your time. I want to recognize the important contributions of Steve Post, Steve Stewart, Seamus Bruner, and Hannah Scott, who all contributed to ensure we had an accurate and well-researched book. In the monumental task of exposing government waste, fraud, and abuse, I work with the best of the best. I can't thank Peter and his team enough for their skill, integrity, and professionalism.

We had numerous sources, some of whom we cannot name, and many who were willing to provide their insight and expertise.

Mike Howell and I have worked together for years, first at the Oversight and Government Reform Committee and then at the Oversight Project at the Heritage Foundation. He is a fountain of ideas and one of the best-networked people in Washington, DC.

Many thanks to Andrew Young for bravely sharing his experience as a motion picture animator and standing up for his values.

Erik McCauley was very helpful to my understanding the real-world repercussions of cybersecurity for American small business owners.

Similarly, Spencer Brown shared his expertise in cybersecurity, charting the challenges that lie ahead for companies wishing to secure their networks.

Scott Volmar offered a wealth of knowledge on the history and limitations of the World Wide Web, sharing out-of-the-box solutions that might be considered to secure it.

Many thanks to Tristan Leavitt for his tenacious career dedicated to helping whistleblowers. I first met Tristan when he worked with us at the Oversight and Government Reform Committee. He continues to be a good friend and confidant.

I also want to thank Brett Tolman. He has always been available for advice and counsel on the federal courts and our system of justice. He is a good friend, a compassionate warrior, and dedicated to the goodness of liberty, freedom, and the United States of America.

Finally, I want to thank you for taking the time to read or listen to this book. It is an honor to be trusted with your time and attention.

I am frequently asked by people what they can do to make a difference. It's very simple. First, we all need to look beyond the narratives we're being fed by mainstream media to gain a more complete understanding of what's happening around us. Then we need to collectively come together to support efforts to move our country in the right direction. I hope this book helps provide a better understanding of how our data has been used to work against our interests. I am a huge advocate of the reality that sunlight is the best disinfectant. More importantly, I'm more optimistic than ever that real, positive changes are coming.

I love this country and I'm very blessed to have a voice to share these perspectives with you. I truly hope you enjoyed it.

Thank you.

Notes

Preface

1. Representative Jason Chaffetz, "Rep. Jason Chaffetz (R-Utah) on SOPA: 'Bring in the Nerds,'" Center for Democracy and Technology, December 20, 2011, YouTube, 1 min., 26 sec., https://www.youtube.com/watch?v=xrrj9Wc2L84.

Chapter 1: The Power Imperative

1. Heritage Oversight Project, "New Document Highlights Partisan Application of Biden's FedGov Get-Out-The-Vote Operation," May 1, 2024, https://oversight.heritage.org/OP_Memo_on_EO_14019_Partisan_Implementation_5.1.2024.pdf.

2. Sam Starnes, "A Leader in the Fight for Rights," Rutgers University Foundation, April 9, 2024, https://rutgersfoundation.org/news/leader-fight-rights.

3. Mollie Hemingway, "Yes, Biden Is Hiding His Plan to Rig the 2022 Midterm Elections," Federalist, June 23, 2022, https://thefederalist.com/2022/06/23/yes-biden-is-hiding-his-plan-to-rig-the-2022-midterm-elections.

4. Seamus Bruner, *Controligarchs: Exposing the Billionaire Class, Their Secret Deals, and the Globalist Plot to Dominate Your Life* (New York: Penguin, 2024), xii.

5. White House, "Executive Order 14019: Promoting Access to Voting," March 7, 2021, *Federal Register* 86, no. 45 (March 10, 2021): 13623–625.

6. "Biden Bucks: Executive Order 14019," Heritage Foundation, May 16, 2024, https://www.heritage.org/the-oversight-project/election-integrity/biden-bucks-executive-order-14019.

7. Leadership Conference (@civilrightsorg), "Wade Henderson, interim president and CEO of The Leadership Conference on Civil and Human Rights, issued the following statement on the Biden administration's executive order promoting competition in the American economy," Twitter, July 8, 2021, 6:34 p.m., https://twitter.com/civilrightsorg/status/1413266085130952711.

8. Ibid.; "Biden Bucks: Executive Order 14019," Heritage Foundation.

9. "About," Demos, accessed December 30, 2024, https://www.demos.org/about.

10. Ibid.; "Biden Bucks: Executive Order 14019," Heritage Foundation.

11. Ibid.

12. White House, "Executive Order 14019: Promoting Access to Voting," 13623.

13. Tarren Bragdon and Stewart Whitson, "Voter Drive: What's Biden Hiding?" *Wall Street Journal*, April 19, 2022, https://www.wsj.com/articles/voter-drive-whats-biden-hiding-justice-department-freedom-of-information-foia-transparency-corruption-lawsuit-foundation-for-government-accountability-11650403740.

14. "FGA Files Lawsuit Against Biden Administration Demanding Answers on Executive Order 14019," press release, Foundation for Government Accountability, accessed December 30, 2024, https://thefga.org/press/fga-files-lawsuit-against-biden-answers-on-executive-order-14019/.

15. Fred Lucas, "DOJ Cites 'Public Confusion' as Reason to Keep Documents on Biden Order Secret," Daily Signal, October 21, 2022, https://www.dailysignal.com/2022/10/21/doj-cites-public-confusion-as-reason-to-keep-documents-on-biden-order-secret.

Chapter 2: The Privacy Trade-off

1. "2024–2025 Action Plan for the Establishment of the Social Credit System," China Law Translate, accessed January 28, 2025, https://www.chinalawtranslate.com/en/2024-2025social-credit-plan.

2. Antonio Graceffo, "From Cyberspace IDs to Digital Yuan: Communist China's Expanding Grip on Online Freedom," *Epoch Times*, August 28, 2024, updated September 2, 2024, https://www.theepochtimes.com/opinion/from-cyberspace-ids-to-digital-yuan-communist-chinas-expanding-grip-on-online-freedom-5710876.

3. Ibid.; Roger Huang, "A 2024 Overview of the E-CNY: China's Digital Yuan," *Forbes*, July 15, 2024, https://www.forbes.com/sites/digital-assets/2024/07/15/a-2024-overview-of-the-e-cny-chinas-digital-yuan.

4. "The Chinese Firewall," Internet Society, accessed January 28, 2025, https://www.internetsociety.org/resources/internet-fragmentation/the-chinese-firewall.

5. Ibid.; Graceffo, "From Cyberspace IDs to Digital Yuan."

6. US District Court for the District of Columbia, *Statement of Facts, Case No. 1:21-cr-00065-CRC, Document 1-1*, filed October 3, 2020, https://www.documentcloud.org/documents/22088133-1-1-statement-of-facts.

7. "Privacy Policy," Kia Motors UK, accessed January 28, 2025, https://www.kia.com/uk/privacy; "How Cars Spy on You: Most Shocking Takeaways from Mozilla's Report," *AdGuard Blog*, accessed January 28, 2025, https://adguard.com/en/blog/car-spying-mozilla-privacy-report.html.

8. Jess Weatherbed, "Biden Administration Is Investigating Security Threats from Chinese Vehicles," Verge, February 29, 2024, https://www.theverge.com/2024/2/29/24086490/us-biden-administration-investigation-chinese-vehicles-security-threat.

9. Akiko Fujita, "Chinese EVs Are 'Driving into Mexico'—and It's Starting to Worry the US," Yahoo Finance, June 15, 2024, https://finance.yahoo.com/news/chinese-evs-are-driving-into-mexico--and-its-starting-to-worry-the-us-210133299.html.

10. James A. Lewis, "Connected Cars and Spying," Center for Strategic and International Studies, October 1, 2024, https://www.csis.org/analysis/connected-cars-and-spying.

11. Bradley A. Thayer, "For Chinese Firms, Theft of Your Data Is Now a Legal Requirement," *The Hill*, January 7, 2021, https://thehill.com/opinion/cybersecurity/532583-for-chinese-firms-theft-of-your-data-is-now-a-legal-requirement.

12. US Congress, House, *Infrastructure Investment and Jobs Act. H.R. 3684, 117th Congress*, introduced June 4, 2021, https://www.congress.gov/bill/117th-congress/house-bill/3684/text.

13. Jon Miltimore, "The Feds' Vehicle 'Kill Switch' Mandate Is a Gross (and Dangerous) Violation of Privacy," Foundation for Economic Education, November 22, 2023, https://fee.org/articles/the-feds-vehicle-kill-switch-mandate-is-a-gross-and-dangerous-violation-of-privacy.

14. Ulysses Group, "Telematics Enabled Intelligence," accessed December 30, 2024, https://s3.documentcloud.org/documents/20515640/ulysses-document.pdf; Joseph Cox, "Cars Have Your Location. This Spy Firm Wants to Sell It to the U.S. Military," Vice, March 17, 2021, https://www.vice.com/en/article/car-location-data-telematics-us-military-ulysses-group.

15. "Florida Is Selling Drivers' Personal Information to Private Companies and Marketing Firms," WXYZ, updated July 11, 2019, https://www.wxyz.com/news/national/florida-is-selling-drivers-personal-information-to-private-companies-and-marketing-firms.

16. "Executive Order on Collecting Information About Citizenship Status in Connection with the Decennial Census," Trump White House Archives, July 11, 2019, https://trumpwhitehouse.archives.gov/presidential-actions/executive-order-collecting-information-citizenship-status-connection-decennial-census.

17. US Census Bureau, "U.S. Census Bureau Statement on State Data Sharing Agreements," news release, October 15, 2019, https://www.census.gov/newsroom/press-releases/2019/state-data-sharing-agreements.html.

18. "New Docs from Deep State Committee Reveal How January 6 and the Raid at Mar-a-Lago Emboldened DHS to Expand Monitoring of Americans," America First Legal, June 24, 2024, https://aflegal.org/exclusive-new-docs-from-deep-state-committee-reveal-how-january-6-and-the-raid-at-mar-a-lago-emboldened-dhs-to-expand-monitoring-of-americans.

Chapter 3: The New Blacklist

1. "105 Organizations Demand Banks Stop Financing Industrial Livestock Production that Fuels the Climate Crisis," Friends of the Earth, September 12, 2024, https://foe.org/news/banks-industrial-livestock.

2. US House of Representatives Committee on Oversight and Government Reform, *Report: DOJ's Operation Choke Point Secretly Pressured Banks to Cut Ties with Legal Business*, May 29, 2014, https://oversight.house.gov/release/report-dojs-operation-choke-point-secretly-pressured-banks-cut-ties-legal-business/.

3. Allysia Finley, "Debanking and the Return of Operation Choke Point," *Wall Street Journal*, December 15, 2024, https://www.wsj.com/opinion/debanking-and-the-return-of-operation-choke-point-finance-money-government-8d507083.

4. "The Truth About Account Closures," Bank Policy Institute, December 13, 2024, https://bpi.com/wp-content/uploads/2024/12/The-Truth-About-Account-Closures.pdf.

5. Ibid.; Finley, "Debanking and the Return of Operation Choke Point."

6. Timothy Two Project International, https://www.timothytwo.org, accessed January 28, 2025; "Timothy Two Project International," Charity Navigator, accessed January 28, 2025, https://www.charitynavigator.org/ein/453052440.

7. Steve Curtis, "Why Is Bank of America Canceling the Accounts of Religious Organizations?" *Washington Examiner*, November 12, 2023, https://www.washingtonexaminer.com/opinion/beltway-confidential/2748853/why-is-bank-of-america-canceling-the-accounts-of-religious-organizations.

8. Ibid.; Helena Kelly, "Debanking Row Breaks as Bank of America Shuts Account of Ultra-Conservative Christian Charity Serving Impoverished Ugandans," *Daily Mail*, August 22, 2023, https://www.dailymail.co.uk/yourmoney/banking/article-12417653/Debanking-row-breaks-Bank-America-shuts-account-ultra-conservative-Christian-charity-serves-impoverished-Ugandans.html.

9. Ibid.

10. Ibid.; Curtis, "Why Is Bank of America Canceling the Accounts of Religious Organizations?"

11. US House Committee on the Judiciary, *Financial Surveillance in the United States*, December 6, 2024, https://judiciary.house.gov/sites/evo-subsites/republicans-judiciary.house.gov/files/2024-12/2024-12-05-Financial-Surveillance-in-the-United-States.pdf.

12. Joel Schoffstall, "Republican AGs Demand Wells Fargo Answer for Abruptly Closing Gun Dealer's Account, Other Woke Policies," Fox Business, March

6, 2024, https://www.foxbusiness.com/fox-news-politics/republican-ags -demand-wells-fargo-answer-for-abruptly-closing-gun-dealers-account-other -woke-policies.

13. "Instances of Viewpoint-Based De-Banking," Viewpoint Diversity Score, March 27, 2024, https://www.viewpointdiversityscore.org/resources /instances-of-viewpoint-based-de-banking.

14. Select Subcommittee on the Weaponization of the Federal Government, *Financial Surveillance in the United States: How the Federal Government Weaponized the Bank Secrecy Act to Spy on Americans*, December 6, 2024, https://judiciary.house.gov/sites/evo-subsites/republicans-judiciary.house. gov/files/2024-12/2024-12-05-Financial-Surveillance-in-the-United-States .pdf.

15. Ibid., 30.

16. "Bankrolling Bigotry: An Overview of the Online Funding Strategies of American Hate Groups," Institute for Strategic Dialogue, 2020, https://www .isdglobal.org/wp-content/uploads/2020/10/bankrolling-bigotry-3.pdf.

17. Ibid.

18. Tyler O'Neil, "Conservatives Wrongly Demonized as 'Hate Groups' May Get Justice at Last," Heritage Foundation, April 25, 2023, https://www.heritage .org/crime-and-justice/commentary/conservatives-wrongly-demonized-hate -groups-may-get-justice-last.

19. Tyler O'Neil, "Far-Left Group Puts Moms for Liberty on Map With KKK Chapters," Daily Signal, June 6, 2023, https://www.dailysignal.com/2023/06/06 /breaking-southern-poverty-law-center-adds-parental-rights-groups-hate -map; "Tucker Carlson," Extremist Files, Southern Poverty Law Center, accessed January 30, 2025, https://www.splcenter.org/resources/extremist-files /tucker-carlson.

20. "Center for Immigration Studies," Extremist Files, Southern Poverty Law Center, accessed January 30, 2025, https://www.splcenter.org/resources /extremist-files/center-immigration-studies; "Number of Hate Groups Continues to Rise," Southern Poverty Law Center, accessed January 30, 2025, https:// www.splcenter.org/resources/reports/number-hate-groups-continues-rise.

21. "American College of Pediatricians," Extremist Files, Southern Poverty Law Center, accessed January 30, 2025, https://www.splcenter.org/resources /extremist-files/american-college-pediatricians.

22. Select Subcommittee on the Weaponization of the Federal Government, *Letter to Noah Bishoff*, January 17, 2024, https://judiciary.house.gov/sites/evo-subsites /republicans-judiciary.house.gov/files/evo-media-document/2024-01-17-jdj -to-bishoff-re-ti-request.pdf.

23. *Financial Surveillance in the United States*, 21.

24. Sam Brownback and Jeremy Tedesco, "Stop the Troubling Trend of Politically Motivated Debanking," *Newsweek*, March 15, 2023, https://www.newsweek.com/stop-troubling-trend-politically-motivated-debanking-opinion-1787639.

25. Sheldon Whitehouse, *Letter to Charles Rettig*, January 19, 2021, https://www.whitehouse.senate.gov/wp-content/uploads/imo/media/doc/Whitehouse%20IRS%20Letter%20re%20Turning%20Point%20USA.pdf.

26. "Press Release: Politicized IRS Opens Investigation into American Accountability Foundation After Exposing Biden Nominees," American Accountability Foundation, November 6, 2023, https://americanaccountabilityfoundation.com/blog/2023/11/06/press-release-politicized-irs-opens-investigation-into-american-accountability-foundation-after-exposing-biden-nominees.

27. Treasury Inspector General for Tax Administration, "Inappropriate Criteria Were Used to Identify Tax-Exempt Applications for Review," May 14, 2013, archived June 12, 2013, https://web.archive.org/web/20130612132155/http://www.treasury.gov/tigta/auditreports/2013reports/201310053fr.pdf.

28. Office of Public Affairs, "Attorney General Jeff Sessions Announces Department of Justice Has Settled with Plaintiff Groups Improperly Targeted by IRS," news release, October 26, 2017, https://www.justice.gov/opa/pr/attorney-general-jeff-sessions-announces-department-justice-has-settled-plaintiff-groups.

29. Katie Lobosco, "IRS Plans to Increase Audit Rates of Wealthy Taxpayers by 50%," CNN, May 2, 2024, https://www.cnn.com/2024/05/02/politics/irs-audit-tax-rates-wealthy.

30. US Department of the Treasury, "Secretary of the Treasury Janet L. Yellen Sends Letter to IRS Commissioner in Support of Funding for IRS to Improve Taxpayer Service & Combat Evasion by High Income Earners and Corporations," news release, April 7, 2022, https://home.treasury.gov/news/press-releases/jy0918.

31. United States Senate Committee on Finance, "Crapo Statement on Protecting Taxpayers Earning Under $400,000 from Increased IRS Scrutiny," August 11, 2022, https://www.finance.senate.gov/ranking-members-news/crapo-statement-on-protecting-taxpayers-earning-under-400000-from-increased-irs-scrutiny.

32. "IRS Ramps Up New Initiatives Using Inflation Reduction Act Funding to Ensure Complex Partnerships, Large Corporations Pay Taxes Owed, Continues to Close Millionaire Tax Debt Cases," Internal Revenue Service, January 12, 2024, https://www.irs.gov/newsroom/irs-ramps-up-new-initiatives-using-inflation-reduction-act-funding-to-ensure-complex-partnerships-large-corporations-pay-taxes-owed-continues-to-close-millionaire-tax-debt-cases.

33. Alan Rappeport, "I.R.S. Deploys Artificial Intelligence to Catch Tax Evasion,"

New York Times, September 8, 2023, https://www.nytimes.com/2023/09/08/us/politics/irs-deploys-artificial-intelligence-to-target-rich-partnerships.html.

34. Committee on Oversight, "Hearing Wrap Up: IRS Whistleblowers Expose How Bidens Were Treated Differently," news release, July 19, 2023, https://oversight.house.gov/release/hearing-wrap-up-irs-whistleblowers-expose-how-bidens-were-treated-differently.

35. Luke Rosiak, "IRS Employees Owe $50 Million in Back Taxes, Audit Finds," Daily Wire, July 29, 2024, https://www.dailywire.com/news/irs-employees-owe-50-million-in-back-taxes-audit-finds.

36. White House, "Executive Order on Further Advancing Racial Equity and Support for Underserved Communities Through the Federal Government," news release, February 16, 2023, archived December 28, 2024, http://web.archive.org/web/20241228035708/https://www.whitehouse.gov/briefing-room/presidential-actions/2023/02/16/executive-order-on-further-advancing-racial-equity-and-support-for-underserved-communities-through-the-federal-government.

37. Michael Washburn, "Legal Foundation Demands Answers from IRS Over Risk of 'Discriminatory' Audits," *Epoch Times*, February 22, 2023, https://www.theepochtimes.com/us/legal-foundation-demands-answers-from-irs-over-risk-of-discriminatory-audits-5076851; Jack Phillips, "IRS Sued for Illegally 'Concealing' Records on 'Race-Based Tax Audits,'" *Epoch Times*, April 19, 2024, https://www.theepochtimes.com/us/irs-sued-for-illegally-concealing-records-on-race-based-tax-audits-5633013.

38. Select Subcommittee on the Weaponization of the Federal Government, *Letter to Janet Yellen*, March 20, 2024, https://judiciary.house.gov/sites/evo-subsites/republicans-judiciary.house.gov/files/evo-media-document/2024-03-20%20JDJ%20HH%20to%20IRS%20re%20AI%20surveillance.pdf.

39. "Polselli v. Internal Revenue Service," Case Files, *SCOTUSblog*, accessed January 30, 2025, https://www.scotusblog.com/case-files/cases/polselli-v-internal-revenue-service.

40. Select Subcommittee on the Weaponization of the Federal Government, *Letter to Janet Yellen.*

41. Executive Office of the Governor, "Governor Ron DeSantis Signs Legislation to Protect Floridians' Financial Future & Economic Liberty," news release, May 2, 2023, archived October 6, 2024, http://web.archive.org/web/20241006195131/https://www.flgov.com/2023/05/02/governor-ron-desantis-signs-legislation-to-protect-floridians-financial-future-economic-liberty.

42. Andrew Schwartz, "Religion, Politics, Fossil Fuels: Bank Customers Get New Protections Against Discrimination in Tennessee," *Chattanooga Times Free Press*, April 23, 2024, https://www.timesfreepress.com/news/2024/apr/23/religion-politics-fossil-fuels-bank-customers-get.

43. "Debanking Treats Law-Abiding Citizens Like Criminals, but States Can Set Them Free," Foundation for Government Accountability, March 15, 2024, https://thefga.org/blog/debanking-treats-law-abiding-citizens-like-criminals-but-states-can-set-them-free.

Chapter 4: Purging the Heretics

1. Alayna Treene, Annie Grayer, Hannah Rabinowitz, and Jeremy Herb, "FBI Director Wray Faces Off with His Harshest Critics at Heated Congressional Hearing," CNN, July 12, 2023, https://www.cnn.com/2023/07/12/politics/christopher-wray-hearing-house-judiciary/index.html.

2. Committee on the Judiciary, *Interview of Jennifer Leigh Moore*, April 24, 2023, 10, 116, https://judiciary.house.gov/sites/evo-subsites/republicans-judiciary.house.gov/files/evo-media-document/2023_04_24_Moore%20Transcript_Redacted.pdf.

3. Select Subcommittee on the Weaponization of the Federal Government, *FBI Whistleblower Testimony Highlights Government Abuse, Misallocation of Resources, and Retaliation*, May 18, 2023, 42, 48, https://judiciary.house.gov/sites/evo-subsites/republicans-judiciary.house.gov/files/evo-media-document/2023-05-17-fbi-whistleblower-testimony-highlights-government-abuse-misallocation-of-resources-and-retaliation-sm.pdf.

4. Committee on the Judiciary, "Jim Jordan Explains the 14 FBI Whistleblowers: 'Frankly, We Anticipate More,'" news release, August 17, 2022, https://judiciary.house.gov/media/press-releases/jim-jordan-explains-the-14-fbi-whistleblowers-frankly-we-anticipate-more.

5. "Whistleblower Protection: DOJ and FBI Need to Improve Employees' Awareness of Rights," Government Accountability Office, November 12, 2024, https://www.gao.gov/products/gao-25-106547.

6. Ibid., 51.

7. Committee on the Judiciary, *Interview of Jennifer Leigh Moore*, 119.

8. Ibid., 175.

9. Steven Richards and John Solomon, "FBI Suffers a New Black Eye, Accusing the Wrong Agent of Leaking," Just the News, July 23, 2024, https://just-thenews.com/accountability/whistleblowers/fbi-withheld-evidence-about-whistleblower-congress-leading-erroneous.

10. Select Subcommittee on the Weaponization of the Federal Government, *FBI Whistleblower Testimony Highlights Government Abuse, Misallocation of Resources, and Retaliation*, 9.

11. Christopher Wray, "Threats to the Homeland: Evaluating the Landscape 20 Years After 9/11," statement before the Senate Homeland Security and

Governmental Affairs Committee, September 21, 2021, https://www.fbi.gov
/news/testimony/threats-to-the-homeland-evaluating-the-landscape-20
-years-after-911-wray-092121; Merrick Garland, "Remarks: Domestic Terrorism Policy Address," speech, June 15, 2021, https://www.justice.gov/opa
/speech/attorney-general-merrick-b-garland-remarks-domestic-terrorism
-policy-address.

12. Committee on the Judiciary, *Interview of Jennifer Leigh Moore*, 111.

13. Department of Justice Office of the Inspector General, *Management Advisory
Memorandum 24-067*, May 2024, 3, https://oig.justice.gov/sites/default/files
/reports/24-067.pdf.

14. Empower Oversight, *Letter to Inspector General Horowitz*, June 8, 2024,
https://empowr.us/wp-content/uploads/2024/06/2024-06-08-TL-to-DOJ
-OIG-Protected-Disclosure-FINAL-REDACTED.pdf.

15. Christy Matino, "'I Never Sought This Life': FBI Whistleblower Stephen
Friend Writes Tell-All Book," *Washington Examiner*, February 25, 2023,
https://www.washingtonexaminer.com/news/935548/i-never-sought-this-life
-fbi-whistleblower-stephen-friend-writes-tell-all-book.

16. Christopher Wray, "FBI Oversight Hearing on Trump Assassination Attempt
and Agency Oversight, Part 2," C-SPAN, July 24, 2024, 2 hrs., 5 min., 45 sec.,
1:11, https://www.c-span.org/program/public-affairs-event/fbi-oversight
-hearing-on-trump-assassination-attempt-and-agency-oversight-part-2/645405.

17. Representative Jason Chaffetz, H.R. 5790, July 14, 2016, https://oversight
.house.gov/wp-content/uploads/2016/12/HR-H5790.pdf.

18. Kerry Picket, "Justice Department Kept FBI Employees in the Dark for Years
About Whistleblower Protections," *Washington Times*, November 12, 2024,
https://www.washingtontimes.com/news/2024/nov/12/justice-department
-kept-fbi-employees-dark-years-w.

19. Miranda Devine, "30 Ex-FBI Agents Stand Up to Support Whistleblower
Who Exposed Agency's Political Bias," *New York Post*, September 28,
2022, https://nypost.com/2022/09/28/30-ex-fbi-agents-stand-up-to-support
-whistleblower-who-exposed-agencys-political-bias/.

20. Nicole Parker, "Why I Left the FBI," Fox News, January 12, 2023, https://
www.foxnews.com/opinion/why-left-fbi.

21. Ibid.

22. Drew Lunt, "Interviewing Applicants: 6 Questions to Avoid," Employment Law
Handbook, accessed January 30, 2025, https://www.employmentlawhandbook
.com/prohibited-practices/6-questions-to-avoid.

23. Matthew Continetti, "Kamala Harris's Outrageous Assault on the Knights of
Columbus," *National Review*, January 12, 2019, https://www.nationalreview

.com/2019/01/kamala-harris-knights-of-columbus-religious-test/; Adam O'Neal, "Harris vs. the Knights of Columbus," *Wall Street Journal*, August 20, 2020, https://www.wsj.com/articles/harris-vs-the-knights-of-columbus-11597966256.

24. Ibid.

25. Samantha Kamman, "Christian Infantry Officer Stripped of Position, Accused of Expressing 'Hatred' for LGBT People," Christian Post, August 26, 2024, https://www.christianpost.com/news/christian-infantry-officer-stripped-of -position-complaint.html.

26. Ibid.

27. Liberty Counsel, *Letter to the Office of the Governor*, August 15, 2024, https:// lc.org/PDFs/Attachments2PRsLAs/2024/081924LtrtoIdahoGovernorreIdaho InfantryOfficerandIDARNG%20Recommendations08152024_Redacted .pdf.

28. Samuel Alito Jr., *Statement on Missouri Department of Corrections v. Jean Finney*, February 20, 2024, https://www.supremecourt.gov/opinions/23pdf /23-203_1co6.pdf.

29. Ibid.

30. Mark Pattison, "Knights' Leader Takes Umbrage at Senate Questioning of Judge Nominee," Archdiocese of Baltimore, January 4, 2019, https://www .archbalt.org/knights-leader-takes-umbrage-at-senate-questioning-of-judge -nominee.

31. Jessica Hockett, "Who Is Teaching Your Children? How DEI Policies Influence K–12 Educator Hiring in America," National Opportunity Project, August 2023, archived June 10, 2024, http://web.archive.org/web/20240610071913 /https://www.nationalopportunity.org/wp-content/uploads/2023/08/NOP -Report-DEI-Teacher-Hiring-August-2023.pdf.

32. Grace Toohey, "SoCal District to Pay $360K to Teacher Who Was Fired after Refusing to Follow Transgender Policies," *Los Angeles Times*, May 15, 2024, https://www.latimes.com/california/story/2024-05-15/california-district-to -pay-360k-to-teacher-who-was-fired-after-refusing-to-follow-transgender -policies.

33. Aaron Sibarium, "Study: Diversity Statements Required for One-Fifth of Academic Jobs," Washington Free Beacon, November 8, 2021, https://freebeacon .com/campus/study-diversity-statements-required-for-one-fifth-of-academic -jobs.

34. Robert Maranto and James D. Paul, "Other Than Merit: The Prevalence of Diversity, Equity, and Inclusion Statements in University Hiring," American Enterprise Institute, November 8, 2021, https://www.aei.org/research-products /report/other-than-merit-the-prevalence-of-diversity-equity-and-inclusion

-statements-in-university-hiring; Andrew Gillen, "The Impact of the Left's Takeover of Academia on the Quality of Higher Education," Areo, April 29, 2020, archived May 21, 2024, http://web.archive.org/web/20240521110653 /https://areomagazine.com/2020/04/29/the-impact-of-the-lefts-takeover-of -academia-on-the-quality-of-higher-education.

35. Abigail Thompson, "The University's New Loyalty Oath," *Wall Street Journal*, December 19, 2019, https://www.wsj.com/articles/the-universitys-new -loyalty-oath-11576799749.

36. Breccan F. Thies, "Taxpayer-Funded Truman Scholarship Has Massive Anti-Conservative Bias, Lawmakers Say," *Washington Examiner*, May 20, 2024, https://www.washingtonexaminer.com/policy/education/3009936/truman -scholarship-massive-anti-conservative-bias.

37. Ibid.

38. Puneet Cheema, "Biden Must Purge Military and Law Enforcement of White Nationalists," Slate, January 19, 2021, https://slate.com/news-and -politics/2021/01/biden-purge-military-white-nationalist-capitol-riots.html.

39. US Department of Defense, "Secretary of Defense Austin Announces Immediate Actions to Counter Extremism in the Military and the Establishment of the Countering Extremism Working Group," news release, April 9, 2021, https://www.defense.gov/News/Releases/Release/Article/2567545/secretary -of-defense-austin-announces-immediate-actions-to-counter-extremism-in.

40. Daniel Greenfield, "Bishop Garrison: Biden's Racist Tool for a Military Purge," FrontPage Magazine, June 9, 2021, https://www.frontpagemag.com /bishop-garrison-bidens-racist-tool-military-purge-daniel-greenfield.

41. Natalie Winters, "Biden's Counter-Extremism Committee Includes CCP Advocates and Far-Left Twitter Trolls," National Pulse, May 20, 2021, https:// thenationalpulse.com/archive-post/biden-extremism-committee-includes -ccp-advocates.

42. Jack Poso (@JackPosobiec), "BREAKING: Biden Pentagon to welcome discredited, anti-Christian SPLC activists to advise Counter Extremism Working Group," Twitter (now X), May 19, 2021, https://x.com/JackPosobiec/status /1395115836545945609.

43. "Pete Hegseth: Meet Bishop Garrison, the Pentagon's 'Newly Minted MAGA Purge Man,'" Fox News, May 6, 2021, https://www.foxnews.com/media /pete-hegseth-meet-bishop-garrison-the-pentagons-newly-minted-maga -purge-man.

44. Darren Beattie, "Critical Race Theory Zealot in Charge of Purging Patriots from the U.S. Military," *Bannon's War Room*, Rumble, May 6, 2021, 1 min., 28 sec., https://rumble.com/vgm7p7-critical-race-theory-zealot-in-charge-of -purging-patriots-from-the-u.s.-mil.html.

45. Ibid.; "Pete Hegseth: Meet Bishop Garrison, the Pentagon's 'Newly Minted MAGA Purge Man'"; John Knefel, "Anatomy of a Smear Campaign: How Right-Wing Media Neutralized a Pentagon Effort to Address White Supremacy in the Military," Media Matters for America, May 25, 2023, https://www.mediamatters.org/fox-news/anatomy-smear-campaign-how-right-wing-media-neutralized-pentagon-effort-address-white.

46. Lisa Lerer, "How Republican Vaccine Opposition Got to This Point," *New York Times*, July 17, 2021, updated September 12, 2021, https://www.nytimes.com/2021/07/17/us/politics/coronavirus-vaccines-republicans.html; John Burnett, "The Number of Americans Who Say They Won't Get a COVID Shot Hasn't Budged in a Year," NPR, May 10, 2022, https://www.npr.org/sections/health-shots/2022/05/10/1091053850/the-number-of-americans-who-say-they-wont-get-a-covid-shot-hasnt-budged-in-a-yea; Yasmin Tayag, "How Many Republicans Died Because the GOP Turned Against Vaccines?" *Atlantic*, December 23, 2022, https://www.theatlantic.com/health/archive/2022/12/covid-deaths-anti-vaccine-republican-voters/672575.

47. William Galston, "For COVID-19 Vaccinations, Party Affiliation Matters More than Race and Ethnicity," Brookings Institution, October 1, 2021, https://www.brookings.edu/articles/for-covid-19-vaccinations-party-affiliation-matters-more-than-race-and-ethnicity.

48. Lynn V (@lynnv38), "Well I guess the White Supremacy leaning military members will be choosing the Proud Boys, Boogaloo Boys, Q-Anon, & MAGA armies instead of getting vaxxed. The mandate is gonna be a good way of getting those folk out of our military," Twitter (now X), August 9, 2021, https://x.com/lynnv378/status/1424833980831051780.

49. Meghann Myers, "The Fallout of the Military's COVID-19 Vaccine Mandate," Military Times, March 27, 2023, https://www.militarytimes.com/news/your-military/2023/03/27/the-fallout-of-the-militarys-covid-19-vaccine-mandate.

50. Heather Hunter, "Trump Says He Would Rehire Military Members Fired over Vaccine Mandate with Back Pay," *Washington Examiner*, August 21, 2024, https://www.washingtonexaminer.com/policy/defense/3130384/trump-rehire-military-members-fired-vaccine-mandate-back-pay.

51. Nicholas Ballasy and Natalia Mittelstadt, "Biden DOD Firing Vax Refuseniks to 'Purge Conservative Service Members': House Armed Services Member," Just the News, March 9, 2023, https://justthenews.com/government/congress/banks-biden-admin-seeking-purge-conservative-unvaccinated-service-members.

52. "Project 2025," Office of Kamala D. Harris, archived January 15, 2025, http://web.archive.org/web/20250115003044/https://kamalaharris.com/project2025.

53. Joe Davidson, "National Security Prime Target of Trump's Plan to Weaken Civil

Service," *Washington Post*, September 27, 2024, https://www.washingtonpost
.com/politics/2024/09/27/trump-schedule-f-national-security.

54. Miles Taylor, "I Am Part of the Resistance Inside the Trump Administration,"
New York Times, September 5, 2018, https://www.nytimes.com/2018/09/05
/opinion/trump-white-house-anonymous-resistance.html.

55. James Sherk, "The President Needs the Power to Fire Bureaucrats," *Wall
Street Journal*, August 8, 2022, https://www.wsj.com/articles/the-power-to
-fire-insubordinate-bureaucrats-schedule-f-executive-order-trump-deborah
-birx-at-will-civil-service-removal-appeals-11659989383.

56. Ibid.

57. White House, *Executive Order on Creating Schedule F in the Excepted Service*, October 21, 2020, https://trumpwhitehouse.archives.gov/presidential
-actions/executive-order-creating-schedule-f-excepted-service.

58. US Office of Personnel Management, "RELEASE: OPM Issues Final Rule
to Reinforce and Clarify Protections for Nonpartisan Career Civil Service,"
archived January 19, 2025, http://web.archive.org/web/20250119230838
/https://www.opm.gov/news/releases/2024/04/release-opm-issues-final-rule
-to-reinforce-and-clarify-protections-for-nonpartisan-career-civil-service/.

59. Jacob Sagert and James Sherk, "New Biden Rule Aims to Entrench the Deep
State Forever," Federalist, May 14, 2024, https://thefederalist.com/2024/05/14
/new-biden-rule-aims-to-entrench-the-deep-state-forever/.

60. US Office of Personnel Management, "RELEASE: OPM Issues Final Rule to
Reinforce and Clarify Protections for Nonpartisan Career Civil Service"; Committee on Oversight, *Comer: OPM's Final Rule Insulates the Federal Workforce from Accountability*, April 4, 2024, https://oversight.house.gov/release
/comer-opms-final-rule-insulates-the-federal-workforce-from-accountability/.

Chapter 5: The Need to Win

1. Brianna Herlihy, "Biden's Get-Out-the-Vote Executive Order Challenged,
Heading to Supreme Court: 'Target Welfare Populations,'" Fox News, April
4, 2024, https://www.foxnews.com/politics/a-lawsuit-challenging-bidens-get
-out-the-vote-executive-order-will-soon-head-to-the-supreme-court.

2. "Jennifer Kim," SBA Leadership, US Small Business Administration, archived
January 18, 2025, http://web.archive.org/web/20250118092918/https://www
.sba.gov/person/jennifer-kim; "Executive Overreach: Examining the SBA's
Electioneering Efforts with Associate Administrator of Office of Field Operations," 118th Cong. (2024), statement of Jennifer Kim, Associate Administrator of Office of Field Operations, https://democrats-smallbusiness.house.gov
/uploadedfiles/07-24-24_associate_administrator_jennifer_kim_testimony
.pdf.

3. Ibid.

4. "Examining the SBA's Electioneering Efforts with Associate Administrator Jennifer Kim," hearing, published July 24, 2024, YouTube, 1 hr., 2 min., 42 sec., 51:27, https://www.youtube.com/watch?v=FdAPFRf4TI4.

5. Congresswoman Maria Elvira Salazar, "Salazar Exposes SBA's Voter Registration Scheme in Michigan Before 2024 Elections," news release, June 5, 2024, https://salazar.house.gov/media/press-releases/salazar-exposes-sbas-voter -registration-scheme-michigan-2024-elections.

6. "Isabel Casillas Guzman," SBA Leadership, US Small Business Administration, https://www.sba.gov/person/isabel-casillas-guzman.

7. Jason Cohen, "Isabel Guzman Was Scheduled to Attend 17 'Equity' Meetings in Less Than One Year," Daily Caller, March 14, 2024, https://dailycaller .com/2024/03/14/exclusive-biden-agency-head-scheduled-attend-17-equity -meetings-less-than-one-year.

8. "Van Duyne: 'Executive Overreach: Examining the SBA's Electioneering Efforts with Associate Administrator of Office of Field Operations, Jennifer Kim,'" House Committee on Small Business, July 24, 2024, https://smallbusiness.house .gov/news/documentsingle.aspx?DocumentID=407045.

9. House Committee on Small Business, "Chairman Williams, Senator Ernst Issue Statements on Release of SBA-Michigan MOU," news release, May 23, 2024, https://smallbusiness.house.gov/news/documentsingle.aspx?Document ID=406005.

10. "Van Duyne: 'Executive Overreach,'" House Committee on Small Business.

11. Hans A. von Spakovsky, "Why Does DHS Want to Designate Election Booths 'Critical Infrastructure?'" Heritage Foundation, August 17, 2016, https://www.heritage.org/election-integrity/commentary/why-does-dhs-want -designate-election-booths-critical-infrastructure.

12. David Samuels, "The Aspiring Novelist Who Became Obama's Foreign-Policy Guru," *New York Times Magazine*, May 5, 2016, https://www .nytimes.com/2016/05/08/magazine/the-aspiring-novelist-who-became -obamas-foreign-policy-guru.html.

13. Spakovsky, "Why Does DHS Want to Designate Election Booths 'Critical Infrastructure?'"

14. Tami Abdollah, "US Designates Election Infrastructure as 'Critical,'" Associated Press, January 6, 2017, https://apnews.com/united-states-government -64a7228c974d43009cdfc2b98766320b.

15. Ibid.

16. "HSE Oversight—Election Cybersecurity' Part," hearing, C-SPAN, Sep-

tember 28, 2016, 1 hr., 53 min., 51 sec., 1:36:00, https://www.c-span.org/video/?415978-1/hse-oversight-election-cybersecurity-part.

17. White House, Executive Order on Promoting Access to Voting, archived January 19, 2025, https://web.archive.org/web/20250119115551/https://www.whitehouse.gov/briefing-room/presidential-actions/2021/03/07/executive-order-on-promoting-access-to-voting/.

18. Violet Jackson correspondent, email messages to James Harvey, "FW: Request for Information Promoting Voting at AJCs," https://oversight.heritage.org/09_Combine%20PDF%20File%20-%20Attachments%20FOIA%20 2024-F-04627.pdf.

19. "Van Duyne: 'Executive Overreach,'" House Committee on Small Business.

20. "Chairman Williams Discusses Investigation into the Biden Harris SBA's Voter Registration Scheme," House Committee on Small Business, July 23, 2024, YouTube, 8 min., 55 sec., https://www.youtube.com/watch?v=wz88wyBvlbQ.

21. Secretary Miguel Cardona (@SecCardona), "🔒STOP SCROLLING🔒 I'm sending 40 million borrowers info on student debt relief this morning. Here's a quick overview but read the email to get more information about potential relief!" Twitter (now X), August 1, 2024, https://x.com/SecCardona/status/1819055056764740088.

22. Ibid.; US Department of Education, "Biden-Harris Administration Takes Next Step Toward Additional Debt Relief for Tens of Millions of Student Loan Borrowers This Fall," news release, archived January 19, 2025, https://web.archive.org/web/20250119014406/https://www.ed.gov/about/news/press-release/biden-harris-administration-takes-next-step-toward-additional-debt-relief-for-tens-of-millions-of-student-loan-borrowers-this-fall.

23. Amy Howe, "Supreme Court Strikes Down Biden Student-Loan Forgiveness Program," *SCOTUSblog*, June 30, 2023, https://www.scotusblog.com/2023/06/supreme-court-strikes-down-biden-student-loan-forgiveness-program.

24. Paul Teas, "Explaining the Partisan Gap in Support for Student Loan Forgiveness," YouGov, May 10, 2024, https://today.yougov.com/politics/articles/49386-explaining-partisan-gap-support-student-loan-debt-forgiveness-poll.

25. Fred Lucas, "HUD Pushes Voter Registration Drives in Public Housing Under Biden's Executive Order," Daily Signal, April 27, 2022, https://www.dailysignal.com/2022/04/27/hud-pushes-voter-registration-drives-in-public-housing-under-bidens-executive-order.

26. Letter to executive director, Office of Public & Indian Housing, February 9, 2022, https://nlihc.org/sites/default/files/PIH_Announcement.pdf.

27. Kevin Stocklin, "Behind Massive Mail-In Ballot Push Is a Little-Noticed Executive Order," *Epoch Times*, September 15, 2024, https://www.theepochtimes

.com/article/mail-in-ballots-for-inmates-how-the-federal-government-is
-targeting-new-voters-5578741.

28. Naomi F. Sugie, "Punishment and Welfare: Paternal Incarceration and Families' Receipt of Public Assistance," *Social Forces* 90, no. 4 (2012): 1403–27, https://doi.org/10.1093/sf/sos055.

29. Ashley Nellis, "The Color of Justice: Racial and Ethnic Disparity in State Prisons," Sentencing Project, October 13, 2021, https://www.sentencingproject .org/reports/the-color-of-justice-racial-and-ethnic-disparity-in-state-prisons -the-sentencing-project.

30. Ruth Igielnik, Scott Keeter, and Hannah Hartig, "Behind Biden's 2020 Victory," Pew Research Center, June 30, 2021, https://www.pewresearch.org /politics/2021/06/30/behind-bidens-2020-victory.

31. Nicole Lewis and Christina Cauterucci, "Trump's Surprising Popularity in Prison," Marshall Project, data analysis by Anna Flagg, March 21, 2020, https://www .themarshallproject.org/2020/03/12/trump-s-surprising-popularity-in-prison.

32. Dan Gooding, "Donald Trump Won More Black Voters than Any Republican in 48 Years—Analyst," *Newsweek*, updated November 9, 2024, https://www .newsweek.com/donald-trump-black-voters-gains-results-1982939.

33. Jonathan Swan, "Government Workers Shun Trump, Give Big Money to Clinton," *The Hill*, October 26, 2016, https://thehill.com/homenews /campaign/302817-government-workers-shun-trump-give-big-money-to -clinton-campaign.

34. Laura Counts, "Study Finds the Cost of Partisanship Among Federal Workers," Haas School of Business, University of California, Berkeley, April 20, 2021, https://newsroom.haas.berkeley.edu/research/study-finds-the-cost-of -partisanship-among-federal-workers.

35. Ibid.

36. Ralph R. Smith, "Political Donations and Federal Employees in 2020 Elections," FedSmith, updated August 25, 2021, https://www.fedsmith .com/2021/02/12/political-donations-and-federal-employees.

37. Anna V. Smith, "How Indigenous Voters Swung the 2020 Election," *High Country News*, November 6, 2020, https://www.hcn.org/articles/indigenous -affairs-how-indigenous-voters-swung-the-2020-election/.

38. "Biden Bucks: Executive Order 14019," Heritage Foundation.

39. Robert Schmad, "Biden Admin Weighed Using 'School Children' to Help Register Dem-Leaning Voters, Emails Show," Daily Caller, June 24, 2024, https://dailycaller.com/2024/06/24/biden-voter-registration-native-american -children.

40. "Biden Bucks: Executive Order 14019," Heritage Foundation.

41. Lance Purvis correspondent, email message to David Bossie, "RE: Citizens United v. U.S. Dept. of the Interior, Civil Action No. 22-2443 (CRC) FOIA Request #SOL-2022-004127," February 24, 2023, https://oversight.heritage .org/23_CU-Interior-Dept-Voting-EO-FOIA-Production-3.pdf.

42. US District Court for the District of Kansas, Plaintiff's Complaint for Declaratory and Injunctive Relief, August 13, 2024, https://mcusercontent .com/08cb3e52aa1308600f84d49ea/files/8827e8ea-0eb8-123c-23b9 -5d39b2e8c0e4/1_2024_08_13_Complaint.pdf.

43. Ibid.

44. Tamara Keith, "How Democrats Learned to Love Project 2025," NPR, August 19, 2024, https://www.npr.org/2024/08/19/nx-s1-5052064/democratic -national-convention-project-2025.

45. Adriana Gomez Licon, "Biden Assails Project 2025, a Plan to Transform Government, and Trump's Claim to be Unaware of It," Associated Press, updated July 6, 2024, https://apnews.com/article/trump-project-2025-biden-9d372469 033d23e1e3aef5cf0470a2e6.

46. Poli Alert (@polialertcom), "Rep. #AyannaPressley: Project 2025 is a thousand page, far-right manifesto of extremist policies that would uproot every government agency and disrupt every American life," Instagram, May 29, 2024, https://www.instagram.com/polialertcom/reel/C7kAFlRPu1L.

47. Kevin D. Roberts, "The Stories Democrats Tell About Project 2025," Heritage Foundation, September 4, 2024, https://www.heritage.org/conservatism /commentary/the-stories-democrats-tell-about-project-2025.

48. Ted Budd, Claudia Tenney, and Mike Garcia et al. to Shalanda Young, January 19, 2022, https://tenney.house.gov/sites/evo-subsites/tenney.house.gov /files/evo-media-document/1.19.22_Letter%20to%20OMB%20on%20 Voting%20EO_Final.pdf.

49. "Executive Action to Advance Democracy: What the Biden-Harris Administration and the Agencies Can Do to Build a More Inclusive Democracy," Demos, https://www.demos.org/sites/default/files/2020-12/Executive%20Action% 20to%20Advance%20Democracy.pdf.

50. Parker Thayer and Hayden Ludwig, "Shining a Light on Zuck Bucks in the 2020 Battleground States," Capital Research Center, May 28, 2024, https://capitalresearch.org/article/shining-a-light-on-zuck-bucks-in-key -states.

51. "Dr. Alister Martin, MD MPP," A Healthier Democracy, https://ahealthierde-mocracy.org/alister-martin.

52. Kay Lazar, "They Come for Health Care. They Leave Ready to Vote," *Boston Globe*, updated October 14, 2022, https://www.bostonglobe.com/2022/10/14/ metro/they-come-health-care-they-leave-ready-vote/?event=event12.

53. Gabe Kaminsky, "Inside the Left-Wing Dark Money Voter Turnout Operation Targeting Vulnerable Patients," *Washington Examiner*, May 9, 2024, https://www.washingtonexaminer.com/news/investigations/2993671/left-wing-dark-money-voter-turnout-patients; "Tides Foundation," Influence Watch, https://www.influencewatch.org/non-profit/tides-foundation.

54. Farah Stockman, "In Era of Sickness, Doctors Prescribe Unusual Cure: Voting," *New York Times*, July 25, 2020, https://www.nytimes.com/2020/07/25/us/in-era-of-sickness-doctors-prescribe-unusual-cure-voting.html.

55. Aaron Sibarium, "Meet the Little-Known Activist Group That Has Tens of Thousands of Doctors Registering Patients to Vote," Washington Free Beacon, August 6, 2024, https://freebeacon.com/elections/meet-the-little-known-activist-group-that-has-tens-of-thousands-of-doctors-registering-patients-to-vote/.

56. Ibid.

Chapter 6: What the Government Knows

1. Eric Revell, "Apple to Pay $95 Million in Siri Spying Lawsuit," Fox Business, January 3, 2025, https://www.foxbusiness.com/markets/apple-pay-95-million-siri-spying-lawsuit.

2. Marie Boran, "Is Your Phone Really Listening to You? Here's What We Know," *Newsweek*, updated September 7, 2024, https://www.newsweek.com/phone-voice-assistants-active-listening-consent-targeted-ads-1949251.

3. "Is Meta Listening to My Conversations?" Privacy Center, https://privacycenter.instagram.com/dialog/does-meta-listen-to-convo.

4. Emily Price, "Cox Deletes 'Active Listening' Ad Pitch After Boasting That It Eavesdrops Through Our Phones," *Fast Company*, December 15, 2023, https://www.fastcompany.com/90999277/cox-cmg-active-listening-phones-targeted-advertising.

5. Tim Hinchliffe, "Humankind Is Transitioning into 'The Intelligent Age,' a New Dawn for Civilization: Klaus Schwab, World Governments Summit," *The Sociable* (blog), February 12, 2024, https://sociable.co/government-and-policy/humankind-the-intelligent-age-new-dawn-civilization-klaus-schwab-world-governments-summit.

6. Aaron Kliegman, "AI Expert Doubtful DC Prepared for New Tech: 'Well, They Put Kamala Harris in Charge,'" Fox News, June 3, 2023, https://www.foxnews.com/politics/ai-expert-doubtful-dc-prepared-new-tech-they-put-kamala-harris-charge.

7. Bob Pisani, "It's Google vs. Amazon to Create the Biggest Database in History," CNBC, updated April 27, 2016, https://www.cnbc.com/2016/04/26/its-google-vs-amazon-to-create-the-biggest-data-base-in-history.html.

8. Marc Wheat, "New SEC Database Violates Privacy and Freedom of Association," *Washington Examiner*, October 13, 2024, https://www .washingtonexaminer.com/opinion/3186124/new-sec-database-violates -privacy-freedom-association.

9. Brianna Herlihy, "SEC Hit with New Lawsuit Alleging 'Mass Surveillance' of Americans Through Stock Market Data," Fox News, April 21, 2024, https:// www.foxnews.com/politics/sec-hit-new-lawsuit-alleging-mass-surveillance -americans-stock-market-data.

10. Ibid.

11. William P. Barr, "The Securities and Exchange Commission is Watching You," *Wall Street Journal*, April 15, 2024, https://www.wsj.com/articles/the -securities-and-exchange-commission-is-watching-you-surveillance-4e782f82.

12. Ibid.

13. Wheat, "New SEC Database Violates Privacy and Freedom of Association."

14. Dell Cameron, "The Next US President Will Have Troubling New Surveillance Powers," *Wired*, April 22, 2024, https://www.wired.com/story/section -702-reauthorization-expansion.

15. "Statement by the President on FISA Amendments Reauthorization Act of 2017," Trump White House Archives, National Archives, January 19, 2018, https://trumpwhitehouse.archives.gov/briefings-statements/statement -president-fisa-amendments-reauthorization-act-2017.

16. Rebecca Beitsch, "Trump on Warrantless Surveillance Reauthorization: 'KILL FISA,'" *The Hill*, April 10, 2024, https://thehill.com/policy/national -security/4584988-trump-on-warrantless-surveillance-reauthorization-kill-fisa.

17. Senator Ron Wyden, "Wyden Releases Documents Confirming the NSA Buys Americans' Internet Browsing Records; Calls on Intelligence Community to Stop Buying U.S. Data Obtained Unlawfully from Data Brokers, Violating Recent FTC Order," news release, January 25, 2024, https://www.wyden .senate.gov/news/press-releases/wyden-releases-documents-confirming -the-nsa-buys-americans-internet-browsing-records-calls-on-intelligence-c ommunity-to-stop-buying-us-data-obtained-unlawfully-from-data-brokers -violating-recent-ftc-order.

18. Andrew Thornbrooke, "NSA Buying Illegally Sourced Data on Americans Without Warrants," *Epoch Times*, January 27, 2024, https://www .theepochtimes.com/us/nsa-buying-illegally-sourced-data-on-americans -without-warrants-5574602.

19. Glenn Greenwald and Ewen MacAskill, "NSA Prism Program Taps In to User Data of Apple, Google and Others," *Guardian*, June 7, 2013, https://www .theguardian.com/world/2013/jun/06/us-tech-giants-nsa-data.

20. Scott Shane and Colin Moynihan, "Drug Agents Use Vast Phone Trove, Eclipsing NSA's," *New York Times*, September 1, 2013, https://www.nytimes.com/2013/09/02/us/drug-agents-use-vast-phone-trove-eclipsing-nsas.html.

21. Barton Gellman and Ashkan Soltani, "NSA Collects Millions of E-mail Address Books Globally," *Washington Post*, October 14, 2013, https://www.washingtonpost.com/world/national-security/nsa-collects-millions-of-e-mail-address-books-globally/2013/10/14/8e58b5be-34f9-11e3-80c6-7e6dd8d22d8f_story.html.

22. Ron Wyden to Merrick B. Garland, November 20, 2023, https://www.wyden.senate.gov/imo/media/doc/wyden_hemisphere_surveillance_letter_112023.pdf.

23. Dell Cameron, "Secretive White House Surveillance Program Gives Cops Access to Trillions of US Phone Records," *Wired*, November 20, 2023, https://www.wired.com/story/hemisphere-das-white-house-surveillance-trillions-us-call-records.

24. US Foreign Intelligence Surveillance Court, document regarding Section 702 2018 Certification, October 18, 2018, https://int.nyt.com/data/documenthelper/1880-fisa-rulings/40a12372947056b0dc08/optimized/full.pdf.

25. Charles Savage, "FBI Practices for Intercepted Emails Violated 4th Amendment, Judge Ruled," *New York Times*, October 8, 2019, https://www.nytimes.com/2019/10/08/us/politics/fbi-fisa-court.html.

26. Tommy Beer, "Trump Suddenly Loses 220,000 Twitter Followers—First Big Drop in 5 Years," *Forbes*, updated December 15, 2020, https://www.forbes.com/sites/tommybeer/2020/12/05/trump-suddenly-loses-220000-twitter-followers-first-big-drop-in-5-years.

27. Brandi Vincent, "How NARA's Preserving More than 20 Terabytes of Trump Social Media Data," Nextgov/FCW, January 22, 2021, https://www.nextgov.com/digital-government/2021/01/how-naras-preserving-more-20-terabytes-trump-social-media-data/171582.

28. Matthew Impelli, "Did Jack Smith Investigate Trump's Twitter Followers? What We Know," *Newsweek*, updated November 29, 2023, https://www.newsweek.com/did-jack-smith-investigate-trumps-twitter-followers-what-we-know-1848167.

29. Victor Nava, "Heavily Redacted Documents Related to Search Warrant for Trump's Twitter Account Released," *New York Post*, November 27, 2023, https://nypost.com/2023/11/27/news/heavily-redacted-documents-related-to-search-warrant-for-trumps-twitter-account-released.

30. US District Court for the District of Columbia, "Warrant by Telephone or Other Reliable Electronic Means," November 27, 2023, https://storage.courtlistener.com/recap/gov.uscourts.dcd.259110/gov.uscourts.dcd.259110.22.1.pdf.

31. Supreme Court of the United States, Petition for Writ of Certiorari, May 2024, https://www.supremecourt.gov/DocketPDF/23/23-1264/311993/20240 530144316325_23-xxxx%20-%20X%20Corp.%20v.%20United%20 States%20-%20cert.%20petition.pdf.

32. ACLU, "You Don't Sacrifice Your Privacy Rights When You Use Twitter," March 6, 2013, https://www.aclu.org/press-releases/you-dont-sacrifice-your -privacy-rights-when-you-use-twitter.

33. Ibid.

34. "Review of Four FISA Applications and Other Aspects of the FBI's Crossfire Hurricane Investigation," Office of the Inspector General, December 2019, https://www.justice.gov/storage/120919-examination.pdf.

35. US Foreign Intelligence Surveillance Court, *In Re Accuracy Concerns Regarding FBI Matters Submitted to the FISC*, December 17, 2019, https://www.fisc .uscourts.gov/sites/default/files/MIsc%2019%2002%20191217.pdf.

36. Ibid.

37. US Foreign Intelligence Surveillance Court, *In Re Accuracy Concerns Regarding FBI Matters Submitted to the FISC: Response to the Court's Order Dated December 17, 2019*, January 10, 2020, https://www.fisc.uscourts .gov/sites/default/files/Misc%2019%2002%20Response%20to%20the%20 Court%27s%20Order%20Dated%20December%2017%202019%20200110 .pdf.

38. Cameron, "The Next US President Will Have Troubling New Surveillance Powers."

39. Charlie Savage, "Secret Rift Over Data Center Fueled Push to Expand Reach of Surveillance Program," *New York Times*, updated April 17, 2024, https:// www.nytimes.com/2024/04/16/us/fisa-surveillance-bill-program.html.

40. Jennifer Valentino-DeVries, "'Stingray' Phone Tracker Fuels Constitutional Clash," *Wall Street Journal*, updated September 22, 2011, https://www.wsj .com/articles/SB10001424053111904194604576583112723197574.

41. Gretchen Smail, "This Netflix Doc Shows How an IRS Scammer Uncovered Secret Spy Technology," Bustle, June 16, 2022, https://www.bustle.com /entertainment/where-daniel-rigmaiden-is-now-web-of-make-believe.

42. Valentino-DeVries, "'Stingray' Phone Tracker Fuels Constitutional Clash."

43. Smail, "This Netflix Doc Shows How an IRS Scammer Uncovered Secret Spy Technology."

44. Committee on Oversight, "Bipartisan Committee Staff Report: Clear Guidelines Needed for 'Stingray' Devices," news release, December 19, 2016, https://oversight.house.gov/report/bipartisan-committee-staff-report-clear -guidelines-needed-stingray-devices.

45. Beryl Lipton and Cooper Quintin, "The Next Generation of Cell-Site Simulators Is Here. Here's What We Know," Electronic Frontier Foundation, June 12, 2024, https://www.eff.org/deeplinks/2024/06/next-generation-cell-site-simulators-here--heres-what-we-know

46. Committee on Oversight, "Bipartisan Committee Staff Report: Clear Guidelines Needed for 'Stingray' Devices"; Jake Laperruque, "Issue Brief: The Cell-Site Simulator Warrant Act," Project on Government Oversight, November 22, 2021, https://www.pogo.org/fact-sheets/issue-brief-the-cell-site-simulator-warrant-act.

47. Committee on Oversight, "Bipartisan Committee Staff Report: Clear Guidelines Needed for 'Stingray' Devices."

48. "US Congress HR6194 Cell-Site Simulator Warrant Act of 2023," TrackBill, accessed January 30, 2025, https://trackbill.com/bill/us-congress-house-bill-6194-cell-site-simulator-warrant-act-of-2023/2453094.

49. Dell Cameron, "The Post Office Is Spying on the Mail. Senators Want to Stop It," *Wired*, May 17, 2023, https://www.wired.com/story/usps-mail-surveillance-letter.

50. "Global Data Broker Market Size, Share, Opportunities, and Trends by Data Type (Consumer Data, Business Data), by End-User (BFSI, Retail, Automotive, Construction, Others), and by Geography—Forecasts from 2025 to 2030," Knowledge Sourcing Intelligence, December 2024, https://www.knowledge-sourcing.com/report/global-data-broker-market.

51. Elizabeth Goitein, "The Government Can't Seize Your Digital Data. Except by Buying It," *Washington Post*, April 26, 2021, https://www.washingtonpost.com/outlook/2021/04/26/constitution-digital-privacy-loopholes-purchases.

52. Joe Lancaster, "Biden Opposes Bill That Would Keep Cops and Feds From Buying Your Data," *Reason*, April 17, 2024, https://reason.com/2024/04/17/biden-opposes-bill-that-would-keep-cops-and-feds-from-buying-your-data.

53. Goitein, "The Government Can't Seize Your Digital Data. Except by Buying It."

54. Lancaster, "Biden Opposes Bill That Would Keep Cops and Feds from Buying Your Data."

55. Michael Dorgan, "Facebook Let Netflix Peek into User DMs, Explosive Court Docs Claim," Fox Business, April 2, 2024, https://www.foxbusiness.com/technology/facebook-let-netflix-peek-user-dms-explosive-court-docs-claim.

56. Lorenzo Franceschi-Bicchierai, "Facebook Snooped on Users' Snapchat Traffic in Secret Project, Documents Reveal," TechCrunch, March 26, 2024, https://techcrunch.com/2024/03/26/facebook-secret-project-snooped-snapchat-user-traffic.

57. Ashley Belanger, "Amazon Finally Admits Giving Cops Ring Doorbell Data without User Consent," ArsTechnica, July 14, 2022, https://arstechnica.com/tech-policy/2022/07/amazon-finally-admits-giving-cops-ring-doorbell-data-without-user-consent.

58. Breck Dumas, "Chase Allowing Advertisers to Target Customers Based on Purchases," Fox Business, April 3, 2024, https://www.foxbusiness.com/markets/chase-allowing-advertisers-target-customers-based-purchases.

59. Jing Wang, "Clear: A Speedy Way to Get Through Security Checkpoints, and More—at the Cost of Your Data Privacy," *Science and Technology Law Review* (blog), January 17, 2022, https://journals.library.columbia.edu/index.php/stlr/blog/view/418.

60. Ariel Zilber, "Grindr Sold Users' Location Data for Years, May Have Outed Catholic Priest: Report," *New York Post*, May 2, 2022, https://nypost.com/2022/05/02/grindr-sold-data-about-users-precise-locations-for-years-report.

61. Jay Peters, "Grindr Has Been Sold by Its Chinese Owner After the US Expressed Security Concerns," Verge, March 6, 2020, https://www.theverge.com/2020/3/6/21168079/grindr-sold-chinese-owner-us-cfius-security-concerns-kunlun-lgbtq.

62. "Tinder, Bumble, Grindr, Spy: Which Dating App Wants Your Data the Most?" Surfshark, February 7, 2022, https://surfshark.com/blog/dating-tracking-app.

63. Joseph Cox, "Muslim Pro Stops Sharing Location Data After Motherboard Investigation," Vice, November 17, 2020, https://www.vice.com/en/article/muslim-pro-location-data-military-xmode.

64. Justin Sherman, "Data Brokers and Sensitive Data on U.S. Individuals," Duke University Sanford School of Public Policy, 2021, https://techpolicy.sanford.duke.edu/wp-content/uploads/sites/4/2021/08/Data-Brokers-and-Sensitive-Data-on-US-Individuals-Sherman-2021.pdf.

65. Barr, "The Securities and Exchange Commission Is Watching You."

66. "RFK Jr. and Aubrey Marcus in the Interview THEY Don't Want You to See!" *WEin5DTarot* (podcast), Rumble, 2 hrs., 3 min., 41 sec., 24:00, https://rumble.com/v477470-january-15-2024.html.

Chapter 7: The Encyclopedia of Faces

1. Brandon Vigliarolo, "Harvard Duo Hacks Meta Ray-Bans to Dox Strangers on Sight in Seconds," Register, October 4, 2024, https://www.theregister.com/2024/10/04/harvard_engineer_meta_smart_glasses; AnhPhu Nguyen (@AnhPhuNguyen1), "Are we ready for a world where our data is exposed at a glance? @CaineArdayfio and I offer an answer to protect yourself here," Twitter (now X), September 30, 2024, 2 min., 34 sec., 00:54, https://x.com/AnhPhuNguyen1/status/1840786336992682409.

2. AnhPhu Nguyen and Caine Ardayfio, "I-XRAY: The AI Glasses That Reveal Anyone's Personal Details—Home Address, Name, Phone Number, and More—Just from Looking at Them."

3. Neil J. Rubenking, "The Best Personal Data Removal Services for 2025," *PC Magazine*, updated February 28, 2024, https://www.pcmag.com/picks/the -best-personal-data-removal-services.

4. Kashmir Hill, "Clearview AI Used Your Face. Now You May Get a Stake in the Company," *New York Times*, June 13, 2024, https://www.nytimes .com/2024/06/13/business/clearview-ai-facial-recognition-settlement.html.

5. Mike Swift, "Clearview AI Has Reached 'Turning Point' with US Legal Challenges, CEO Says, but Won't Return to EU, UK," MLex, January 24, 2024, https://mlex.shorthandstories.com/exclusive-interview-clearview-ai-founder -hoan-ton-that-on-weathering-global-privacy-storm/index.html.

6. Jessica Mudditt, "Meet the CEO of the World's Most Controversial Company, ClearviewAI," *Forbes*, November 24, 2022, https://www.forbes.com.au/covers /innovation/the-photos-that-speak-volumes.

7. Swift, "Clearview AI Has Reached 'Turning Point' with US Legal Challenges, CEO Says, but Won't Return to EU, UK."

8. Juliette Pearse, "Clearview AI: Innovating Facial Recognition," *Time*, April 26, 2021, https://time.com/collection/time100-companies/5953748/clearview-ai.

9. Mudditt, "Meet the CEO of the World's Most Controversial Company, ClearviewAI."

10. "U.S. Commission on Civil Rights: Statement from Hoan Ton-That, CEO Clearview AI," Clearview AI, March 8, 2024, https://www.clearview.ai/us -commission-on-civil-rights.

11. "Facial Recognition Market Size, Share & Trends Analysis Report by Technology (2D, 3D, Facial Analytics), by Application (Access Control, Security & Surveillance), by End-use, by Region, and Segment Forecasts, 2023–2030," Grand View Research, https://www.grandviewresearch.com/industry-analysis /facial-recognition-market.

12. Derek Hawkins, "Researchers Use Facial Recognition Tools to Predict Sexual Orientation. LGBT Groups Aren't Happy," *Washington Post*, September 12, 2017, https://www.washingtonpost.com/news/morning-mix/wp/2017/09/12 /researchers-use-facial-recognition-tools-to-predict-sexuality-lgbt-groups -arent-happy.

13. Ibid.

14. Sam Levin, "Face-Reading AI Will Be Able to Detect Your Politics and IQ, Professor Says," *Guardian*, September 12, 2017, https://www.theguardian.com /technology/2017/sep/12/artificial-intelligence-face-recognition-michal-kosinski.

15. Devin Coldewey, "Facial Recognition Reveals Political Party in Troubling New Research," TechCrunch, January 13, 2021, https://techcrunch.com/2021/01/13/facial-recognition-reveals-political-party-in-troubling-new-research.

16. Michael Kosinski, Poruz Khambatta, and Yilun Wang, "Facial Recognition Technology and Human Raters Can Predict Political Orientation from Images of Expressionless Faces Even When Controlling for Demographics and Self-Presentation," *American Psychologist* 79, no. 7 (2024): 942–55, https://doi.org/10.1037/amp0001295.

17. *Lie to Me*, https://lietome.com.

18. Kristina Suchotzki and Matthias Gamer, "Detecting Deception with Artificial Intelligence: Promises and Perils," *Science & Society* 28, no. 6 (2024): 481–83, https://doi.org/10.1016/j.tics.2024.04.002.

19. Federal Trade Commission, "FTC Warns About Misuses of Biometric Information and Harm to Consumers," news release, May 18, 2023, https://www.ftc.gov/news-events/news/press-releases/2023/05/ftc-warns-about-misuses-biometric-information-harm-consumers.

20. Ben Fischer, "Big Changes Coming in NFL Stadium Credentials," *Sports Business Journal*, July 25, 2024, https://www.sportsbusinessjournal.com/Articles/2024/07/25/nfl-stadium-credential-tech.

21. Estelle Atkinson, "Las Vegas Sheriff Backs Police Union Against NFL Facial Recognition Policy," *Las Vegas Review-Journal*, September 11, 2024, https://www.reviewjournal.com/news/politics-and-government/las-vegas/las-vegas-sheriff-backs-union-against-nfl-facial-recognition-policy-3167184.

22. Paul Bischoff, "CCTV Surveillance in the Most Populated Cities in the United States," Comparitech, updated January 8, 2024, https://www.comparitech.com/blog/vpn-privacy/us-surveillance-camera-statistics.

23. Matthew Lysiak, "Don't Look Up! 'Orwellian' AI Traffic Cameras Raise Privacy Concerns," *Epoch Times*, updated August 30, 2023, https://www.theepochtimes.com/us/dont-look-up-orwellian-ai-traffic-cameras-raise-privacy-concerns-5482829.

24. Nicholas Cecil, "Keir Starmer: We Can Make London the AI Capital of the World. The Opportunities to Create Wealth Are Endless," *London Evening Standard*, September 26, 2024, https://www.standard.co.uk/news/politics/keir-starmer-london-ai-wealth-b1184299.html.

25. "Nearly 300 of London's ULEZ Cameras Sabotaged Ahead of Expansion, Police Say," ITV News, August 18, 2023, https://www.itv.com/news/london/2023-08-18/nearly-300-of-londons-ulez-cameras-sabotaged-ahead-of-expansion-police-say.

26. Josh Salisbury, "Anti-Ulez Vigilantes Hang Up Bat Boxes on Camera Poles in Latest Disruptive Tactic," *London Evening Standard*, March 25, 2024, https://

www.standard.co.uk/news/london/ulez-cameras-tfl-fixed-bat-boxes-sadiq
-khan-b1147557.html.

27. Joseph Robertson, "'Blade Runners' Warn ULEZ Camera Sabotage Will Increase," *Epoch Times*, updated January 17, 2024, https://www .theepochtimes.com/world/exclusive-blade-runners-warn-ulez-camera -sabotage-will-increase-5474802.

28. Jack Simpson, "TfL Seizes 1,400 Vehicles from Drivers Who Ignore London Ulez Fines," *Guardian*, October 16, 2024, https://www.theguardian.com /environment/2024/oct/16/tfl-seizes-vehicles-drivers-ignore-london-ulez-fines.

29. Sean Hollister, "Here's the Letter from 14 Senators Slamming TSA Facial Recognition in Airports," Verge, May 3, 2024, https://www.theverge .com/2024/5/3/24148346/tsa-facial-recognition-airports-us-senators-oversight.

30. "RFK Jr. and Aubrey Marcus in the Interview THEY Don't Want You to See!" *WEin5DTarot*.

31. Paul Mozur, "One Month, 500,000 Face Scans: How China Is Using AI to Profile a Minority," *New York Times*, April 14, 2019, https://www.nytimes.com/2019 /04/14/technology/china-surveillance-artificial-intelligence-racial-profiling.html.

32. Chris Buckley, "China Is Detaining Muslims in Vast Numbers. The Goal: 'Transformation,'" *New York Times*, September 8, 2018, https://www.nytimes .com/2018/09/08/world/asia/china-uighur-muslim-detention-camp.html.

33. Sarah Dai, "Chinese Police Test Gait-Recognition Technology from AI Start-Up Watrix That Identifies People Based on How They Walk," *South China Morning Post*, updated February 27, 2019, https://www.scmp.com /tech/start-ups/article/2187600/chinese-police-surveillance-gets-boost-ai -start-watrix-technology-can.

34. Bischoff, "CCTV Surveillance in the Most Populated Cities in the United States."

35. Vera Demertzis, "Flushed Out: China Installs Toilet Timers to Broadcast How Long Subjects Are in the Loo Amid Sinister Rise of 'Social Credit' System," *Sun*, updated June 12, 2024, https://www.thesun.co.uk/news/28461355/china -installs-toilet-timers-to-broadcast-time-spent.

36. Tim Hinchliffe, "US Spy Community Looks to Autonomously Track People & Vehicles with AI, Video Data," *The Sociable* (blog), February 9, 2024, https:// www.sociable.co/government-and-policy/us-spy-community-autonomously -track-people-vehicles-ai-video.

37. "Proposer's Day—VideoLINCS," SAM.gov, https://sam.gov/opp/64446a6a80 9e49238d1346eb8b462bb9/view.

38. John Mac Ghlionn, "A Chilling Threat to Americans' Privacy," *Epoch Times*, updated February 25, 2024, https://www.theepochtimes.com/opinion/a -chilling-threat-to-americans-privacy-5587208.

39. Committee on Oversight, "Law Enforcement's Use of Facial Recognition Technology," March 22, 2017, https://www.govinfo.gov/content/pkg/CHRG -115hhrg28689/html/CHRG-115hhrg28689.htm.

40. Ibid.; Government Accountability Office, "Face Recognition Technology: FBI Should Better Ensure Privacy and Accuracy," report, May 2016, 10, https:// www.gao.gov/assets/gao-16-267.pdf.

41. Ibid.; Committee on Oversight, "Law Enforcement's Use of Facial Recognition Technology."

42. RealClearInvestigations, "RealClearInvestigations' Jan. 6-BLM Riots Comparison," September 9, 2021, https://www.realclearinvestigations.com/articles /2021/09/09/realclearinvestigations_jan_6-blm_comparison_database_ 791370.html.

43. "U.S. House Passes Fourth Amendment Not for Sale Act!" Project for Privacy & Surveillance Accountability, April 17, 2024, https://www.protectprivacynow .org/news/us-house-passes-fourth-amendment-not-for-sale-act.

44. Ibid.

Chapter 8: Securing Data at the Speed of Government

1. William Mauldin and Keith Zhai, "Xi Jinping Meets Antony Blinken as U.S., China Resume High-Level Engagement," *Wall Street Journal*, updated June 19, 2023, https://www.wsj.com/articles/xi-jinping-to-meet-blinken -monday-as-u-s-china-resume-high-level-engagement-c898f541?mod =article_inline.

2. Mohit Kumar, "China Finally Admits It Has Army of Hackers," Hacker News, March 20, 2015, https://thehackernews.com/2015/03/china-cyber-army.html.

3. Dustin Volz and William Mauldin, "Chinese Hackers Breached Email of Commerce Secretary Gina Raimondo and State Department Officials," *Wall Street Journal*, updated July 12, 2023, https://www.wsj.com/politics/chinese -hackers-spied-on-state-department-13a09f03.

4. Jason Chaffetz, Mark Meadows, and Will Hurd, "The OPM Data Breach: How the Government Jeopardized Our National Security for More than a Generation," report, Committee on Oversight and Government Reform, September 7, 2016, https://oversight.house.gov/wp-content/uploads/2016/09 /The-OPM-Data-Breach-How-the-Government-Jeopardized-Our-National -Security-for-More-than-a-Generation.pdf.

5. Graham Cluley, "Report Claims National Security Was Put at Risk by the OPM Data Breach," Fortra, September 8, 2016, https://www.tripwire.com/ state-of-security/report-claims-national-security-was-put-at-risk-by-the -opm-data-breach.

6. Zack Whittaker, "The Biggest Data Breaches in 2024: 1 Billion Stolen Records and Rising," TechCrunch, October 14, 2024, https://techcrunch.com/2024/06/29/2024-in-data-breaches-1-billion-stolen-records-and-rising.

7. Zack Whittaker, "Change Healthcare Confirms Ransomware Hackers Stole Medical Records on a 'Substantial Proportion' of Americans," TechCrunch, June 21, 2024, https://techcrunch.com/2024/06/21/change-healthcare-confirms-ransomware-hackers-stole-medical-records-on-a-substantial-proportion-of-americans.

8. Rebecca Schneid, "Ticketmaster Data Breach May Affect More than 500 Million Customers. What to Know," *Time*, June 2, 2024, https://time.com/6984811/ticketmaster-data-breach-customers-livenation-everything-to-know.

9. Waqas, "Ticketmaster Hackers Leak 30K Ticket Barcodes, Share Counterfeit Tutorial," HackRead, July 8, 2024, https://hackread.com/ticketmaster-hackers-leak-ticket-barcodes-tutorial.

10. Drew FitzGerald and Sadie Gurman, "AT&T Says Hacker Stole Cell, Text Data on Nearly All Its Wireless Customers," *Wall Street Journal*, updated July 12, 2024, https://www.wsj.com/business/telecom/at-t-says-hacker-stole-data-on-nearly-all-its-wireless-customers-32d6969d.

11. Vilius Petkauskas, "Mother of All Breaches Reveals 26 Billion Records: What We Know So Far," Cybernews, updated January 29, 2024, https://cybernews.com/security/billions-passwords-credentials-leaked-mother-of-all-breaches.

12. "Police Software Vendor Breach Exposes Personal Data, Raid Plans," *Government Technology*, January 23, 2023, https://www.govtech.com/security/police-software-vendor-breach-exposes-personal-data-raid-plans.

13. Ibid.

14. "The Unhackable Internet," National CIO Review, https://nationalcioreview.com/bookshelf/the-unhackable-internet-how-rebuilding-cyberspace-can-create-real-security-and-prevent-financial-collapse.

15. "Scott M. Volmar," biography, George Mason University, https://care.gmu.edu/wp-content/uploads/Scott-Bio.pdf.

16. Donna Levalley, "Nearly 3 Billion People Hacked in National Public Data Breach. What You Need to Know," Kiplinger, updated August 19, 2024, https://www.kiplinger.com/personal-finance/billions-hacked-in-national-public-data-breach.

17. Gintaras Radauskas, "After Breach of Billions of Records, National Public Data Files for Bankruptcy," Cybernews, updated October 11, 2024, https://cybernews.com/news/national-public-data-breach-social-security-bankruptcy.

18. Paul Bischoff, "A Recent History of US Government Breaches—Can You Trust

Them with Your Data?" Comparitech, updated November 28, 2023, https://www.comparitech.com/blog/vpn-privacy/us-government-breaches.

19. "Cyber Threat Snapshot," Committee on Homeland Security, https://homeland .house.gov/wp-content/uploads/2024/11/11.12.24-Cyber-Threat-Snapshot.pdf.

20. Bischoff, "A Recent History of US Government Breaches."

21. James Rundle, "Cyber Insurers Warn Catastrophic Hacks Will Require Government Help," *Wall Street Journal*, November 27, 2023, https://www .wsj.com/articles/cyber-insurers-warn-catastrophic-hacks-will-require -government-help-645a2b41.

22. "High-Risk Series: Federal Government Needs to Urgently Pursue Critical Actions to Address Major Cybersecurity Challenges," US Government Accountability Office, March 24, 2021, https://www.gao.gov/products/gao-21-288.

23. Jen Easterly and Tom Fanning, "The Attack on Colonial Pipeline: What We've Learned & What We've Done Over the Past Two Years," Cybersecurity and Infrastructure Security Agency, May 7, 2023, https://www.cisa.gov/news -events/news/attack-colonial-pipeline-what-weve-learned-what-weve-done -over-past-two-years.

24. Zachary Cohen, Geneva Sands, and Matt Eagen, "What We Know About the Pipeline Ransomware Attack: How It Happened, Who Is Responsible and More," CNN, updated May 10, 2021, https://www.cnn.com/2021/05/10 /politics/colonial-ransomware-attack-explainer/index.html.

25. US Department of Justice, "Department of Justice Seizes $2.3 Million in Cryptocurrency Paid to the Ransomware Extortionists Darkside," news release, Office of Public Affairs, June 7, 2021, https://www.justice.gov/opa/pr /department-justice-seizes-23-million-cryptocurrency-paid-ransomware -extortionists-darkside.

26. Reuven Avi-Yonah, "A Five-Year Prison Sentence for a Public Hero," *American Prospect*, May 21, 2024, https://prospect.org/justice/2024-05-21-five -year-sentence-public-hero-charles-littlejohn.

27. House Judiciary Committee Republicans, "Chairman Jordan Opens Inquiry into DOJ's Sweetheart Deal for Trump Tax Return Leaker," news release, February 8, 2024, https://judiciary.house.gov/media/press-releases/chairman -jordan-opens-inquiry-dojs-sweetheart-deal-trump-tax-return-leaker.

28. Rosiak, "IRS Employees Owe $50 Million in Back Taxes, Audit Finds."

29. Cybersecurity and Infrastructure Security Agency Act of 2018, H.R. 3359, 115th Cong. (2017–18), https://www.congress.gov/bill/115th-congress/house -bill/3359.

30. Cynthia Brumfield, "What Is the CISA? How the New Federal Agency Protects Critical Infrastructure from Cyber Threats," CSO, July 1, 2019, https://

www.csoonline.com/article/567457/what-is-the-cisa-how-the-new-federal
-agency-protects-critical-infrastructure-from-cyber-threats.html.

Chapter 9: The Right to Be Wrong

1. Mike Benz, "The National Science Foundation's 'Convergence Accelerator Track F' Is Funding Domestic Censorship Superweapons," Foundation for Freedom Online, January 29, 2023, https://foundationforfreedomonline.com /the-national-science-foundations-convergence-accelerator-track-f-is -funding-domestic-censorship-superweapons.

2. "Award Abstract # 2137530," Awards, US National Science Foundation, accessed January 30, 2025, https://www.nsf.gov/awardsearch/showAward ?AWD_ID=2137530.

3. Committee on the Judiciary and the Select Subcommittee on the Weaponization of the Federal Government, *The Weaponization of the National Science Foundation: How NSF Is Funding the Development of Automated Tools to Censor Online Speech 'At Scale' and Trying to Cover Up Its Actions*, report, February 5, 2024, 11n51, https://judiciary.house.gov/sites/evo-subsites/republicans-judiciary .house.gov/files/evo-media-document/NSF-Staff-Report_Appendix.pdf.

4. Ibid., Appendix D, 5.

5. Ibid., 22

6. Ibid., 11n51.

7. Joy Pullmann, "AI Censorship Targets People Who Read Primary Sources to Fact-Check the News," Federalist, March 7, 2024, https://thefederalist .com/2024/03/07/ai-censorship-targets-people-who-read-primary-sources-to -fact-check-the-news.

8. Tim Pearce, "Senate GOP Probe National Science Foundation over 'Brazen Attempt' to Censor Free Speech," Daily Wire, February 23, 2024, https:// www.dailywire.com/news/senate-gop-probe-national-science-foundation -over-brazen-attempt-to-censor-free-speech.

9. Edward Murrow, CBS radio broadcast from London, October 27, 1947, quoted on Goodreads.com, https://www.goodreads.com/quotes/149332-no -government-ever-voluntarily-reduces-itself-in-size-government-programs.

10. Pullmann, "AI Censorship Targets People Who Read Primary Sources to Fact-Check the News."

11. Global Disinformation Index, "Disinformation Risk Assessment: The Online News Market in the United States," December 2022, https://reason.com/wp -content/uploads/2023/02/gdi_us-mmr-22.pdf.

12. Joseph Vasquez, "MRC Exposes NewsGuard for Leftist Bias Third Year in a Row," MRC NewsBusters, December 12, 2023, https://www.newsbusters

.org/blogs/free-speech/joseph-vazquez/2023/12/12/mrc-exposes-newsguard
-leftist-bias-third-year-row.

13. Paul Farhi, "The Washington Post Corrects, Removes Parts of Two Stories Regarding the Steele Dossier," *Washington Post*, November 12, 2021, https:// www.washingtonpost.com/lifestyle/style/media-washington-post-steele -dossier/2021/11/12/f7c9b770-43d5-11ec-a88e-2aa4632af69b_story.html.

14. "NY Times Still Can't Admit Hunter Biden's Laptop Is Real! What's It Going to Take?" *New York Post*, June 12, 2024, https://nypost.com/2024/06/12 /opinion/ny-times-still-cant-admit-hunter-bidens-laptop-is-real-whats-it -going-to-take.

15. Jonathan Turley, "The GARMs Race: The House Moves Forward with Its Investigation of Blacklisting Company," *Jonathan Turley* (blog), August 6, 2024, https://jonathanturley.org/2024/08/06/the-garms-race-the-house-moves -forward-with-its-investigation-of-blacklisting-company.

16. "Trendsetters: Rob Rakowitz Outlines at Davos New Actions from the Global Alliance for Responsible Media," Internationalist, http://the-internationalists .com/trendsetters/Trendsetter_1-26-20-more.html.

17. Turley, "The GARMs Race."

18. Brent Scher, "GARM Exposed: House Judiciary Report Says Ad Coalition Likely Broke Law to Silence Conservatives," Daily Wire, July 10, 2024, https:// www.dailywire.com/news/garm-exposed-house-judiciary-report-says-ad -coalition-broke-law-to-silence-conservatives.

19. House Committee on the Judiciary, "GARM's Harm: How the World's Biggest Brands Seek to Control Online Speech," report, July 10, 2024, 17, https:// dw-wp-production.imgix.net/2024/07/2024-07-10-GARMs-Harm-How-the -Worlds-Biggest-Brands-Seek-to-Control-Online-Speech.pdf.

20. Scher, "GARM Exposed."

21. Linda Yaccarino (@lindayaX), "An Open Letter to Advertisers," Twitter (now X), August 6, 2024, https://x.com/lindayaX/status/1820838134470328676.

22. Charles Gasparino, "Trump Nominee for Antitrust Chief Testifies Anti-Conservative Advertising Trade Group Engaged in Collusion," Fox Business, December 11, 2024, https://www.foxbusiness.com/media/trump-nominee -antitrust-chief-testifies-anti-conservative-advertising-trade-group-engaged -collusion.

23. Shawna Chen, "Obama: 'I Underestimated' Disinformation's Threat to Democracies," Axios, April 6, 2022, https://www.axios.com/2022/04/06/obama -disinformation-democracy.

24. James Bamford, "Every Move You Make," *Foreign Policy*, September 7, 2016, https://foreignpolicy.com/2016/09/07/every-move-you-make-obama-nsa

-security-surveillance-spying-intelligence-snowden; Kate Tummarello, "Obama Expands Surveillance Powers on His Way Out," Electronic Frontier Foundation, January 12, 2017, https://www.eff.org/deeplinks/2017/01/obama-expands -surveillance-powers-his-way-out; Rowan Scarborough, "Govt. Documents Show Six Examples of Obama Administration Spying on Trump Camp," *Washington Times*, August 20, 2020, https://www.washingtontimes.com/news/2020 /aug/20/six-examples-obama-administration-spying-trump-cam.

25. Mike Benz, "DHS Censorship Agency Had Strange First Mission: Banning Speech That Casts Doubt on 'Red Mirage, Blue Shift' Election Events," Foundation for Freedom Online, November 9, 2022, https:// foundationforfreedomonline.com/dhs-censorship-agency-had-strange -first-mission-banning-speech-that-casts-doubt-on-red-mirage-blue-shift -election-events.

26. Margot Cleveland, "Meet the Partisans Who Wove the Censorship Complex's Vast and Tangled Web," Federalist, February 28, 2023, https://thefederalist .com/2023/02/28/meet-the-partisans-who-wove-the-censorship-complexs -vast-and-tangled-web.

27. Greg Piper, "Federal Censorship Machine Started Years Before COVID, Involved Military Contractors: Whistleblower," Just the News, November 29, 2023, https://justthenews.com/government/federal-agencies/federal -censorship-machine-started-years-covid-involved-military; Michael Shellenberger, Alex Gutentag, and Matt Taibbi, "CTIL Files #1: US And UK Military Contractors Created Sweeping Plan for Global Censorship in 2018, New Documents Show," November 28, 2023, https://www.congress.gov/118 /meeting/house/116615/documents/HHRG-118-FD00-20231130-SD001 .pdf.

28. Piper, "Federal Censorship Machine Started Years Before COVID, Involved Military Contractors."

29. Shellenberger, Gutentag, and Taibbi, "CTIL Files #1."

30. "Significant Cyber Incidents," Center for Strategic and International Studies, https://www.csis.org/programs/strategic-technologies-program/significant -cyber-incidents.

31. Subcommittee on Oversight, Investigations, and Accountability, *Censorship Laundering: How the U.S. Department of Homeland Security Enables the Silencing of Dissent*, May 11, 2023, 6, https://www.congress.gov/118/chrg /CHRG-118hhrg54079/CHRG-118hhrg54079.pdf.

32. Ibid., 2.

33. Brianna Lyman, "YouTube Won't List the Full Trump Podcast with Joe Rogan in Its Search Results," Federalist, October 28, 2024, https://thefederalist .com/2024/10/28/youtube-wont-list-the-full-trump-podcast-with-joe-rogan -in-its-search-results.

34. John Solomon, "Congress Opens Probe into Whether Google Search Misled Americans on Trump Assassination Attempt," Just the News, updated August 14, 2024, https://justthenews.com/accountability/congress-opens-probe-whether-google-search-misled-americans-trump-assassination.

35. Ariel Zilber, "Facebook Admits It Wrongly Censored Iconic Photo of Bleeding Trump Pumping His Fist After Assassination Attempt: 'This Was an Error,'" *New York Post*, July 29, 2024, https://nypost.com/2024/07/29/business/facebook-admits-it-wrongly-censored-iconic-photo-of-bleeding-trump.

36. Bobby Burack, "Google Blames 'Error' For Discrepancy Showing Poll Locations for Kamala, but Not Trump," OutKick, updated November 5, 2024, https://www.outkick.com/analysis/google-blames-error-discrepancy-showing-poll-locations-kamala-not-trump.

37. Sam Dean, "Google CEO Sandar Pichai Says Yes to Privacy Laws, No to Political Bias and Maybe to China," *Los Angeles Times*, December 11, 2018, https://www.latimes.com/business/technology/la-fi-tn-google-congress-pichai-20181211-story.html.

38. Evan Halper, "Studying Google's Effects on Voters," *Los Angeles Times*, March 27, 2019, https://enewspaper.latimes.com/infinity/article_share.aspx?guid=b9954d51-cf81-489f-a4b3-f410d75321a4.

39. "Google and Censorship Through Search Engines, Before the U.S. Senate Judiciary Subcomm. on the Constitution," 114th Cong. (2019), testimony of Robert Epstein, senior research psychologist for the American Institute for Behavioral Research and Technology, https://www.judiciary.senate.gov/imo/media/doc/Epstein%20Testimony.pdf.

40. Catherine Salgado, "Alarming: Guess Who Google Is Targeting with Its 'Go Vote' Reminders?" MRC NewsBusters, November 5, 2024, https://newsbusters.org/blogs/free-speech/catherine-salgado/2024/11/05/alarming-guess-who-google-targeting-its-go-vote.

41. Ibid.; "Google and Censorship Through Search Engines."

42. Craig Timberg, "Could Google Rankings Skew an Election? New Group Aims to Find Out," *Washington Post*, March 14, 2017, https://www.washingtonpost.com/news/the-switch/wp/2017/03/14/could-google-rankings-skew-an-election-new-group-aims-to-find-out.

43. Peter Schweizer, "Election Interference Nobody Is Talking About," *The Drill Down*, posted September 12, 2023, YouTube, 29 min., 29 sec., https://www.youtube.com/watch?v=N8YwZXOzZpk.

44. Ibid.

45. Thomas Fujiwara, Karsten Müller, and Carlo Schwarz, "The Effect of Social Media on Elections: Evidence from the United States," *Journal of the European Economic Association* 22, no. 3 (2024): 1495–1539, https://doi.org/10.1093/jeea/jvad058.

46. Matt Taibbi, "Capsule Summaries of All Twitter Files Threads to Date, with Links and a Glossary," Racket News, January 4, 2023, https://www.racket.news/p /capsule-summaries-of-all-twitter; State of Missouri et al. v. Joseph R. Biden Jr. et al. (W.D. La. 2022), deposition of Elvis Chan, November 11, 2022, 100, https:// www.documentcloud.org/documents/23379650-elvis-chan-deposition/.

47. Taibbi, "Capsule Summaries of All Twitter Files Threads to Date," part 6.

48. Julia Shapero, "Former NYT Columnist Bari Weiss Releases 'Twitter Files Part Two,'" ABC27, updated December 9, 2022, https://www.abc27.com/hill -politics/former-nyt-columnist-bari-weiss-releases-twitter-files-part-two.

49. Taibbi, "Capsule Summaries of All Twitter Files Threads to Date."

50. Committee on the Judiciary and the Select Subcommittee on the Weaponization of the Federal Government, *The Censorship-Industrial Complex: How Top Biden White House Officials Coerced Big Tech to Censor Americans, True Information, and Critics of the Biden Administration*, report, May 1, 2024, 3, https://judiciary.house.gov/sites/evo-subsites/republicans-judiciary.house.gov /files/evo-media-document/Biden-WH-Censorship-Report-final.pdf.

51. Ibid., 6.

52. Ibid., 3–7.

53. Kaia Hubbard and Melissa Quinn, "Supreme Court Orders New Look at Social Media Laws in Texas and Florida," CBS News, updated July 1, 2024, https:// www.cbsnews.com/news/supreme-court-social-media-laws-florida-texas.

Chapter 10: The Social Engineering of Children

1. Ian Failes, "'Antz' Hits 20: Re-Visiting PDI's Tech from 20 Years Ago," Cartoon Brew, October 4, 2018, https://www.cartoonbrew.com/feature-film/antz-hits -20-re-visiting-pdis-tech-from-20-years-ago-164870.html.

2. Andrew Young, "They Are Deliberately Adding These Disturbing Scenes into Kids Movies," interview by Greg Matsen, Cwic Media, posted October 5, 2023, YouTube, 1 hr., 20 min., 3 sec., 00:12, https://www.youtube.com /watch?v=4FFgERZAR_M.

3. "The Family: A Proclamation to the World," Church of Jesus Christ of Latter-day Saints, September 23, 1995, https://www.churchofjesuschrist.org/study /scriptures/the-family-a-proclamation-to-the-world.

4. Young, "They Are Deliberately Adding These Disturbing Scenes into Kids Movies."

5. Marc Graser, "End of an Era for PDI as DreamWorks Animation Closes Studio," *Variety*, January 22, 2015, https://variety.com/2015/film/news/end-of-an-era -for-pdi-as-dreamworks-animation-closes-studio-1201412629.

6. Alex Sherman, "Disney CEO Bob Iger Says Company's Movies Have Been Too Focused on Messaging," CNBC, updated November 30, 2023, https://www.cnbc.com/2023/11/30/disney-ceo-bob-iger-says-movies-have-been-too-focused-on-messaging.html.

7. "National Association for Media Literacy Education (NAMLE)," Influence Watch, https://www.influencewatch.org/non-profit/national-association-for-media-literacy-education-namle.

8. "Tides Foundation," Influence Watch.

9. Tyler O'Neil, "Woketopus: USAID's Troubling Ties to Woke Nonprofits That Called the Shots in Biden Administration," Daily Signal, February 16, 2025, https://www.dailysignal.com/2025/02/16/woketopus-usaids-troubling-ties-woke-nonprofits-called-shots-biden-administration/.

10. "Collaborative for Academic, Social, and Emotional Learning (CASEL)," Influence Watch, https://www.influencewatch.org/non-profit/collaborative-for-academic-social-and-emotional-learning-casel/; "NoVo Foundation," Influence Watch, https://www.influencewatch.org/non-profit/novo-foundation.

11. Reagan Reese, "School District Shells Out Thousands on Controversial Emotional Survey Program with Ties to Merrick Garland," *The Lion*, Herzog Foundation, May 8, 2023, https://readlion.com/school-district-shells-out-thousands-on-controversial-emotional-survey-program-with-ties-to-merrick-garland; "Xan Tanner," Influence Watch, https://www.influencewatch.org/person/xan-tanner.

12. Sarah Shapiro and Catherine Brown, "A Look at Civics Education in the United States," *American Educator*, 2018, https://www.aft.org/ae/summer2018/shapiro_brown.

13. Matt Barnum, "Mark Zuckerberg Tried to Revolutionize American Education with Technology. It Didn't Go as Planned," Chalkbeat, October 4, 2023, https://www.chalkbeat.org/2023/10/4/23903768/mark-zuckerberg-czi-schools-personalized-learning-technology-summit.

14. Warner Todd Huston, "Former Disney Exec Blames Hollywood's Collapse on Woke DEI Policies Forced by Investment Firms," Breitbart, November 2, 2024, https://www.breitbart.com/entertainment/2024/11/02/former-disney-exec-blames-hollywoods-collapse-on-woke-dei-policies-forced-by-investment-firms.

15. Jon McGowan, "Conservative Outrage over ESG and DEI Fueled by 2017 BlackRock CEO Video," *Forbes*, June 5, 2023, https://www.forbes.com/sites/jonmcgowan/2023/06/05/conservative-outrage-over-esg-and-dei-fueled-by-2017-blackrock-ceo-video.

16. Andy Kroll, "Meet the New George Soros," *Mother Jones*, May/June 2013, https://www.motherjones.com/politics/2013/05/jeffrey-katzenberg-dreamworks-barack-obama-fundraiser.

17. Peter White, "The Obamas & 'Doc McStuffins' Creator Chris Nee Team on Animated Preschool Series for Netflix," Deadline, October 1, 2020, https://deadline.com/2020/10/the-obamas-doc-mcstuffins-creator-chris-nee -preschool-series-netflix-1234589487.

18. Oscar Buynevich, "DHS-Funded Video Game Pits 'Superhero' Government Against 'Disinformation,'" Foundation for Freedom Online, June 6, 2024, https://foundationforfreedomonline.com/dhs-funded-video-game-pits -superhero-government-against-disinformation.

19. Office of American Spaces, "*Cat Park*: A Seriously Fun Game to Counter Disinformation," digital campaign toolkit, October 2022, https://americanspaces .state.gov/wp-content/uploads/sites/292/22-Cat-Park-Toolkit.pdf; Jon Roozenbeek and Sander Van Der Linden, "Breaking Harmony Square: A Game That 'Inoculates' Against Political Misinformation," *Misinformation Review*, Harvard Kennedy School, November 6, 2020, https://misinforeview.hks.harvard .edu/article/breaking-harmony-square-a-game-that-inoculates-against -political-misinformation.

20. iCivics, https://vision.icivics.org; CASEL, https://casel.org; Cyber Civics, https://www.cybercivics.com.

21. Ramona Bessinger, "DHS Is Training Teachers to Develop Student 'Disinformation' Informers—I Know, I Took the Training," Legal Insurrection Foundation, February 19, 2024, https://legalinsurrection.com/2024/02/dhs-is-training-teachers -to-develop-student-disinformation-informers-i-know-i-took-the-training.

22. Ibid.

23. "Putting Media Literacy on the Public Policy Agenda," Media Literacy Now, https://medialiteracynow.org/impact/current-policy.

24. Ben Weingarten, "The Problematic Rise of Media Literacy Education," RealClearInvestigations, March 22, 2023, https://www.realclearinvestigations .com/articles/2023/03/22/media_literacy_ed_the_true-or-false_question _that_schools_might_blow_on_the_big_test_888153.html.

25. "'Media Literacy' and 'Digital Citizenship': Smuggling Censorship and Indoctrination Into Schools," Foundation for Freedom Online, June 13, 2024, https://foundationforfreedomonline.com/media-literacy-and-digital -citizenship-smuggling-censorship-and-indoctrination-into-schools.

26. "Content Partners," Newsela, https://preauthenticated-site. newsela.com/about/ content/content-partners; Foundation for Freedom Online, "Analysis: Newsela Is the 'Media Literacy' Provider Active in 90 Percent of American Schools," *Ohio Star*, August 13, 2024, https://theohiostar.com/news/analysis-newsela-is-the-media -literacy-provider-active-in-90-percent-of-american-schools/ffo/2024/08/13..

27. "New: Anti-Bias, Anti-Racism Lessons in the Newsela SEL Collection," Newsela, January 22, 2021, https://preauthenticated-site.newsela.com/about /blog/anti-bias-anti-racism-lessons-newsela-sel.

28. Corinne Weaver, "Google Funds Anti-Conservative 'Hate Watch' Group Southern Poverty Law Center," MRC NewsBusters, January 23, 2019, https://www.newsbusters.org/blogs/free-speech/corinne-weaver/2019/01/23/google-funds-anti-conservative-hate-watch-group; Jalaya Liles Dunn, "Learning for Justice: Teaching Tolerance Changes Its Name to Reflect Evolving Work in the Struggle for Radical Change in Education and Community," Southern Poverty Law Center, February 3, 2021, https://www.splcenter.org/news/2021/02/03/learning-justice-teaching-tolerance-changes-its-name-reflect-evolving-work-struggle-radical.

29. Weingarten, "The Problematic Rise of Media Literacy Education."

30. John D. Sailer, "Media Literacy's False Promise," *City Journal*, August 16, 2021, https://www.city-journal.org/article/media-literacys-false-promise.

31. Panorama Education, "Panorama Social-Emotional Learning Survey: Topics and Questions for Students, Teachers, and Staff," user guide, 29, https://cdn01.dailycaller.com/wp-content/uploads/2023/05/SEL-User-Guide-1.pdf.

32. Masooma Haq, "Parents Warn That Social-Emotional Learning Is Not What It Appears," *Epoch Times*, updated July 27, 2023, https://www.theepochtimes.com/us/in-depth-parents-warn-that-social-emotional-learning-is-not-what-it-appears-5423919.

33. Panorama Education, "How Panorama Works," 2015, https://panorama-www.s3.amazonaws.com/files/product/product-tour.pdf.

34. Brittany Brunell, "Unpacking the Origins of Social Emotional Learning: A Brief Background Guide," *Everyday Speech* (blog), https://everydayspeech.com/sel-implementation/unpacking-the-origins-of-social-emotional-learning-a-brief-background-guide; Max Eden, "The Trouble with Social Emotional Learning," American Enterprise Institute, April 6, 2022, https://www.aei.org/research-products/testimony/the-trouble-with-social-emotional-learning.

35. Max Eden, "Smuggling in Radical Instruction," *City Journal*, May 19, 2022, https://www.city-journal.org/article/smuggling-in-radical-instruction.

36. "The Fatal Flaw of the 1619 Project Curriculum," History Education, American Revolution Institute, archived October 5, 2024, https://web.archive.org/web/20241005091635/https://www.americanrevolutioninstitute.org/fatal-flaw-of-the-1619-project-curriculum/.

37. Kenin M. Spivak, "Perverting 'Civics,'" American Mind, April 29, 2022, https://americanmind.org/salvo/perverting-civics.

38. Shapiro and Brown, "A Look at Civics Education in the United States."

39. Jason Bedrick, "Beware Civics Education's 'Wolf in Sheep's Clothing,'" Daily Signal, February 9, 2024, https://www.dailysignal.com/2024/02/09/beware-civics-educations-wolf-in-sheeps-clothing.

40. Dr. Joseph Mercola, "Google Is Like 'a Stranger Watching Your Child Through Their Bedroom Window,'" Defender, Children's Health Defense, September 22, 2022, https://childrenshealthdefense.org/defender/google-watching-children-schools-chromebooks-personal-data; Lucas Rockett Gutterman, "Chromebook Churn," U.S. PIRG Education Fund, revised May 2023, https://publicinterestnetwork.org/wp-content/uploads/2023/05/PIRG-Chromebook-Churn-Full-Report-May-1.pdf.

41. "Privacy and Security FAQ," Google for Education, https://edu.google.com/intl/ALL_us/why-google/privacy-security/frequently-asked-questions.

42. "Google News," AllSides, https://www.allsides.com/news-source/google-news-media-bias.

43. Hazem Ibrahim, Nouar Aldahoul, and Sangjin Lee et al., "YouTube's Recommendation Algorithm Is Left-Leaning in the United States," PNAS Nexus 2, no. 8 (2023): 264, https://doi.org/10.1093/pnasnexus/pgad264.

44. Douglas Murray, "Google's Push to Lecture Us on Diversity Goes Beyond AI," New York Post, February 22, 2024, https://nypost.com/2024/02/22/opinion/googles-push-to-lecture-us-on-diversity-goes-beyond-ai.

45. Dan Milmo and Alex Hern, "Google Chief Admits 'Biased' AI Tool's Photo Diversity Offended Users," Guardian, February 28, 2024, https://www.theguardian.com/technology/2024/feb/28/google-chief-ai-tools-photo-diversity-offended-users.

46. Umar Shakir, "Google Will Let You Make AI Clip Art for Your Documents," Verge, November 15, 2024, https://www.theverge.com/2024/11/15/24297524/google-docs-gemini-ai-image-generator-clip-art.

47. Elizabeth Elkind, "House of Representatives Politics: Youngest House Republican-Elect Reveals How GOP Won Back America's Youth," Fox News, November 18, 2024, https://www.foxnews.com/politics/youngest-house-republican-elect-reveals-how-gop-won-back-americas-youth.

48. "Thomas Sowell on Education," Liberty.org, August 25, 2023, https://www.liberty.org/education/thomas-sowell-on-education.

49. Bridget Bowman and Joe Murphy, "Democrats Flooded with Cash in Fight for Congress as the GOP Tries to Stretch Its Money," NBC News, updated October 16, 2024, https://www.nbcnews.com/politics/2024-election/democrats-flooded-cash-fight-congress-gop-stretch-money-rcna175636.

Chapter 11: Game Changers on the Horizon

1. Bowman and Murphy, "Democrats Flooded with Cash in Fight for Congress as the GOP Tries to Stretch Its Money."

2. Fredreka Schouten and Edward-Isaac Dovere, "Kamala Harris Has Raised $1 Billion Since Launching Presidential Campaign," CNN, October 9, 2024, https://edition.cnn.com/2024/10/09/politics/harris-billion-fundraising-election/index.html.

3. "Who's Funding the 2024 Election?" USAFacts, updated August 2, 2024, https://usafacts.org/articles/whos-funding-the-2024-election.

4. Rich Noyes, "TV Hits Trump with 85% Negative News vs. 78% Positive Press for Harris," MRC NewsBusters, October 28, 2024, https://www.newsbusters.org/blogs/nb/rich-noyes/2024/10/28/tv-hits-trump-85-negative-news-vs-78-positive-press-harris.

5. Alicja Hagopian, "How Shifts Among Key Demographic Voting Groups Sealed Trump's 2024 Election Victory," *Independent*, November 8, 2024, https://www.the-independent.com/news/world/americas/us-politics/election-trump-harris-demographic-breakdown-b2643412.html.

6. Ian Smith, "Chaffetz: It's Time to Get Federal Agencies Out of Washington," FedSmith, updated January 17, 2017, https://www.fedsmith.com/2017/01/12/chaffetz-its-time-to-get-federal-agencies-out-of-washington.

7. Tristan Justice, "Media Accuse Trump of Hatch Act Violations While Ignoring Democrats," Federalist, August 27, 2020, https://thefederalist.com/2020/08/27/media-accuse-trump-of-hatch-act-violations-while-ignoring-democrats/; "Ethics Handbook for On and Off-Duty Conduct," Justice Management Division, US Department of Justice.

8. Deirdre Shesgreen, "13 High-Level Trump Officials Violated Hatch Act, Using Government Office for Partisan Activity, Watchdog Probe Finds," *USA Today*, November 9, 2021, https://www.usatoday.com/story/news/politics/2021/11/09/mike-pompeo-kellyanne-conway-more-trump-officials-violated-hatch-act/6354972001/.

9. US Office of Special Counsel, "Investigation of Political Activities by Senior Trump Administration Officials During the 2020 Presidential Election."

10. Josh Gerstein, "Ethics Agency Says HUD Chief Castro Violated Hatch Act," *Politico*, July 18, 2016, https://www.politico.com/story/2016/07/julian-castro-ethics-hud-hatch-225732; Jennifer Haberkorn, "Report: Sebelius Violated Hatch Act," *Politico*, updated September 13, 2012, https://www.politico.com/story/2012/09/osc-report-sebelius-violated-hatch-act-081122.

11. Lesley Kennedy, "What Is the Hatch Act and Why Was It Established in 1939," History Channel, September 22, 2020, https://www.history.com/news/hatch-act-fdr-politics.

12. Ibid.

13. "Union Arbitrators Overturn Most Federal Employee Dismissals," America First Policy Institute, September 14, 2022, https://americafirstpolicy.com/issues/20220914-union-arbitrators-overturn-most-federal-employee-dismissals.

14. Daren Bakst and Gabriella Beaumont-Smith, "Five Conservative Principles to Apply Against Weaponized Antitrust," Heritage Foundation, August 5, 2021, https://www.heritage.org/government-regulation/report/five-conservative-principles-apply-against-weaponized-antitrust.

15. Zo Ahmed, "Oracle CEO Safra Catz Unpacks TikTok Data Security, Generative AI's Promise, and Tech Diversity," TechSpot, May 13, 2024, https://www.techspot.com/news/102977-oracle-ceo-safra-catz-unpacks-tiktok-data-security.html.

16. Bree Fowler, "Apple's Tim Cook Says the Fight to Protect Privacy Is a Crucial One," CNET, April 12, 2022, https://www.cnet.com/news/privacy/tim-cook-says-the-fight-to-protect-privacy-is-a-crucial-one.

17. Ben Gould, "Privacy vs Free Speech: Challenges with Adopting the European Union's Right to Be Forgotten in the United States," International Law and Policy Brief, George Washington University Law School, February 28, 2023, https://studentbriefs.law.gwu.edu/ilpb/2023/02/28/privacy-vs-free-speech-challenges-with-adopting-the-european-unions-right-to-be-forgotten-in-the-united-states.

18. Ronald Reagan, address on behalf of Senator Barry Goldwater (R-AZ), "A Time for Choosing," October 27, 1964, quoted on Goodreads.com, https://www.goodreads.com/quotes/149332-no-government-ever-voluntarily-reduces-itself-in-size-government-programs.

About the Author

JASON CHAFFETZ is an American politician and Fox News contributor. He was elected as a US representative from Utah in 2008 after spending sixteen years in the local business community. When he left Congress in 2017, he was the chairman of the United States House Committee on Oversight and Government Reform. He currently is a fellow at the Government Accountability Institute.